JESUS
THE MESSIAH

CUNNINGHAM LECTURES

JESUS
THE MESSIAH

THE SYNOPTIC TRADITION OF THE REVELATION OF GOD IN CHRIST: WITH SPECIAL REFERENCE TO FORM-CRITICISM

BY

WILLIAM MANSON

D.D. (Knox Coll., Toronto), D.D. (Glasgow)

PROFESSOR OF NEW TESTAMENT LANGUAGE, LITERATURE,
AND THEOLOGY IN THE UNIVERSITY OF EDINBURGH

HODDER AND STOUGHTON
LIMITED   LONDON

FIRST PUBLISHED . . NOVEMBER, 1943
FIFTH IMPRESSION . . MAY, 1948

PRINTED IN GREAT BRITAIN FOR HODDER AND STOUGHTON LTD., LONDON,
AT THE UNIVERSITY PRESS, ABERDEEN

PREFACE

THE present work incorporates a course of public lectures undertaken by the writer at the invitation of the Cunningham Lectureship Trustees and delivered in New College, Edinburgh, at the close of 1940. Advantage has been taken of the interval since then to revise and complete the substance of the book, to give the argument a closer relation to some of the broad questions of New Testament theology as a whole, and to add a number of appendices, including an inquiry into the Iranian Redemption Myth hypothesis, so far as the latter may be thought to have a bearing on late Jewish and early Christian religious ideas.

It is not the primary intention of the book to handle afresh the problem of the Messianic consciousness of Jesus, but rather to show how, on the basis of the confession of Jesus as Messiah, the early Church built up the structure of its distinctive witness to the Christian revelation of God. In working out this purpose, however, I have been obliged by the nature of the material to cross the borders of the other problem, and to formulate at least the outlines of an approach to its solution. I have assumed on what seems adequate grounds, that the tradition of the Church from the beginning embodied a substantial core of authentic historical reminiscence of the word and work of its Founder, and the plan which I have followed has been to segregate and, as far as possible, to consider by themselves the various strata or levels of tradition embodied in the Synoptic material—e.g. the ' signs ' of Jesus, his religious and ethical teaching, his utterances regarding his mission and person, and his predictions of his Passion— and from these to work down to the underlying character of the mind regarding God and man in which Christianity had its origin. Inevitably the argument has had to take account of the theories and pronouncements of the school of Form-Criticism which at the present day stands guard over all the approaches to the Synoptic literature. This will explain the constancy of the reference in certain sections to Dr. Rudolf Bultmann's *Geschichte der Synoptischen Tradition*, to which I acknowledge a very real debt. If at many points I have dissented from the findings of that book, it is because I take a different view of historical probability from Dr. Bultmann, and there I must simply leave the matter.

I have not in fact been able to accept the tacit assumption of the Form-Critics that the images and ideas by aid of which the post-resurrection Church represented to itself the person and work of its Lord were necessarily of the nature of makeshifts, the product of its own thought and life, and not of his. The evidence compels me to believe that the Messianic ideas of Israel were the medium through which not the Church alone but Jesus interpreted the urgency and finality of the religious revelation with which he knew himself to be charged.

In the course of the book I have had occasion to question certain presuppositions of other schools of criticism which think to discover new roads of approach to Jesus by explorations in the field of late Jewish apocalyptic Midrash or in the remoter terrain of Graeco-Oriental religious mysticism. We owe much to such investigations, and I trust I have not failed in justice towards the one theory of this kind which I have had specially to handle, the theory associated with the name of Dr. R. Reitzenstein. It must, nevertheless, be insisted that all Messianic ideas, from whatever source derived, underwent a total change in being appropriated to Jesus the Crucified, so that for our understanding of Christianity we start from the Crucified, and not from these ideas. Moreover, the real background of the mind of Jesus, to judge from the tradition, was not Jewish apocalyptic or ethnic gnosis but the prophetic religion of the Old Testament. There is in the latter a very definite structure of thought : an intense apprehension of the living God in His transcendence and holiness leads to, and throws up the supernatural conception of the kingdom of heaven and the apocalyptic view of history. In the teaching of Jesus, even in some of his single utterances, the same order of ideas is discernible : but in Jesus a consciousness of God surpassing that of the prophets presses to conclusions in which, alike as regards his proclamation of the kingdom and the ultimate definition of his personal calling, all merely prophetic norms are left behind.

I have, in working out the plan of these studies, given a large place to the teaching of Jesus, recognizing its supreme significance as revelation of God to the human spirit. The massive incorporation of this teaching in the tradition through the Q source may well appear the most important single event in the history of early Christian thought. In Chapters IV and V the nature of the human encounter with Jesus in the matter of his teaching is analysed, and in Chapter VIII I have tried to bring out the supra-historical aspect of the experience.

If here or elsewhere the method which has been followed should seem to suggest new lines of approach to the Synoptic tradition or to indicate fresh aspects of its significance, it will more than justify to my own mind the putting of the book into print. By a renewed placing of the tradition against the background of the Old Testament religion I have come to a deepened sense of its historical and revelational value. At the same time I am more conscious of having raised critical or exegetical problems in this region than of having solved them, but this is a matter which I must leave to the judgement of others. The extent of my debt to the literature of the subject will be amply apparent from the citations and references in the book itself. My colleagues, Principal W. A. Curtis, D.Litt., D.D., and Professor John Baillie, D.D., D.Litt., and the Rev. A. K. Walton, D.D., have been good enough to read some of the following pages in typescript, and I am grateful to them for practical suggestions and criticism.

W. MANSON.

University of Edinburgh,
    6th March, 1943.

CONTENTS

xi

Chapter I

THE PRIMITIVE CHRISTIAN CONFESSION

IF the problem of Christian origins is not easily resolved by the methods of historical analysis, the cause lies less in the meagreness than in the complexity of the documentary evidence.

The ancient material which has been handed down to us in the Gospels of Mark, Matthew, and Luke is indeed fragmentary both in range and in character. It represents at best an exiguous survival from a once larger body of tradition. But it is at the same time highly complex, for its survival was determined in large part by its adaptation to the practical necessities and interests of the first Christian generation. The material has thus become deeply inwoven with the thought, the life, the point of view of the Christian Church.

In the intensive use to which the tradition of Jesus was put in the evangelistic and missionary activity of the apostolic age the older forms of some of its parts have been covered over. Conceptions rooted in the primitive Judean stratum—such as Son of God and Son of Man—have taken to themselves a fuller revelational significance from contact with the thought of the larger world. Later insights have imposed themselves on earlier, and a variorum of ideas has resulted in which it is possible not infrequently to distinguish primary, secondary, and even tertiary levels of meaning.

Such developments are not surprising when regard is had to the intense activity of religious thought and imagination in the first Christian generation. Within the area of the Synoptic tradition the developing and interpreting principle continued, as I believe, to express the mind and spirit of Jesus himself, as these were alive and at work in the community. Even so, there is imposed on the historian the necessity of an always watchful and critical procedure. If he is to achieve a synthesis of ideas entitled to rank as a first chapter to a history of Christian doctrine, he will not aim immediately at a complete integration of the Synoptic material as it stands. Rather will he seek to work back from this highly composite product to simpler states and levels of the Church's tradition.

Fortunately, for the starting-point of the historical task it is not necessary to await the results of so complicated a process of analysis. There are facts which antedate the rise of the Church's tradition as we have it, and which as such stand above the tides and the ever-shifting currents of critical opinion on the Gospels.

The first of these—and it is as reasonably certain as any fact of history—is that before any of the acts or words of Jesus were proclaimed to mankind as the sign or proof of a divine redemption offered to the world in him, in other words before the tradition as we have it had begun to crystallize, Jesus was already acknowledged as the Messiah of Israel, the coming Son of Man. This confession stands so near to the beginning of Christian history that beside it no other starting-point is perceptible. Dating as public proclamation from the Easter days of the primitive community, it is the absolute presupposition of the Church's tradition and the substratum of the Christian theology in all later forms of its development.

A second fact—not perhaps so generally admitted but upon analysis just as incontestable—is that the confession in question, by the very circumstance of its being made with reference to a Jewish teacher who had died a death of shame upon a cross, cannot have originated except upon grounds already given in the life and mind of the Crucified himself.

At these points historical analysis takes us to positions lying well behind the lines of the literary criticism of the Gospels, and the latter cannot, save at its peril, omit them from its reckoning. Yet so imperfectly is this recognized in modern reconstructions of early Christian thought and belief that a detailed statement of the grounds on which the claims for the two theses are advanced would seem to be necessary.

The Messianic Confession the Presupposition of the Church's Tradition

We take first the historical relation of the Messianic confession to the Christian tradition as a whole. Here investigation fails to discover any hiatus or interval of time between the completion of the course of Jesus and the first making public of the faith of his adherents. Had such an interval existed, or had any significant group or body of persons claiming to be followers of Jesus withheld assent from the common Christian confession, it is hardly conceivable that some trace of this hesitation or dividedness of opinion would not have persisted in some part of our records, if not also in some indurated historical cleavage within the Church itself.

Of such divergence or division there is, however, no convincing evidence. No stratum of tradition capable of being isolated by the methods of literary analysis reveals a non-Messianic basis. In the first generation indeed there still existed, singly or in groups, a small number of 'disciples,' who had been impressed by the teaching of Jesus or by reports concerning his work, but who did not apparently know him in the character in which he was preached as Messiah. These, however, flourished only on the circumference of the Christian movement where inadequate opportunities existed for becoming acquainted with the full Christian message, and in any case these strays were quickly absorbed into the main body of the Church's life.

The most interesting example of the eccentric type of Christian here under review is perhaps Apollos, the erudite Jew of Alexandria who, according to the at first sight confused story in Acts, was instructed in 'the way of the Lord' and preached and taught 'the things concerning Jesus' but understood only 'the baptism of John' (Acts xviii. 24-28).[1] If we take this curious description as it stands, without devaluation of its terms or resort to theories of source-conflation, a window is opened on a temporary phase of religious life of which there may have been other instances in the history of the apostolic generation.

Apollos, an adherent of the religious movement inaugurated by John the Baptist, had in some manner come to know of the work and teaching of Jesus, but, interpreting the mission of Jesus apparently in terms of the work of John, he had proclaimed him as, like John, a prophet of the last days, a herald or precursor of the coming Son of Man. In course of time he comes to Ephesus where, being apprised of the real character of the Christian message, he becomes an enthusiastic convert to the new movement and preaches Jesus no longer as a Messianic prophet, but as himself the Messiah, the Son of Man (Acts xviii. 28). The Christian writer's statement that before his conversion Apollos had been instructed in 'the way of the Lord' falls into its proper perspective when we observe that from the Christian standpoint John's teaching was altogether a preparation of 'the way of the Lord' (Mk. i. 2-4, Mt. xi. 10, etc.), and on one signal occasion

---

[1] See Appendix A on Apollos.

had led to the propounding of capital questions with regard to Jesus (Mt. xi. 2-6, Lk. vii. 18-23).

If this is a credible interpretation of the Apollos incident, a similar explanation may be offered with regard to the episode which is bracketed with it in the Acts narrative. The ' disciples ' at Ephesus, who had not heard of the Holy Spirit (Acts xix. 1-7), were possibly converts whom Apollos had made when he first came to labour at that centre and who, like their teacher, had thought of Jesus only as a prophet of the things to come. The reason why these disciples had not heard of the Holy Spirit was, as the intervention of St. Paul makes clearly evident, because the Holy Spirit in Christian belief was never dissociated from the confession of Jesus as *the Messiah* and from baptism into his name.

We seem, then, to witness a process by which in the first generation individuals or groups of individuals on the circum-ference of the Christian movement pass from a vaguer to a more exact confession of faith. The existence of such imperfect types of Christian witness may possibly underlie and account for the form of the Synoptic passage in which Jesus, before putting to his disciples the intimate question, " Who do you say that I am ? " is declared to have asked them, " Who do men say that I am ? " and to have received the answer : " Some say John the Baptist, others Elias, and others one of the prophets " (Mk. viii. 27-29, etc.). Against the same background we may justifiably set the recurring formula or pattern of thought, so characteristic of the Fourth Gospel, according to which individuals who are brought into contact with Jesus or who receive blessing at his hands—the Samaritan woman for example (Jn. iv. 19, 25-26), or the man born blind (Jn. ix. 17, 35-38)—confess him first to be a ' prophet,' and then are brought to register a higher verdict. But while this progress from a less to a more articulate faith was taking place on the frontiers of the Christian movement there is no reason to suppose that the original nucleus of Christians in Jerusalem ever trod this path or thought of Jesus in other than Messianic terms. Such a conclusion would not only run counter to the main extant evidence of our sources, but would have to face insuperable difficulties in another quarter, as becomes apparent when we pass to the second of our questions. This concerns the real ground of the Messianic confession of Christianity.

THE SELF-DISCLOSURE OF JESUS AS THE MESSIAH

How did the conviction that Jesus was the Messiah originate in the circle of the first disciples ? Can we explain it as a belief to which they came of themselves before or after his death and without suggestion or warrant from him ? This hypothesis has been freely advanced, and in a qualified form it provides the starting-point of Dr. Wilhelm Bousset's reconstruction of early Christian history in his work *Kyrios Christos*.[1] According to Bousset, the motive which impelled the followers of Jesus to define the significance of his person and function was the incomparably powerful and indestructible impression wrought by the personality of Jesus upon their spiritual nature, an impression which no force of public shame and obloquy, torment, insult, and death could efface. When their first instinctive hopes that their leader would prove the national Messiah perished through his death, they found a substitute and compensation in the transcendent Son of Man conception of contemporary apocalyptic thought. They cast the ready-to-hand royal mantle of the Son of Man around the person of their Master, set the highest of crowns upon his head, and confessed themselves disciples of one who through suffering and death had entered into glory. So arose the Christian Church and its doctrine of the person of Christ. Is this at all a credible hypothesis ? If the personal relation of Jesus to the Messianic expectations of his disciples was, as Bousset holds, quite indeterminate, can we suppose that these expectations would survive his death, and indeed take a new and loftier flight from the fact of that death ? It is difficult to think so.

While the humility and comparative obscurity of Jesus on earth would present no insuperable obstacle to enthusiasts whose hopes of a Messianic future he had unconsciously kindled, while the paradox involved in his earthly fortunes might under certain circumstances even attract their Israelitish hearts, it is by no means clear that the same would hold true of the calamity of his end, seeing that this could hardly be construed by them as a mere point of earthly humiliation, but exposed the Sufferer to the grave accusation of being, from the standpoint of the law and religion of Israel, an excommunicate from God, one who had borne the curse of sin (Deut. xxi. 23, Acts v. 30, Gal. iii. 13).

It is indeed at this point that all theories which explain the Messianic confession of the primitive Church from the outside as

[1] Sec. ed. (1921), pp. 17 ff.

an aureole which an enthusiastic body of Jewish religionists cast around the head of Jesus call for serious scrutiny. If Jesus had set no higher interpretation on his calling than that of a teacher of righteousness, a prophet to his times, a herald of the divine Kingdom, or a witness to the coming of the Son of Man ; if he had said nothing which in any way identified his fortunes with those of the Christ or Son of Man ; is it thinkable that the love and devotion of his followers would, after the event on Calvary, have taken the acutely paradoxical form of investing him with the Messianic sceptre and glory ? Would even the persuasion of his resurrection have led beyond the certainty that he lived with God to the further assurance that he would return as the predicted Son of Man ?

As a way of escape from this position for those who do not accept that Jesus himself directly inspired the faith of his followers, it is argued that Scriptural or doctrinal ideas known to the community turned the death of Jesus into the very mark or sign by which they identified him as the Messiah or Son of Man.

But when appeal is made in defence of this hypothesis to the ' Suffering Servant ' passage in Isa. liii, to which advocates of the theory ordinarily point as the real ground of the community's faith, and to which the pre-Pauline Christian tradition also undoubtedly referred in its deliverance that " Christ died for our sins according to the Scriptures " (I Cor. xv. 3), it is by no means certain that the Biblical passage in question will stand the weight of the construction here put upon it. *While in or behind the Deutero-Isaianic conception of the Suffering Servant we may, and in my judgement ought to recognize a genuinely Messianic figure in whose person the older Davidic conception of the king of righteousness had become infiltrated with the idea of suffering, with what Psalm cxxxii calls the ' afflictions ' of David,[1] it is by no means clear that the first disciples of Jesus, who followed either nationalistic or apocalyptic ideas of the coming Messiah, had or could have attained to this height of insight unaided.* At this point, in fact, we seem to be faced by a real dilemma. If the followers of Jesus were not accustomed to think of the Servant as the Messiah, how should the parallel between the fortunes of Jesus and those of the Servant yield a Messianic conclusion in favour of Jesus ? If, on the other hand, they identified the Servant with the Messiah, why should they wish to connect a Jesus, who *ex hypothesi* had made no personal Messianic claim, with the Servant ?

[1] See Appendix C.

The mere martyr-fate of Jesus would hardly of itself afford the identification-sign. For here the official teaching of the Synagogue, which ordinarily fixed the sense in which Scripture was received and understood by the rank and file of Jews, must have failed the associates of Jesus at the crucial point. While the Targums, which embody substantially the traditional Synagogue teaching, discover the Messiah abundantly on almost every page of the Old Testament, and while the Targum on the prophets on four several occasions (Isa. xlii. 1, xliii. 10, lii. 13, liii. 10) expressly identifies him with the Servant, the same authority in its paraphrase of Isa. liii definitely signs away the element of *suffering* from the Messiah to the nation of Israel or to the heathen peoples.[1] Even if this Targumic exclusion of suffering and shame from the concept of the Messiah should be set down to later Jewish bias against the Messianic doctrine of the Nazarenes, it would still remain that nothing in Isa. liii suggests that the martyred Servant there depicted suffers and dies as one who bears the curse of God. It is only men in their blindness who esteem the Servant to be smitten of God and afflicted. It cannot therefore be convincingly established that influences proceeding from this quarter would of themselves have enabled the first Christian disciples to put a *Messianic* interpretation on the sufferings and death of Jesus.

In fact, Isa. liii says either too much or too little to lend itself to the Christian interpretation of Jesus if Jesus had not himself defined his mission as Messianic.

As an alternative it is suggested that doctrinal ideas centering in the conception of the apocalyptic ' Son of Man ' formed the medium through which the Christian society came to its recognition of the Crucified as the Messiah. This argument too is not exempt from criticism. In the famous passage in Daniel, in which the conception of the Son of Man first rises above the horizon of Israel, the apocalyptist says :

" I saw in the night visions, and behold, there came with the clouds of heaven one like a son of man, and he came even unto the Ancient of Days. . . . And there was given him dominion and glory and a kingdom " (Dan. vii. 13-14).

Nothing in this passage suggests that the transcendent figure here introduced makes his entrance on his glory through humiliation and suffering, not to say through abandonment by God and

[1] See Appendix B on the Targum on Isa. liii.

death. The powers of evil are indeed present in the context of the vision. They appear in the guise of the symbolic beast-figures which are contrasted with the transcendent Heavenly Man (Dan. vii. 2-12). But while St. Paul from his Christian standpoint can speak of the ' princes ' or rulers of the present world-æon as having crucified the Lord of glory (I Cor. ii. 8), and while he teaches that Jesus in dying disarmed or rid himself for ever of these principalities and powers (Col. ii. 15), no ideas of this kind are hinted at in Daniel or in those sections of the Jewish books of I Enoch and IV Ezra which continue and develop the Daniel tradition. It is, however, contended in some quarters that, according to some esoteric development of doctrine which was current at the time and known to Jews and Christians, the Son of Man or apocalyptic Redeemer was to come among men *incognito*, and after varied fortunes and great sufferings on earth to be revealed in his true character by an heavenly exaltation or apotheosis.[1] The development of this hypothesis we owe for the most part to the erudition and ingenuity of Dr. R. Reitzenstein.

In a series of works this scholar has expounded to our age the grandiose myth of the Heavenly Man or Son of Man Redeemer. Relying chiefly upon recently discovered documents of Manichæan and Mandæan origin, but finding support for his views also in widely scattered fields of Oriental and Hellenistic religious belief, Reitzenstein lays bare a sequence of ideas, constituting a redemption-mystery, which he considers to have exercised a powerful influence on the minds of the Eastern peoples bordering on Palestine from a period earlier than the rise of Christianity. These ideas he traces ultimately to an Iranian myth transmitted not by the channels of normal orthodox Zoroastrianism but through a filter-bed, so to speak, of Babylonian and Syrian mysticism. A fuller account of the origin and alleged diffusion of the myth may be reserved for separate treatment at a later stage of the present work.[2] Suffice here to say that the heart of the doctrine, as Reitzenstein expounds it, lies in the idea that the soul or inner essence of man is a divine nature which is imprisoned in a world of darkness and evil and which has to be liberated and restored to the world of light.

This nature man has from a primal Heavenly or Divine Man who, being sent forth from God at the beginning of time, fell a

[1] See Appendix D on " The Heavenly Man Redemption Myth."

[2] See Appendix D where also the literature of the subject will be found noted.

prey to the powers of darkness and was victimized by them to the extent that, though raised by the Father again to divinity in the realm of light, he left behind him in the world a part of his heavenly elements or panoply, from which in turn the soul, the heavenly part of man's being, is descended. In consequence, alike as regards his origin, his present fortunes in the world, and his ultimate hope of redemption, man stands in a relation of dependence upon the Primal or God Man, whose deliverance and exaltation to God is the sign of man's final salvation.

A mystery-religion so frankly Manichæan and Gnostic in its expression is not easily reconciled with the terms of the New Testament doctrine of Christ as we know it. Reitzenstein, however, would argue that conceptions of redemption of an essentially similar type were already current in the age of Jesus and St. Paul and had influenced the people of the Bible. He thinks that from its origin-point in the Persian story of the first man Gayomart the myth acquired in Babylonia and Syria a redemptorial significance. The primal man became a Redeemer Man. In this form, uniting a revelation regarding the origin of man and the cosmos with a message of final redemption, the doctrine, like other beliefs of Iranian provenance, found its way into Judaism and into early Christianity. The Heavenly Man appears first in Judaism in the person of the " One like a son of man " whom the author of Daniel sees coming with the clouds of heaven, and he emerges again in a more substantial form in the Jewish books of I Enoch and IV Ezra, in the Gospel tradition, and in the Pauline doctrine of Christ. In Daniel, indeed, the function of the Heavenly Man is limited to his appearance at the end of history, and it is as final judge and deliverer that he chiefly interests the authors of the other Jewish writings referred to. But as in I Enoch he is also one who *pre-existed* with God before the ages, and as in the Pauline teaching the Christ who is revealed as the Man from Heaven was with the Father from before creation, Reitzenstein ventures the opinion that more came into Judaism with the idea of the Son of Man than appears in Daniel or in the Jewish doctrine of the last things. Overtones of the myth entered, and already in the age of Jesus, he thinks, it was current doctrine that the Heavenly Man first descends into the world in his own person or in that of his messengers, and lives a wandering and suffering life on earth in order to exalt mankind, as sharers of his own life, to God.

It is a bold assumption which is made when ideas characteristic

of the Manichæan religion, itself influenced by Christianity, are
held to lie at the root of the Christian doctrine of the Son of
Man.   Here we are concerned not with the general validity of
the theory but with one supposed deduction from it.   Was it the
influence of some such doctrine that enabled the first disciples of
Jesus to surmount the offence of the Cross and to recognize the
heavenly Son of Man in the Galilean teacher who toiled and
suffered on earth, not having where to lay his head ?   The theory
has against it that nowhere in the Synoptic tradition is such a
doctrine of the Son of Man attributed to anyone except to Jesus
himself.

> " For he taught his disciples, and said to them : the Son of Man
> is delivered into the hands of men, and they shall kill him ; and
> when he is killed . . . he will rise again " (Mk. ix. 31.   Cf. Lk. xvii.
> 25, Mk. ix. 12b, etc.).

But whereas Jesus is said to have taught this doctrine, the evangelist Mark openly declares that the death and resurrection of the
Son of Man was not an idea known to the disciples (Mk. ix. 10).
They did not understand when Jesus spoke of it, and they were
afraid to ask him for an explanation (Mk. ix. 32).   If some
esoteric doctrine of the Heavenly Man had served the early community as the clue to the sufferings of Jesus, if it had supplied
the reagent, so to speak, which revealed the meaning of the
death of Jesus and enabled him to be recognized as the heavenly
Messiah, we should have expected clearer traces of the fact to
have stamped themselves on the tradition, and we should have
found St. Mark working with a different theory of the Messianic
secret from that which he has actually employed.   In other
words Mark, if he had had any knowledge of the real course of
events, would have said, not that the disciples failed to understand mysteries which Jesus announced before his death, but
that after the resurrection they understood mysteries which Jesus
had *not* announced—a very different thing, and one which is
nowhere hinted in Mark, not even in the passage :

> " He charged them that they should tell no man what things
> they had seen, save when the Son of Man should have risen again
> from the dead.   And they kept hold of the saying, questioning
> among themselves what the rising again from the dead should mean "
> (ix. 9-10).

But even if too great a stress should not be laid on features of the
Markan representation at this point, it is scarcely likely that any

form of the supposed Son of Man myth, in portraying the loneliness and suffering of the Heavenly Man, went so far as to predict death for him, not to say a death of the kind endured by Jesus. Had such an idea established itself even in esoteric circles in Judaism, it is difficult to think that St. Paul, who better than most others knew what Gnostic ideas were playing on the margin of Jewish apocalypticism, and who shared not a few of these ideas himself, would have affirmed so dogmatically that the ' word of the Cross,' the doctrine of a ' Messiah Crucified,' was to the Jews a ' scandal ' and an incredibility (I Cor. i. 23).

The conclusion to which the above argument has tended, viz. that *somewhere, somehow, Jesus before his death stood self-revealed to his disciples as the Messiah,* will be resisted by all to whom it is axiomatic that we can know little or nothing of the historical Jesus, and that the offence of the Cross and all similar ideas are only figments of the Christian imagination, mere by-products of its ideology. But if the character and structure of the Christian tradition do not display the smoothness which we would expect to find in a purely ideological creation, if on the contrary the Messianic ideas of which it makes use have been patently forced at numberless points to new shapes and uses, it will be seen that history in the sense of the objective factors conditioning the Christian transformation of these ideas cannot be dismissed as something irrelevant to Christian faith, nor yet as something incapable of being inferred from the Christian shape of the ideas. If, however, a principle of sufficient force to transform the Old Testament and Jewish ideas of the Messiah has thus to be postulated as a condition of Christian history from the beginning, what necessity or ground is there for locating it purely in the mind of the Christian community after the death of Jesus ? If the above argument has any validity, it would seem to show that the source of the power inspiring the Christian community to preach to the world a crucified Christ has to be carried a stage further back. In that case the Christological stamp on the history of Jesus is not something which was imposed upon it at a later time and *ab extra,* but which was inherent in it from the start. We cannot do with less than this minimum of assumption if the place of the Cross in Christianity is to be rendered explicable. On the other hand, we cannot too highly exalt the importance of this minimum, for here the basis of the whole future theological development of Christianity is essentially given, and given in a context of history.

The Historical Life of Jesus and Revelation

In the Christian representation of Jesus, accordingly, two elements, an historical and a supra-historical, blend and intermingle. On the one hand, there is a recitative of events affirmed to have happened on the plane of human and terrestrial existence. On the other hand, a claim of absolute significance is made for these events.

1. An historical claim is asserted and is vital to Christianity. The groundwork of the Gospel is, and continues to be, a human story. It was in a life of earthly humiliation and conflict, the life of a *viator*, that the Messianic destiny of Jesus was disclosed. Hence from the beginning the historical features of that life, if they were remembered at all, would continue to accompany and condition all authentic Christian conceptions of Messianic glory and power, righteousness and wisdom, victory and sovereignty. And that they were remembered, and did so condition the Christian conceptions is proved by the character of the Christian tradition itself.

The Christian tradition of *Jesus* as Messiah and Son of Man has in fact nothing except these titles in common with the Jewish national and apocalyptic visions of the coming Deliverer, nor is its debt any greater to any of the myths of a world-Soter which were current in that age. On the contrary, the content of the tradition evolves essentially from what is presented as a record of the personal experience and fortunes of Jesus, and what from its character as a whole can fairly claim to be such a record. The image of the heavenly Christ has indeed at times superimposed itself on the earthly lineaments of Jesus. The Christian society looked at Jesus in the light of his exaltation, doing herein what St. Paul enjoins when he says in II Cor. v. 16 : " though we have known Christ after the flesh, now we no longer know him so." But what this primarily means is that certain human facts have now become the measure of heavenly glory and Lordship. The historical and human life of Jesus remains the subject of the gospel ; the Messianic titles are the predicate.

> " The life was manifested, and we have seen . . . and declare unto you the eternal life which was with the Father, and was manifested unto us " (I Jn. i. 2).

Through Jesus, as he lived on earth, the hope of the ages had made itself known. The Kingdom of God, hitherto only a vision or dream, a transcendent object of hope or aspiration, had come into immediate and verifiable relation to history. The advent and claim of the End had been registered. Hence around Jesus, and in such a manner as to become permanently associated with his personality, gather the hopes, anticipations, and promises of the Old Testament religion, while upon him are concentrated also all future imaginations of divine purpose, glory, and power. Jesus becomes the presentation-point, so to speak, of the divine working in history, the focus through which all lines of the divine plan connecting the past and the future are drawn. But in all this he remains Jesus, and through its relation to the character and spirit of Jesus the nature of the Christian religion as a personal and spiritual force is decided.

2. An absolute significance is attached to the history. Because the subject of the representation is *the Messiah, the Son of Man,* the revelational significance of the life, word, and spirit of Jesus becomes indefinitely and even infinitely extensible, co-terminous as it now is with the whole saving purpose of God.

Certainly, it is an absolute claim which is made for the Man of Nazareth when we think of his Messiahship in terms of the transcendent Son of Man with whom Jesus is identified. Nor was Christianity slow to develop the potentialities of the predicates here annexed to him. Yet when we consider the actual terms in which the tradition presents the Jesus for whom the claim is made, we see the organic relation in which the absolute of Christianity stands to our human experience of duty and suffering, life and death. Moreover, it is of the essence of our moral experience that it, above all the determinations of our nature, demands an absolute for the full understanding of itself and for the proper regulation of its activity. What the nature of the ethical absolute of Jesus is we shall have to consider later when we come to Chapters V and VIII. Enough meantime that, as an ethic of love, the absolute of Jesus stands nearer to our necessities than any which has ever been formulated in this world of relativities.

It is not the primary purpose of the following pages to investigate analytically what is ordinarily called the ' Messianic Consciousness ' of Jesus but rather to show how, within the area of the evangelical tradition and on the basis of its faith in Jesus as the Messiah, the early Church built up its distinctive conception of the Christian revelation of God, using for this purpose all that was remembered or reported concerning the acts, parables, and teaching of Jesus, his sayings about himself, and the story of his Passion.   We do not see through to the beginnings of the personal consciousness of Jesus.   We see it only in its historical setting, and here some preliminary observations bearing on the general character of the tradition will not be out of place.

(a) The fact that there is no attempt anywhere to withdraw the veil from the mystery of the inner consciousness of Jesus goes far to show that the tradition is not in its essence an ideological creation, the unfolding of a theory, but reflects the characteristics of an objective situation.

(b) The fact that Jesus was disclosed as the Messiah during his earthly course creates the presumption that most or all of the things which the community afterwards remembered of his life and teaching will have had for it the significance of Messianic phenomena.   If, therefore, at certain points, as we shall see, the tradition has missed or all but missed the full Messianic significance of this or that reported saying, parable, or action of Jesus, it will be legitimate to conclude that the community did not always rise to the full height and greatness of the mind of Jesus. We shall not, however, infer—though this is sometimes done— that there was not a real effort on the part of the community to preserve the memory of the history of Jesus.   The facts show in such cases that the community remembered better than it understood.

(c) On the whole, the tendency was to preserve and incorporate only such acts and sayings of Jesus as the community definitely presented to itself as Messianic or Christological.   We should accordingly be on our guard against thinking it possible to isolate within the tradition any substantial core of material which as ' historical ' or non-Messianic can be played off against a ' dogmatic ' element in the rest of the tradition.

JESUS AND THE LAST THINGS

We revert to the confession " Jesus is the Messiah."   It raises important questions of a general nature which have now to be considered.

The first concerns the precise nature of the relation in which Jesus as personal subject stands to the particular Messianic predicates employed by the tradition.   The school of critical thought represented by Dr. Albert Schweitzer in his book, *The*

Quest of the Historical Jesus, which exercised so dominating an influence on New Testament theology at the beginning of the present century, argued in the name of history that the key to the life and to the Messianic consciousness of Jesus is to be found in the complete initial surrender of his mind to the contemporary apocalyptic conceptions of the Kingdom of God and the coming of the Son of Man, ideas which he took over from Jewish or semi-Jewish sources. This interpretation was opposed to the ' liberal ' idea that the Messianic language of Jesus came only as a final and indeed contingent stamp upon a sense of religious vocation which was essentially independent of such forms. It is not possible here to reproduce even in outline the arguments advanced on the two sides of the controversy. The school of Schweitzer has not had it all its own way in claiming the entire Synoptic tradition for the support of its hypothesis, and it has, as it seems to me, thrown too heavy an emphasis on the external and traditional character of the motives determining the mind of Jesus. There are aspects of the tradition which suggest a deeper ground and source for the message of Jesus than any absorption in thoughts of the world's end. Among these may be mentioned such facts as the following :

1. The marked reserve of Jesus in speaking of the glory of the coming Kingdom and of his own person in relation to the Son of Man.

2. His consistent emphasis on the ethical and inward conditions governing man's acceptance with God and his entrance into the life of salvation.

3. The clear recognition by Jesus that the coming of the Kingdom of God depended not on any cosmological calendar or programme of events, but on the immediate will and Fatherly goodness of God ; and, in conjunction with this, his deep and fundamental sense of filial dependence upon God.

4. The circumstance that in the tradition—to judge both from Mark and the Q source—the Messianic claim of Jesus becomes explicit only at a relatively advanced stage in his ministry. Jesus does not start from a position of open self-identification with the Son of Man, but comes to it only with the unfolding of his sense of mission and destiny.

It is not claimed on the strength of any or all of these facts that the message of Jesus was not concerned with the last things, but only that this concern had not an external inspiration. The proclamation by Jesus of the nearness of the End rests on and reflects a prior and more fundamental inward certitude, and for this reason *it is possible that what we call the Messianic consciousness of Jesus registers not the starting-point but rather the climax of his self-expression, the moment of highest tension in the unfolding of his sense of destiny.* If so, the order of things in the mind of Jesus will have corresponded to the structure of thought which comes to light in the prophetic religion of the Old Testament. This is a point of peculiar interest and importance.

In the prophetic religion of Israel, so finely analysed by Dr. Walther Eichrodt,[1] it is an intense awareness of God in His exaltedness and holiness which in the end throws up the apocalyptic vision of the future, the ' eschatological ' conception of the Kingdom of God. The reality of God has laid hold of the prophets, producing a radical revolution in their lives (cf. Isa. vi), and as it has laid hold of themselves, so they see it existentially confronting the nation of Israel and the world, throwing the entire existing life of man under the shadow of sin and affixing to all human works and institutions the question-mark of the last judgement of God. Only as men turn round to face the challenge of the God who draws near to judge the world and to establish His *malkuth* or sovereignty over all mankind is true knowledge of God attained, human personality rightly awakened, ethic raised to its spiritual norm, and the divine purpose in history brought to manifestation and accomplishment. In this manner all righteousness or ' justification ' is denied to, and withdrawn from the present order and existence of things in the world, and is transferred to a world to come, a new age in which the righteous will of God will be the only source and perfect norm of life.

As the vision of this future world, which is the Kingdom of God, takes final form in late Jewish apocalyptic literature, it is seen that foreign ideas from Iranian, Babylonian, and Egyptian sources have contributed to the picture and assisted its development. Iranian influence in particular has helped Israel to frame the vision cosmically, and has imparted structural outlines and some touches of colour to it. But the spirit which dominates the vision as a whole and inspires prophets and righteous men to look to the supernatural intervention of God for the hope of blessedness, the resolution of life's problems, the ending of sin and death, and the final explication of history, is Israel's own spirit nourished by an intense realization of the character of God. As Eichrodt says : " He who knows God knows also God's future."

---

[1] *Die Theologie des Alten Testaments*, Bd. I (1933), pp. 182-209.

If this was the order of things in the religious development of Israel, would it be strange if the mind of Jesus should pass by similar stages to its goal ? In that case we can conceive that an awareness of God deeper than that which possessed the prophets inspired in Jesus a more than prophetic vision of the nearness of the Kingdom, and simultaneously brought to birth a sense of personal vocation which as it developed defined itself in terms of that which prophets and righteous men had indeed desired to see, but had not seen.

CHRISTOLOGY AND COMPARATIVE RELIGION

A second question concerns the relation of the Christian Messiology to the facts adduced by Comparative Religion. Great advances in our knowledge of Oriental and Hellenistic religions and cults in recent years have shown that at many points the ideas of the Old Testament, of late Judaism, and of early Christianity march with ideas indigenous to these ethnic faiths, and theories involving a relation of dependence on one side or the other have been put forward for the explanation of the coincidences. Thus (1) it is contended, and on good grounds, that the early Hebrew prophetic descriptions of the reign of the future king of righteousness have borrowed certain of their idealized features, such as the peace of nature, the marvellous fertility of the earth, and the end of wars from ancient ethnic myths of an age or king of Paradise. Even so careful a theologian as Eichrodt considers that Gressmann and other scholars have here proved their point.[1] (2) It is universally agreed that Israel's apocalyptic outlook in the Persian and late Jewish periods shows an increasing influence of Zoroastrian religious ideas both on its form and content, as for example in its conception of present and future world-æons, its dualism, its angelology and demonology, and its belief in a resurrection of the dead. (3) It is believed by some scholars, as we have already seen, that certain speculative or mystical developments of Zoroastrian religion, embodying one form or another of a Heavenly Man redemption-myth, have contributed to the late Jewish and early Christian apocalyptic conception of the ' Son of Man.'[2] Rudolf Otto and others think that they see in Galilean circles in the time of Jesus a

---

[1] H. Gressmann, *Der Ursprung der Israelitisch-Jüdischen Eschatologie* (1905) ; *Der Messias* (1929).

[2] See Appendix D and the literature there quoted.

vigorous working of such non-Jewish ideas. These had penetrated into the Enoch-literature, and through the Enoch-literature
Otto thinks that they influenced the religious thought of Jesus.[1]

But while the Messianic hope of Israel may thus have thrown
out its roots to many waters, the significance of the borrowed
ideas lies not in their pre-history or antecedents but in Israel's
understanding of them and in the use to which it has put them in
the service of its religion. For example, in the delineations of
the Messiah's reign which we find in the prophets and in the
Psalms the paradise-features are visibly subordinated to the
ethical ideals of judgement and righteousness to which they form,
in the main, only a coloured border. Israel includes these
features in the picture not because it believes in paradise but
because it believes in God and in a supernatural destiny for God's
people. As for the influences at work on Israel's doctrine of the
last things during and after the Exile, the really significant thing
here is not so much that ideas have been taken over from Persian
sources as that contact with Persian thought has enabled Israel's
religion to come to its own and to paint on a vaster canvas its
own distinctive doctrine of the transcendent righteousness of God.
In the atmosphere of Iranian-Babylonian thought Israel's religion
flames up to its full world-significance as Christianity does later
when it comes into contact with Hellenism. Finally, the theories
turning upon a ' Son of Man ' redeemer-myth are too nebulous
and too precarious for much to be built upon them. Despite the
advocacy of notable scholars, I see no real proof that the Heavenly
Man idea acquired a final redemptive significance anywhere
until it did so in apocalyptic Judaism and in Christianity, and
there it is profoundly modified by being united to the pre-existing
conception of Israel's Messiah.

In the same way, when we come to Christianity, the question
which we have to ask is not whether ideas of ethnic origin have
entered into its Christology or cosmology, but to what use it has
turned them. It has been a disservice to true history when from
a basis in the modern study of religions it has been proposed to
' restore ' or touch up the traditional picture of early Christianity
by reading into its ideas the meaning which these ideas bore in
other contexts and in mythology. The only validity and value
which ideas such as the Son of Man have for us as Christians is
the validity which they have when they are predicated of Jesus,
above all when they are predicated of him as crucified. His life,

[1] R. Otto, *The Kingdom of God and the Son of Man*.

his spirit, his self-disclosure, and, above all, his death have profoundly changed all Messianic ideas, producing a new sense of glory and of God. *He* is the subject of the New Testament religion, so that no line of thought connecting ancient Messianic imaginations with our thought or with our exegesis of the gospel is valid if it does not come to us by way of him and of his cross. To ignore this by stepping back to older thresholds of thought or understanding is to reverse the process of history. It is by reference to the mind and outlook of Jesus, and not by reference to ancient history, that we must primarily orient our course when we seek the meaning of the cardinal Christian conceptions, Kingdom of God, Son of God, and Son of Man.

Chapter II

FORM–CRITICISM AND THE GOSPELS

WE see Jesus only through the medium of a tradition which circulated orally in the Christian community before it was collected
and set down in writing. The earliest of written sources, which
was a compilation of the words of Jesus with a minimum of
narrative framework to which scholars give the name Q, may be
assumed to have taken shape by or before the close of the first
Christian generation, and its substance is preserved for us in
certain didactic sections common to our Gospels of Matthew and
Luke. The final redaction of the tradition began towards the
year A.D. 70 with the Gospel which bears traditionally the name
of St. Mark, and was continued during the next two decades in
the two other Synoptic Gospels, which also have traditional
names of the first generation affixed to them, viz. the Gospels of
Matthew and Luke.

THE EARLY ORAL TRADITION IN THE CHRISTIAN COMMUNITY

What was the character of the early oral tradition? To what
extent did it embody, to what extent has it refracted the historical
lineaments of Jesus of Nazareth? We assume, to begin with,
that such a tradition existed, that certain sayings of Jesus and
certain stories reporting acts or incidents in his life were current
in the Church from the earliest days, together with some summary
of the Passion history. This, indeed, cannot be taken absolutely
for granted, since the modern school of Form-Criticism makes a
point of denying it, though on grounds which seem to the present
writer neither adequate nor in accordance with probability.
According to Form-Criticism the tradition incorporated in our
Gospels is, for the most part, a late product, and a product of
the Church's mind at that, which came into existence at a time
when an objective record of the history of Jesus was no longer
possible. Its contents represent a distillation from the life of the
Church, from its preaching, its debates with Jewish opponents,
its ethic, its catechetical activities, its theology, and its cultus.
Its Messianic categories are an attempt, necessarily inadequate,
to state in terms comprehensible to itself the essential mystery of

the personality of Jesus, and are not to be ascribed to him. For the moment, however, we assume that something like an objective tradition of words and acts of Jesus was in existence from the first days, and ask what would be the fortunes of such a tradition at a time when, not yet committed to a fixed form in writing, its contents formed part of the instruction given by apostles and other missionaries in an age of expanding activity and of intense spiritual and intellectual awakening. Obviously the answer to the question how far the tradition has preserved, how far it has refracted the image of Jesus of Nazareth will depend to some extent on the laws governing the transmission of the material in the practical service of the community during this period.

Here, as stabilizing factors making for the preservation of the objective character of whatever real tradition existed, we shall recognize, on the one hand, the reverence which the first community would feel for the words and institutions of Jesus or what were reported to it as such, and, on the other hand, the remarkable tenacity of the Oriental memory. To these two principles may be added the presence in the community of eyewitnesses and others who claimed to speak from personal knowledge of the words and deeds of Jesus. All these factors would make for a maximum of accuracy and fidelity wherever it was a question of simply transmitting things which had been ' received.' Over against these factors, however, we shall have to allow for the undoubted operation of other factors connected not with the simple transmission of the material but with its application and adaptation for practical and missionary purposes. Was it possible for the terms of the tradition to remain unaffected when we consider such facts as the following :

(a) that the community had in its hands the Old Testament which bore striking testimony in advance to the Lord's Messiah from the cradle (cf. Isa. vii. 14) to the grave (cf. Isa. liii. 7-9) ;

(b) that there were prophets in the Church claiming to speak by inspiration of Jesus, and leaving their words in the memory of the hearers ;

(c) that there were controversial purposes to which the debate with Jews or with the followers of John the Baptist or with the civil authorities compelled the teaching and the acts of Jesus to be daily put ;

(d) that there were practical situations to which preachers had continually to apply the commandments or example of Jesus, thus giving their texts an ever-changing point ;

(e) that there were events which as seeming to fulfil predictions of Jesus could not but react on the traditional form of
these predictions ?

Nevertheless, it would be unwise to base an estimate of the
possibilities of the situation purely on general or preconceived
grounds, though Form-Criticism itself is not without sin in this
matter. Form-Criticism has its own preconceived idea of a
' constructive ' principle governing the formation of the tradition.
That is to say, Form-Criticism assumes the existence in the early
Christian community-life of typical situations or activities which
constituted the matrix of the ' form ' of the various elements in
the tradition.[1] It would seem better, however, at this stage to
discard all assumptions of an *à priori* kind, and to concentrate
attention on the nearest-lying objective evidence for the growth
of the tradition, in this case the evidence—indirect in a sense—
of the developmental processes which come to light in the literary
redaction of the Gospels.

LITERARY CRITICISM AND THE ORAL TRADITION

The general position taken by Synoptic scholarship in this
country at the present time may be regarded as that of the late
Canon B. H. Streeter and his followers. The particular development by this school of the ' Proto-Luke ' hypothesis has not
everywhere commanded assent. But there is a general agreement to accept the positions, which Streeter also accepts, that
the Gospel according to Mark in its existing form is the foundation-
document of the Synoptic narrative of Jesus, and that Matthew
and Luke, where they run parallel to Mark, represent revisions
of that document. It is true that a somewhat different line of
approach is advocated by the Continental scholar, Dr. Wilhelm
Bussmann, who sees in Mark not the starting-point but the end
of the redaction-process within the Synoptic literature.[2] According to Bussmann the basic narrative document was a source
which he calls G and which he considers to be best preserved in
those sections of St. Luke which we ordinarily assume to have
been drawn from Mark. G was shorter than Mark, lacking, for
example, the section Mk. vi 46–viii. 26 ; thus Bussmann is able
to explain less artificially than Streeter why Luke has no parallel
to that section of Mark in his Gospel. The original G, however,

---

[1] See M. Dibelius, *From Tradition to Gospel* (1934).
[2] *Synoptische Studien*, Bd. I-III (1925-1931).

which Luke used, had already undergone in a different quarter a revision and amplification which included the matter now found in Mk. vi. 46–viii. 26. This revision Bussmann calls B, and the composite document G + B he considers to have been the narrative on which the Gospels of Matthew and Mark were based. While, however, this theory deserves more attention than it has yet received, it is extremely doubtful whether the placing of Mark at the end of the redactional process will ever be made to seem other than fanciful. On grounds of style Mark would seem to stand altogether nearer to the original source, whatever it was, than the parallel material of Matthew and Luke, and therefore we can still regard the latter two Gospels as representing essentially a later form of the material embodied in Mark.

This being so, is it not possible to regard the modifications which the Mark-material has undergone at the hands of the redactors Matthew and Luke as giving us a key to the kind of development through which the tradition of the acts and words of Jesus passed in the earlier oral period, as giving us in fact a measured base-line from which to calculate the whole trend of tradition-history? If, for example, we find in the later Gospels as compared with Mark a tendency to omit the more human features in the representation of Jesus ; to heighten the miraculous colouring of some of the incidents ; to give to events seen as the fulfilment of Old Testament prophecies a form more exactly assimilated to these prophecies ; to impart to predictions of Jesus regarding the future a preciser expression in accordance with the events in which they were fulfilled ; to lose sight here and there of the original context or meaning of words or actions ; to add to the earlier matter later traditions of an obviously secondary order ; shall we not conclude generally that the same tendencies and the same processes were at work when the tradition was still plastic and circulating on the lips of men?

The answer is that this argument, though valid within measurable limits, is not really applicable over the whole stretch of tradition-history. Certain objections at once suggest themselves.

1. Because there is more miracle in Matthew and Luke than there is in Mark, are we therefore to conclude that there was a stage in the tradition preceding Mark when there was no miracle at all? Because there is much teaching of Jesus in Matthew and Luke and little in Mark, are we to conclude that at a still earlier period the didactic element was entirely absent? It is obvious

that at such points the calculus in question, when applied to the pre-literary tradition, leads to absurdities.

2. Were the changes produced in the pre-literary period greater or less than those in the literary? In favour of the first hypothesis it may be pled that writing imposes a check on free development which is not present where transmission is oral. But is this altogether true, or is it the whole measure of the truth? It is not an unfamiliar experience for forms of words carried in the memory to become suddenly vague and uncertain when the pen is taken in hand. Writing introduces its own changes not only into the form but into the substance of tradition.

3. The development in the tradition from Mark to Matthew and Luke is not by any means a one-direction process. If at points the movement is away from origins, at other points, as we shall see, it is a movement in the reverse direction. The tendency was not everywhere uniform.

The Theoretical Presuppositions of Form–Criticism

The above considerations may help to explain why Form-Criticism, interested in tradition as a vital phenomenon, insists that its peculiar problem is not to be solved within the limits of the literary analysis of the Gospels, but demands to be taken up in other regions of investigation. The evangelical tradition, it is claimed, cannot be truly understood if regard is not had to principles applying to the growth and development of popular tradition in other fields than those of early Christianity. The laws governing the nature of popular tradition generally have to be examined, and its stylistic 'forms' diagnosed and scrutinized. When this is done, it is seen that we are delivered from the bookish problems of the literary critics and from the kind of dilemmas to which, as I have indicated above, their method is ultimately exposed. All popular or communal tradition, it will be found, is essentially a function of the social life and mentality of a community, and its 'forms' are the product and reflection of the situation, the various interests, and the needs of that community. Upon this understanding of the matter, it is to the history of the primitive Church and not to any anterior stratum or body of fact that a real analysis of the Synoptic material takes us back. Gunkel and other scholars having shown that the results won from the study of folk-literature over wide areas can be successfully applied to the investigation of Genesis and other early Old Testament narratives, Form-Criticism sees no reason why the same results should not be accepted as valid in relation to the early Christian evangelical tradition as well.

We postpone for the moment the consideration of the wider bearings of this method of approach to the Synoptic literature. As the Form-Critics conceive the matter, the task of scholarship is (1) to distinguish the various elements in our Gospels which have come from the oral tradition—sayings, parables, miracle-stories, narratives, legends, etc.—and to separate them from the redactional framework in which they are encased, (2) to examine these elements in the light of the knowledge gained elsewhere of the ' forms ' of popular literature, and so to reduce them to their first or tradition shape, (3) to take them back to an origin in the ' living situation ' to which they severally relate, it being an axiom of this school that " the literature in which the life of a community . . . is precipitated springs from definite expressions and needs of the life of this community, producing a definite style." [1] Popular use and repetition, it is argued, impart to what is transmitted from mouth to mouth a regular and recurrent stamp : brevity and pointedness to anecdotal narratives, rhythm and roundedness to didactic utterances and aphorisms, dramatic unity and movement to parables, fulness of detail to stories of the marvellous. Therefore, as the traditional matter of the Gospels shares these characteristics with other kinds of popular literature, it is considered to share with them also a communal origin.

When the analysis is complete, it will be found—so Dr. Bultmann reasons—that the situations from which the original elements of the evangelical tradition emerge and with the character of which they are stamped are situations not in the life of Jesus but in the faith, the evangelistic activities, the worship, and the history of the primitive Christian society. The narrative texture in which the pronouncements of Jesus have come down to us has been largely created by the community out of its own fortunes, circumstances, and relationships, and even the words of Jesus have their source for the most part not in Jesus but in the thought or wisdom of the community. In many cases it is the Christ of faith who speaks, the Risen Lord, not the Jesus who was on earth. Dr. Bultmann would not deny that a certain element of the historical remains within the tradition of the words of Jesus. [2] He regards as authentic those which express a high

[1] Bultmann, *Geschichte der Synoptischen Tradition*, p. 4.   [2] *Ibid.*, p. 110.

degree of concentration on the last things, or which are inspired
by a peculiar energy in their call to repentance, or which demand
newness of spirit. But the Church, argues Bultmann, did not
live by history. It did not preserve any real history. It was not
capable of expressing the mystery of Jesus except in categories of
its own. What it has thrown around Jesus under the guise of
history is really a precipitate of its own experience rather than of
his. And here we come to the real challenge of this critical
method. As Erich Fascher and E. F. Scott have rightly pointed
out, the question is in the end that of the historical validity of
the Gospel record and of the origins of Christianity itself, and
this question it is impossible to ignore.

Hence, while acknowledging that the school of Form-Criticism
has rendered useful technical service by its critical analysis of the
evangelical tradition, we have seriously to interrogate its fundamental assumption that the popular form of the constituent
elements of the tradition provides a clue to the origin and nature
of the substance. It is difficult to see how this can possibly be
established. We can grant, for example, that the popular
addiction to miracle-narratives explains the free development
within the evangelical tradition of elements which have little
relation to the religious purpose and interests of Jesus. But the
point here, as Fascher has rightly observed, is that it is not the
form of the miracle-narratives in the Gospels, the conformity of
their style to that of contemporary Hellenistic tales of the marvellous, that gives rise to the problem of their historicity, but the
substance.[1] So again, while the sayings of Jesus and the reports
of debates in which he was engaged with his Jewish opponents
are relatively free from the imaginative expansions which characterize the miracles, it is not the simplicity or reserve of their
form which wins credence for these sayings or debates, but the
content.

For these reasons, it will not do to think of Form alone as
deciding either for or against the historicity of the subject-matter
of the tradition. Particular form is bound up with particular
substance in the reproduction of the matter of tradition, but it
yields no conclusions as to the truth or origin of that substance.
As Dr. E. F. Scott has pointed out,[2] many sayings of Jesus which
have come down to us in an elevated rhythmic style may have
acquired that form through their use in the worship of the com-

[1] E. Fascher, *Die Form-geschichtliche Methode*, pp. 212-234.
[2] *The Validity of the Gospel Record*, p. 80.

munity where they were conjoined with the reading of Holy
Scripture, but the spirit of worship which has imparted to them
their liturgical and almost incantational form did not necessarily
create their substance.   And the same will hold true of narratives : only, as Fascher notices, in the case of narrative the form
is not rooted in the substance to the same extent as it is in the
case of the sayings of Jesus.   " What Jesus said admitted of being
more easily handed on than what had to be reported concerning
him," [1] and therefore in the formation of the narrative element
the imagination of the community would necessarily be more
drawn upon than in the formation of the discourses.

The question of the historicity of the contents of the tradition
is not, therefore, decided by their form.   So far as it can be
determined it will be upon other grounds.   Here it will be
enough to offer certain criticisms upon the main general presuppositions of the Form-Critical method as a whole.

1. It is an exceedingly dubious analogy which is chosen when
the rise and development of the early Christian tradition is
explained in terms of processes which have worked in the folk-
literature of primitive peoples or in early Hebrew saga.   The
period which divides Jesus from the composition of Mark is little
more than a generation.   In two generations from Jesus the
literary fixation of the tradition in our Gospels was complete.   In
the first generation there were many persons in the Christian
community who had seen and heard the Lord.   What is of even
greater importance at this point is that the level of intelligence in
the original Christian groups and circles must have been relatively
high.   It rested upon Jewish standards of education, and the
conservative mentality of the Beth-ha-Midrash may be considered to offer a closer analogy to that of the Church than the
naive creativeness of a primitive story-telling society.   The
element of wonder or miracle may be strongly developed in the
tradition, but there is no reason for thinking that it was not
rooted in it from the start.

2. It is quite impossible with Form-Criticism to rule out the
influence over the community of commanding personalities,
apostles and others, who had a share in its life.   Communities do
not create, especially where there are leaders upon whom it is
instinctive for them to lean.   In this connection consideration
must be given to the quite extraordinary prestige which the Gospel
of Mark acquired in the Church in the generation in which it

[1] Fascher, p. 222.

appeared. If every centre of Christianity was the seat of a vigorous local communal tradition, how is it that the writer of the Gospel of Matthew, whom there is excellent reason for connecting with Antioch,[1] found nothing better to do than to take over the narrative of Mark *in toto*, adding from local sources only a few narrative traditions of an intrinsically secondary order ? If Antioch had had a rich communal tradition of its own, we should have expected Matthew to be more independent of Mark than it is. How is it, again, that Luke, who had Palestinian, Cæsarean, and Antiochian fields to glean, thought it worth his while to make copious use of the same Mark ? While the Papias-tradition regarding Mark should not be unduly stressed, it remains that the wide acceptance of the Markan document would be more easily explained if, as a whole or in part, it had behind it, as Papias learned that it had, the peculiar authority of the teaching of Peter. Form-Criticism in the interests of its general theory disparages the part played by personal influence in the shaping of the evangelical tradition, but the Petrine hypothesis with regard to the Markan Gospel as stated by so careful a scholar as Johannes Weiss has by no means been discredited.[2]

3. The theory of the Form-Critics represents that the Gospel story, as we have it, springs not so much from a fount of reliable historical reminiscence as from a " myth which the Church had woven, out of a few uncertain traditions, around the life of its Founder." [3] This theory not only leaves us without any adequate explanation of the Church's own existence, but comes into serious conflict with many features of the tradition. If the tradition had unfolded itself smoothly out of the mind or theology of the Church, how do we explain the presence in it of enigmatic words such as the saying in Mt. xi. 12 about the Kingdom of heaven suffering violence, which the Church probably did not understand, or of obscure parables such as that of the Sower, to which it had apparently lost the key, or of utterances like Mk. x. 18, which by seeming to limit the perfect goodness of Jesus must have been offensive to its Christology, or of ethical principles like " Resist not evil " and " Love your enemies," which certainly were not any mere overflow of the Church's moral life ? To these features may be added the frank revelations which the tradition offers on such points as the denial of Christ by Peter or the rebukes administered by Jesus to self-seeking and worldly apostles.

[1] Streeter, *The Four Gospels*, pp. 500 ff.
[2] J. Weiss, *Das älteste Evangelium* (1903).   [3] E. F. Scott, *Validity*, p. 1.

Such things do not look like inventions of the Church in the interest of warning its members against infidelity, but suggest the presence to the Church's mind of a tradition which was not of its own making but which was objectively given to it.   As Origen expressed it, speaking of the evangelists : " If they had not been lovers of truth, but as Celsus opines, compilers of fictions, they would not have recorded that Peter denied or that the disciples were offended at Jesus." [1]

Has the Tradition Lost Contact with History? An Examination of Mark xi. 20-23 and Matthew v. 39-40

The disconnection of the tradition from historical events in place and time is not so absolute as Form-Criticism in some of its expressions would seem to assume.   By way of illustration I shall take two Synoptic passages.   First, in Mk. xi. 20 ff. we read that as Jesus and his disciples were on the road from Bethany to Jerusalem during the last week of Jesus' life, the disciples called their Master's attention to the withered fig-tree by the wayside, and Jesus said :

> " Have faith in God.   Amen I say to you, Whoever shall say to this mountain, Be thou taken up and cast into the sea, and shall not doubt in his heart, but shall believe that what he says comes to pass, he shall have it."

At first sight the transition from the fig-tree in the context to the ' mountain ' in the logion seems abrupt and unnatural.   But as the scene in Mark is laid in the vicinity of the Mount of Olives, there is propriety enough in the allusion to ' this mountain.'   It happens, however, that a doublet of the saying was contained in Q, and has come down to us in Mt. xvii. 20b and Lk. xvii. 6 in different contexts from Mark's.   In Q the word was quite situation-less.   It runs :

> " If you have faith as a grain of mustard-seed, you will say to this mountain (Lk. ' you would say to this sycamine tree '), Remove hence to yonder place (Lk. ' Be rooted up and planted in the sea ') and it shall remove (Lk. ' and it would have obeyed you ')."

Harnack thinks that the Q version, which he finds better represented in Matthew's than in Luke's reproduction, is preferable to Mark's,[2] and Bultmann argues that an independent logion of

[1] Contra Celsum II, 15.   [2] Sayings of Jesus, p. 225.

Jesus has become attached in Mark to the miracle-story of the fig-tree.[1] But there is a point which neither Harnack nor Bultmann has sufficiently noticed or stopped to consider. In Zechariah xiv. 4 it is prophesied that on the Day of the Lord, when Yahweh will fight against the enemies of Jerusalem :

> " His feet shall stand . . . upon the Mount of Olives, which is before Jerusalem on the east, and the Mount of Olives shall cleave in the midst thereof toward the east and toward the west, etc."

This supplies a striking background for the saying in Mark, and gives rise at once to the question whether the original logion of Jesus was not actually uttered on or near the Mount of Olives and with precise reference to it as Mark suggests. In that case a word of Jesus which, as we see by its Q form, had become situation-less and generalized has been reinstated by Mark in its proper historical context. As we can hardly explain this result as accidental, we must either suppose (a) that the tradition known to Mark preserved traces of the original historical context of the word, or (b) that Mark, noticing the pregnant prophetic allusion in the word, connected it with the Mount of Olives on the strength of the Zechariah-prophecy. As, however, there is no explicit allusion either in Mark or in his follower Matthew to the Zechariah-passage, the former alternative seems the better. *Jesus* had the Old Testament passage in mind, and the tradition followed by Mark was here true to history.

If the above reasoning is valid, it would appear (1) that *history in unseen ways controlled the Church's tradition to a greater extent than is commonly recognized*, and (2) that *the development of the tradition was not uniformly away from history, but sometimes led back to historical starting-points.*

The second instance which I take is of a somewhat different type, but it too illustrates the possible preservation or, as the case may be, the restoration of the historical character of a tradition. The problem which is raised in this case has not, so far as I know, been noticed or discussed by any critic or commentator. I refer to the Q passage containing the word of Jesus about not resisting evil.

[1] *Geschichte*, p. 24.

Mt. v. 39-40	Lk. vi. 29
" Resist not him that is evil ; but whosoever smiteth thee on thy right cheek, turn to him the other also. And if any man would go to law with thee and take away thy coat, let him have thy cloak also."	" To him that striketh thee on the one cheek, offer also the other ; and from him that taketh away thy cloak, withhold not thou thy coat also."

Harnack, comparing these parallels with a view to recovering the original text of Q, thinks there can be no question that Matthew has best preserved the language of the source.[1] He points out, that Luke has discarded three Greek expressions—ῥαπίζει, στρέψον, and κριθῆναι—in favour of smoother words. It is important to note these omissions for the sake of their bearing on what now follows. Let us now look again at the Matthew-passage in Greek, placing side by side with it this time a passage from the Septuagint text of Isaiah.

Mt. v. 39-40	Isa. l. 6, 8 (LXX)
ἐγὼ δὲ λέγω ὑμῖν μὴ ἀντιστῆναι τῷ πονηρῷ· ἀλλ' ὅστις σε ῥαπίζει εἰς τήν δεξιὰν σιαγόνα, στρέψον αὐτῷ καὶ τὴν ἄλλην· καὶ τῷ θέλοντί σοι κριθῆναι καὶ τὸν χιτῶνά σου λαβεῖν, ἄφες αὐτῷ καὶ τὸ ἱμάτιον.	τὸν νῶτόν μου δέδωκα εἰς μάστιγας, τὰς δὲ σιαγόνας μου εἰς ῥαπίσματα, τὸ δὲ πρόσωπόν μου οὐκ ἀπέστρεψα . . . ὅτι ἐγγίζει ὁ δικαιώσάς με· τίς ὁ κρινόμενός μοι; ἀντιστήτω μοι ἅμα.

The Isaiah verses are from one of the ' Servant of the Lord ' passages, and the Servant is the speaker. It will be noticed that no less than five distinctive Greek words—the five which are underlined in the texts—are shared by the Matthew version of the commandment of Jesus with the LXX text of the Servant's declaration. How are we to explain this remarkable linguistic coincidence ? We assume, to begin with, that the foundation of the Q logion was a genuine word of Jesus, as even Bultmann admits, and that it was uttered in Aramaic. We have next to ask ourselves whether or not the requirement of non-resistance in its original form was consciously worded by Jesus with allusion to the example of the redeeming Servant of Yahweh in Isaiah. If it was, we may then explain the coincidences in expression between the Greek version of our Lord's word in Matthew and the LXX text of Isaiah in one or other of two ways. We may

[1] *The Sayings of Jesus*, pp. 59 f.

assume (*a*) that the Greek translators of Q observed the allusion
to the Isaianic Servant in the saying of Jesus and reproduced it
in a form reminiscent of the language of the LXX.   In this case
the Q form of the saying is conserved in Matthew and lost to a
large extent in Luke.   Or we may assume (*b*) that the Greek
translators of Q did not pick up the allusion to the Servant, in
which case the Q form would be as in Luke.   In this case, however, we should have to suppose that Matthew noticed the
allusion which Q had missed, and restored the original character
of the word under Septuagintal influences.   *In the one case the
tradition preserves the original colouring of the saying throughout ; in the
other case it restores the colouring after it has been temporarily obscured.*
The remaining alternative that the original word of Jesus contained no allusion of any kind to the Servant, but that this was
read into it in the later course of the tradition is one which, while
not impossible, seems altogether less likely.   But the whole
problem is one of considerable difficulty.

We come back in the end to the position that we see Jesus
only through the tradition of his Church.   What the Johannine
writer says of the ' new commandment ' may be said of the whole
revelation of God in Christ : *which thing is true in him and in you*
(I Jn. ii. 8).   The faith of the Christian society penetrates and
suffuses the matter of the tradition : we see Jesus in the light of
the community's faith and love.   But this glow or aureole in
which the glory of the risen Lord blends to some extent with the
lineaments of the Jesus of history does not mean that the image
of Jesus as he was on earth is so refracted as no longer to appear
in its reality.   It does not mean that because Jesus is Lord we
have no credible glimpse of him as teacher, as healer, as man of
God wrestling with the demonic powers of evil and darkness, as
evangelist seeking the lost, as the friend of sinners and of little
children, as the terrible judge of injustice and hypocrisy.   The
picture which we have in the Gospels is not all, as Form-Criticism
in some quarters teaches, the needy improvisation of a Church
which had no real history to go upon.   Within the tradition the
" I—thou " relation of his word to us is maintained with unmistakable clearness.   The tradition may, as we have suggested,
be a function of the Church's faith and life, but this does not
mean that it has not taken up history into itself and preserved it.

CHAPTER III

THE 'SIGNS' OR 'MIGHTY WORKS' OF JESUS

EVIDENCE OF THE PRIMITIVE DISCOURSES IN ARTS

AT the most ancient level of Christian preaching which is known to us the proclamation of Jesus as Messiah was supported primarily by appeal to the 'signs' attending his ministry. Illustrative instances of this mode of presenting the message are found in the early discourse-material in the Acts of the Apostles, and in particular in two passages, Acts ii. 22 and x. 38, occurring in contexts in which by general consent the archaic colouring of primitive Christian sentiment still shines through like that of some mural fresco in a basilica. In the first of these passages Jesus of Nazareth is presented as

> " A man demonstrated from God to you by mighty works and wonders and signs (δυνάμεσι καὶ τέρασι καὶ σημείοις) which God did by him in your midst."

The second passage shows some confusion in syntax and arrangement, the result possibly of some early disturbance in the text of the source-document. In the most recent of commentaries on Acts [1] it is literally translated as follows :

> " You know the event which happened throughout all Judea, beginning from Galilee after the baptism which John preached, Jesus of Nazareth, how God anointed him with the Holy Spirit and power, who went about doing good, and healing all who were overpowered by the devil because God was with him."

Certain features in the language here used incline the present writer to conjecture that in the source the passage stood as follows : " how God, beginning from Galilee after the baptism which John preached, anointed Jesus of Nazareth, etc." This would explain the unrelated nominative ἀρξάμενος which still sticks in the text, and suggests that the boldness of this construction gave rise to awkward emendations which have left their mark on the present form of the passage. Be that as it may, the emphasis in both statements is on God and on acts of God attending Jesus and investing him outwardly and visibly with revelational significance.

[1] K. Lake and H. J. Cadbury, *The Beginnings of Christianity*, Vol. IV.

There is no reference in these summaries to any manifestation of God made through the doctrine of Jesus. Jesus the Messiah is accredited in this form of the kerygma not by appeal to the divine truth of his teaching or to the transcendent greatness and quality of his person, but externally and phenomenally by the halo of divine signs attending him and authenticating him to Israel as the Deliverer sent by God.

The genuinely ancient character of this type of teaching is attested by its simple correspondence with the Hebrew–Jewish conception of history and of divine revelation in history, according to which God makes Himself known, not through ideas as in the philosophy of Greece, but by mighty acts and by an outstretched arm. For Old Testament prophecy history is the real field of the self-manifestation of God, and His Word is the record of this manifestation. In the same manner primitive Christianity affirms that in the facts in which it had its origin the eternal God has put forth His power for the redemption of mankind. God was with Jesus. It was not Jesus in himself who wrought the mighty works, but God wrought them through him, and the high relief in which these mighty works stand out for Christian faith in the midst of a world in which all past history has been essentially a revelation of God has its ground in the fact that the *whole* purpose of God had not been disclosed in history previous to Jesus. A part, bringing with it the final resolution of the discords of history, had been reserved for a consummation at the end of time : which consummation the Christian society believes to be now announced and on the way to fulfilment in the coming and in the acts of Jesus the Messiah.[1] The prophets of Israel had looked forward to an age when sin and sorrow, confusion and darkness and futility would no longer intercept the vision of God or frustrate His will, but when God would take to Himself His great power and reign. It is the advent of this age, this Reign of God, which the primitive Christian mind regards as signified in the acts of Jesus. His works are ' signs,' they are a demonstration from God that what prophets and righteous men had desired to see is at hand and already in process.

St. Mark a Gospel of the Signs of Jesus

It should now be noted that it is essentially this type of teaching, turning largely upon signs, that dominates the Gospel according

---

[1] See C. H. Dodd, *History and the Gospel*, pp. 33-34.

to Mark, and the same type continues to show itself even in
St. Paul and the Fourth Gospel, though in the Pauline and
Johannine presentations other facets of the revelation of God in
Jesus have come more particularly to the front. If Mark represents Jesus as preaching that " the time is fulfilled, and the
kingdom of God has drawn near " (i. 15), it is because in Jesus
one has stepped on to the stage who, as the chosen of God, is
attended by the power of God, and whose acts are the manifestation of the day of salvation. And it is as witnessing to
this consummation that the message of Jesus is ' good news '
(εὐαγγέλιον), a word specially characteristic of St. Mark's Gospel.

The work of Jesus in Mark appears in fact as an epiphany of
divine Power, a ' mystery ' which is at first veiled to men and
still remains veiled to ' those outside ' (Mk. iv. 11-12), but which
is acknowledged in the supernatural sphere (i. 24, iii. 11, v. 7)
and becomes a revelation to the faithful on earth. This conception of sign or mystery or supernatural revelation covers not only
the acts of Jesus but also his words. Thus at the first mention
of his teaching Mark stresses as its fundamental characteristic
the fact that it was ' with authority ' (κατ' ἐξουσίαν) and that it
astonished the hearers. " They were amazed at his doctrine "
(ἐξεπλήσσοντο ἐπὶ τῇ διδαχῇ αὐτοῦ) is his phrase (i. 21), strange
language for one to use who was thinking of the pure reasonable-
ness or self-evidencing truth of the words of Jesus. But for Mark
the teaching of Jesus is essentially a sign, a Messianic phenomenon.
In the Hellenistic world for which his Gospel was composed the
possession of 'exousia' implied supernatural power based on superhuman wisdom or gnosis.[1] So Mark thinks of the words as well
as the acts of Jesus as signifying a manifestation of God in history.
We may compare Justin Martyr's famous dictum with regard to
the teaching of Jesus : " Short and concise were the words from
him ; for he was no sophist, but his word was power from God "
(Apol. I. 14.5).[2] Only, whereas Justin is stressing the spiritual
reality of the doctrine preached by Jesus over against the dialectical vanities of the philosophers, Mark is thinking of the pheno-
menal dynamic effects of the words pronounced by Jesus. The
Rabbis taught, and nothing happened. Jesus taught, and all
kinds of things happened. He declared sins forgiven, and they
were forgiven ; a paralysed man arose to his feet and walked

[1] R. Reitzenstein, *Poimandres*, p. 48, note 3.

[2] βραχεῖς δὲ καὶ σύντομοι παρ' αὐτοῦ λόγοι γεγόνασι · οὐ γὰρ σοφιστὴς
ὑπῆρχεν, ἀλλὰ δύναμις θεοῦ ὁ λόγος αὐτοῦ ἦν.

(ii. 5, 10-12).   He said that the Sabbath was made for man, and
it was so ; the Jewish Sabbath ceased for all who acknowledged
the power of God in Jesus, the predestined Son of Man (ii. 24,
27-28).   Thus words and acts of Jesus alike are for our earliest
evangelist Messianic phenomena, Messianic events.

No doubt a certain theoretical element enters into the representation through the manner in which Mark subordinates the
content of Jesus' gospel of the Kingdom to the idea of the
' mystery ' which is announced in it.   In iv. 11, for example, the
parables are declared intelligible only to those to whom this
mystery of the Kingdom has been already imparted.   But at
bottom this Markan theorizing rests on the double recognition
(1) that certain parables—those to which the tradition had
already given the special stamp of Similitudes of the Kingdom—
originally signified that in some manner the kingdom of God had
already become actual through the word and in the acts of Jesus ;
and (2) that this significance of the parables had been lost on
the mass of hearers through the deceptive lure of the story-form.
The parables had, in fact, come to be regarded merely as stories,
though originally they were ' signs.'   But while Mark stresses this
idea of a concealed meaning in the acts and in the teaching of
Jesus, it will not do to say with Dr. Bultmann that he has thereby
lost touch with the character of Jesus as a preacher of repentance
and salvation, and has transformed him into something more
nearly resembling the Greek idea of a thaumaturge or ' divine
man,' [1] nor again to account for this metamorphosis by saying
that the original image of Jesus was shaped essentially on the
lines of such Palestinian tradition as we find in Q, whereas in
Mark " Hellenism has made an essential contribution." [2]   This
is a quite untenable distinction.   It is quite plain that the Palestinian tradition had from the beginning definitely connected the
revelation of God in Jesus with the thought of the wonders
wrought by his hands (Acts x. 38), and nowhere is the conception
better attested than in Q itself.   We need only refer to the
answer given by Jesus to John's disciples in Mt. xi. 4-6, Lk. vii.
22-23, to his judgement on the impenitent cities of Galilee in
Mt. xi. 21-24, Lk. x. 13-15, and to his rejoinder to the demand for
a sign in Lk. xi. 29-32, Mt. xii. 38-39.   In every one of these
Q passages it is the mighty works done by Jesus (αἱ δυνάμεις

---

[1] On the θεῖος ἄνθρωπος of the Hellenistic world, see H. Windisch, *Paulus
and Christus* (1934), pp. 25-78.

[2] Bultmann, *Geschichte*, p. 256.

αἱ γενόμεναι ἐν ὑμῖν) that leave men without excuse for not acknowledging in Jesus a revelation of God transcending all earlier revelations. There is therefore no foundation for the assertion that Mark, in order to commend Jesus to the Greeks, has metamorphosed a teacher of righteousness into a wonder-worker, a soter-divinity like Asclepius. Such a charge quite overstates the distinction existing between the popular Palestinian mind and the Hellenistic mind in the age of Jesus and the evangelists.

PARADIGMS OR PRONOUNCEMENT–STORIES IN THE TRADITION

When we go behind Mark and Q and take the evidence of the simplest traditional units into which critical analysis has resolved the Synoptic material, we find this primitive stuff already dyed in the grain with revelational meaning and indeed to a far greater extent than the redactors sometimes have grasped. This becomes plain when we examine some of these very old and easily recognizable stories which scholars of the Form-Criticism school have variously styled ' paradigms ' or ' apothegmata,' but which Dr. Vincent Taylor would prefer to call ' pronouncement-stories.' It is characteristic of these tradition-units that they shape themselves around a central word of Jesus in which some question is answered, some challenge met, or some situation explained, and which has accordingly become an authoritative norm or directive for the Christian society. Normally the narrative framework with which these stories are provided is of the slightest, there being no interest in accentuating anything except the decisive utterance of Jesus himself. In the great majority of cases Bultmann declares the settings to be purely secondary, " ideal scenes " as he describes them, it being his view that the words of Jesus drew to themselves a context in the early debates or controversies of the community and then were handed down to us in these " situations." But while the Synoptic settings of a number of words of Jesus may have been provided in this artificial or *ad hoc* manner, the scepticism which will not allow that any setting has a basis in the historical life of Jesus has not commended itself to the majority even of Form-Critics. Each instance would need, in fact, to be examined on its merits. It ought also to be remembered that if here and there a once " situation-less " word of Jesus has acquired a secondary or " ideal " context in the course of the tradition, it is equally true that a number of once situation-less words have been taken back by the same course of tradition to what look like their original historical settings. We have already noticed one interesting example,[1] and it may be that the number is to be multiplied.

It will be instructive to consider at this point a number of early pronouncement-stories which show not only how deeply ingrained the primitive material was with the sense of a revelation of God in the acts of Jesus, but under what particular aspects the revelation of God in these acts presents itself.

In the Q passage Mt. xi. 2-19, Lk. vii. 18-35, which deals with John the Baptist and Jesus, we find an 'apothegma' or pronouncement-story in verses 2-6 of Mt. and verses 18-23 of Lk. which tells of the imprisoned John sending messengers to question Jesus and of Jesus' answer to them. Round this as nucleus have crystallized a number of words of Jesus bearing on the person and work of John. As regards the story itself, Bultmann would hold that the narrative setting, the statement that John sent messengers to Jesus to ask, " Art thou he who comes ? " is a secondary or ideal element supplied by the Christian community and motived by the desire to uphold the Messiahship of Jesus against the contemporary denials of the followers of John.[2] It may, however, be replied that if this explanation is probable it is just as probable that both question and answer go back to an actual episode in the history of Jesus. The only advantage which Bultmann gains by his historical scepticism is that the necessity of supposing that Jesus himself claimed to be the Jewish Messiah is obviated. The original word of Jesus which forms the nucleus :

> " The blind receive their sight, and the lame walk, the lepers are cleansed, and the deaf hear, and the dead are raised up, and the poor have good tidings preached to them. And blessed is he who shall find no stumbling-block in me,"

had in Bultmann's view nothing to do with personal acts of Jesus. It was a perfectly general allusion to the blessed time of the End which Jesus proclaimed to be now dawning, a time when the calamities wrought by sin under the present order would be removed. On this understanding Jesus did not claim for his own work or time a Messianic character. It was simply as messenger of the approaching End that he wished to be accepted and believed. Bultmann finds support for this view in the fact that the word of Jesus is almost entirely made up of Old Testa-

---

[1] See above, Chapter II, pp. 29-30. [2] Bultmann, *Geschichte*, p. 22.

ment passages (Isa. xxix. 18, xxxv. 5-6, lxi. 1-2). It is built upon past prophecy, not upon present happenings. To all this it may be simply answered that it is not capable of proof that Jesus did not in this and in many other cases appeal to his own works as fulfilling Old Testament predictions of the Messianic salvation. Bultmann's view is a purely imaginative construction.

We take next a pronouncement which is attested both by Mark and by the Q source. It is embedded in the composite passages Mk. iii. 22-30, Mt. xii. 22-37, Lk. xi. 14-23. Bultmann considers the original story to be still recognizable in Mk. iii. 22-26, Mt. xii. 22, 24-26, Lk. xi. 14-15, 17-18.[1] In Q the context was an exorcism (Mt. xii. 22, Lk. xi. 14). In Mark the story runs as follows :

> " The scribes . . . were saying . . . ' it is by the prince of the demons that he casts out the demons.' And he said to them, ' How can Satan cast out Satan ? And if a kingdom is divided against itself, that kingdom cannot stand. Also if a house is divided against itself, that house shall not be able to stand. And if Satan has risen against himself, and is divided, he cannot stand but has an end.' "

It cannot be thought—and Bultmann does not venture to suggest —that the word of Jesus here cited circulated at first as a merely general observation bearing on the strength or integrity of the kingdom of evil, and that it was later given a " situation " by connecting it up with the standard Jewish accusation that Jesus was a sorcerer who was in league with the powers of darkness. There is no reason whatsoever for doubting that the historical Jesus saw in his exorcisms a break-up of the power of Satan and a sign that the Reign of God was not merely already knocking at the door, but had irrupted into the enemy's country. This is brought out in the epexegetic sayings appended to the pronouncement both in Mark and in Q, e.g. in Mk. iii. 27, iii. 28-29, Mt. xii. 27 (Lk. xi. 19), Mt. xii. 28 (Lk. xi. 20).

The pronouncement-story in Mk. xi. 20-23 has already been discussed in certain of its aspects.[2] Here we need only add that the word of Jesus : " Have faith in God. Amen I say to you, Whosoever shall say to this mountain, Be taken up and cast into the sea, and shall not doubt in his heart, but shall believe that what he says comes to pass, he shall have it " implies the consciousness on the part of Jesus that at the moment when he and

---

[1] Bultmann, *Geschichte*, pp. 10-12.   [2] See above, Chapter II, pp. 29-30.

his disciples are going up to Jerusalem the phenomena of the Messianic age (Zech. xiv. 4) are on the point of being fulfilled. What the prophets had predicted about the last days is about to happen. There is no valid reason for not believing Jesus to have held this conviction or for denying the presence of the Zechariah-prophecy to his mind as he crossed the Mount of Olives. This then is a case where the revelational content of the primitive tradition may well have been greater than was later understood. Mark, as we have seen, was led by his particular authority to connect the saying correctly with the Mount of Olives, and so to re-establish its historical and prophetic meaning.

A moment's glance may be directed also to the interesting story in Mk. xi. 28-30 :

> "And they said to him, By what authority doest thou these things ? or who gave thee this authority to do these things ? And Jesus said to them, I will put one question to you, and answer me, and I will tell you by what authority I do these things. The baptism of John, was it from heaven, or from men ? Answer me that."

While Mark locates the incident in the temple-court, it is not certain that the acts of Jesus alluded to as " these things " had originally to do with his expulsion of the traders from the sanctuary, from which it is separated in Mark by an intervening episode. The story may have circulated at first without any connection with the temple-incident : it has even been conjectured on intrinsic grounds that the acts of Jesus in question consisted in the practice of baptism by himself or by the Church acting in his name.[1] However that may be, the answer to the challenge is in effect to say that, as John had his commission from heaven, so also has Jesus. The nature of the commission is not, however, further defined. Does the appeal to ' the baptism of John ' signify in any sense that it was in receiving baptism at John's hands that Jesus became conscious of the extraordinary commission to act and speak for God in Israel which eventuated in his Messianic claim ? It is not impossible. In any case the point is that the ' exousia ' of Jesus to act and teach has corroboration of a heavenly kind.

We take one other instance of pronouncement-story, this time one in which the revelational significance of the work of Jesus comes out in his action in forgiving sins. In the section Mk. ii.

---

[1] Bultmann, *Geschichte*, p. 18.

1-12, which relates the healing of a paralytic, Bultmann fastens on a marked peculiarity in the narration.[1] He notices that in the section as it stands there are two points : (1) there is a miraculous healing, (2) there is the forgiveness of a sinner. As an 'apothegma' or pronouncement-story cannot, while remaining true to type, have more than a single point, Bultmann takes the view that an older miracle-story has here been expanded in the interest of the Christian argument that the forgiveness of sins through Jesus is substantiated by his superhuman power as healer, and he points for proof to the anacoluthon in verse 10 : " But that you may know that the Son of Man has power on earth to forgive sins,—he says to the paralysed man, Arise, etc." The awkward break in the structure of the sentence is evidence that the original course of the narrative has been interrupted. We thus get a story and an addition. The introduction to the composite narrative relates how a paralytic was carried into the presence of Jesus by his friends (verses 1-4), and how Jesus, seeing their faith, spoke to the sick man (verse 5a). In what follows we have to distinguish, according to Bultmann, between the original sequel (A) and the interpolated matter (B). Jesus says :

A. (Mk. ii. 11-12)

(11) " ' I say unto thee, Arise, take up thy bed, and go to thy house.' (12) And he arose, and straightway taking up the bed he went out before them all ; so that all were amazed and glorified God, saying, ' We never saw the like of this before.' "

B. (Mk. ii. 5b-10)

(5b) " ' Son, thy sins are forgiven,' (6) but there were some scribes sitting there and debating in their hearts, (7) ' Why does this man speak like this ? He blasphemes : who can forgive sins except one, and he is God ? ' (8) And immediately Jesus, perceiving in his spirit that they reasoned thus within themselves, says to them : ' Why do you reason about these things in your hearts ? (9) Which is the easier thing, to say to the paralysed man, " Thy sins are forgiven," or to say, "Arise, and take up thy bed, and walk?" But that you may know that the Son of Man has authority on earth to forgive sins, etc.' "

Thus, according to Bultmann, an original miracle-story (A) has been expanded by secondary matter to the extent indicated in B,

---

[1] Bultmann, *Geschichte*, pp. 12 f.

and this B matter originated in the debates of the Christian community with Jewish opponents.   In this way Bultmann gets over what for him is the insuperable difficulty of supposing that in the original tradition Jesus spoke of the Son of Man as being revealed *on earth ;* for verse 10 on this view represents the language not of Jesus but of the Christian Church of a later time, and the statement in the parallel narrative in Mt. ix. 8 that the hearers glorified God who " had given such power to men " is taken by Bultmann to mean that " the authority of Jesus to forgive sins has become the possession of the Church." [1]   But even if we should admit that Mk. ii. 1-12 represents the expansion of an older tradition in a theological interest, Bultmann's delimitation of the original story to verses 1-5*a* and 11-12 is quite unsatisfactory.   He cuts out from it the word of forgiveness in verse 5*b*, assigning this to the accreted matter.   He does so on the ground that " of forgiveness of sins bestowed by Jesus the tradition has nothing to relate " (apart from Lk. vii. 47).   But we may well ask if this is an argument of any real weight.   Was no forgiveness of sins included in the message which drew the tax-gatherers and the harlots rather than the righteous into the kingdom of God ?   Apart from this, if the words in 5*b*, " Son, thy sins are forgiven," were not part of the original story, how did the debate about forgiveness come to be tacked on to this particular section ?   It may be that it had to be inserted somewhere, but surely the likelihood is that it would be attached to an episode in which in one way or another the issue of forgiveness was already raised.   It would seem better, therefore, to retain verse 5*b* and to reconstruct the original pronouncement-story as follows :

(1-4) A paralysed man was carried by his friends into the presence of Jesus.

(5) And Jesus, seeing their faith, says to the paralysed man, " Son, thy sins are forgiven."   (12) And he arose, and straightway took up his bed, and went forth before them all ;   so that all were amazed and glorified God, saying, " We never saw the like of this before."

The point is that it was the declaration of the forgiveness of his sins by Jesus that raised the man to his feet and restored him to life and power.   As the accreted matter shows, the forgiveness of sins is, as such, a sign which proclaims the ' exousia ' of Jesus and carries with it a direct revelational or Messianic significance.

---

[1] Bultmann, *Geschichte*, p. 14.

Miracle-Stories and Their Significance

As several of the above pronouncement-stories have had to do with the revelational character of exorcisms or other healing acts of Jesus, it is not necessary to take up in serial detail the miracle-stories proper to which we now pass. There is this difference between the two types of tradition-unit that, whereas the pronouncement-story is marked by great restraint and brevity of expression, the miracle-narrative is characterized by a very free development of detail, and as the Form-Critics have pointed out, it exhibits a large possession of features shared with non-Christian, especially with pagan Hellenistic narratives. These differences may be accounted for by the fact that, whereas the pronouncement-story centres in a word of Jesus which by its intelligible character and direct appeal to the reason or understanding holds the mind to a firm basis in itself, the miraculous act, as something which is not capable of being reasoned out, engages and indeed demands the exercise of imagination both in the telling and in the hearing or believing. The result is that while the original form of a pronouncement of Jesus may be reckoned upon to preserve itself within reasonable limits in the tradition, it is difficult if not altogether impossible to recover the fact lying behind the tradition of a miracle-act. This is a reason for very great reserve when we are dealing with narratives of this kind, for many or most of which, moreover, there are admittedly close parallels both in Jewish and in Hellenistic-pagan literature.[1]

As to the revelational value for the ancient mind of the miracle type of narrative the tradition leaves us in no uncertainty. In his extremely valuable analysis of the characteristics of the type Bultmann points out that the miracle-stories, despite their free development, are recorded not for their own sakes as marvels but as redemptive acts of Jesus, and not as expressions of the character of Jesus or of any virtue in his own person, but as evidences of a divine power overshadowing and attending him.[2] The instance in Mk. v. 30 where Jesus is represented as " perceiving inwardly that the power (proceeding) from him had gone forth," an expression which Lk. viii. 46 ascribes to Jesus himself in the form, " I perceived that power had gone forth from me," is exceptional and in the Hellenistic rather than in the Synoptic

[1] Reference may be made to the valuable collection of material assembled by Bultmann, *Geschichte*, pp. 247-253.
[2] *Ibid.*, pp. 234-256.

manner. In general, therefore, with all the interest in detail
exhibited by this type of story, there is no " portrait " of Jesus in
the strict sense, and for the most part no motive for his acts is
mentioned, the references to his compassion,[1] for example, or to
his purpose of awakening faith constituting the exception rather
than the rule. Nor is there any awareness in the tradition of a
problem requiring to be solved in the ambiguous relation of
these miracle-acts to Jesus' explicit refusal of a sign to his generation. As a matter of fact, no real problem here existed for the
Christian community, inasmuch as the acts in question, the
exorcisms and the healings wrought by Jesus according to the
tradition, did not signify things willed or designed by Jesus
himself so much as manifestations of the *numen praesens* of the
Holy Spirit (Mt. xii. 28), or of the over-ruling hand of God
(Lk. xi. 20). What is indicated in all these cases is that the
Kingdom of God, the most tremendous of all mysteries, has made
itself known. It is not only near, it is impinging upon present
history : " the kingdom of God has come your length " or " has
lighted upon you " (ἔφθασεν ἐφ᾽ ὑμᾶς).

It is customary to classify the ' mighty works ' of Jesus as
exorcisms, healings, and nature-wonders. That the exorcisms
possessed a peculiar and indeed primary evidential value as part
of the early Christian conception of the revelation of God in
Jesus is shown by the obviously popular development and expansion which some of the exorcism-narratives have undergone.
An interesting instance is the breadth with which the story of the
healing of the Gerasene demoniac is recounted in Mk. v. 1-20.
Bultmann insists rightly on the popular character of the idea,
clearly perceptible in this passage, of the outwitting of the demons
by the power of God in the Messiah.[2] The attractive force
exercised by the same type of narrative is shown by the array
of exponential words appended to the exorcisms in such cases as
Mk. iii. 27 and Mt. xii. 27-28. It is further illustrated by the
tendency of the tradition to assimilate all other acts of healing
and even the nature-miracles to the exorcistic form of procedure.
We may take as instances the cleansing of the leper in Mk. i.
42-44, where it is stated that Jesus rebuked or severely admonished
the leper and " cast him out " (ἐμβριμησάμενος αὐτῷ . . . ἐξέβαλεν
αὐτόν), and the stilling of the storm in Mk. iv. 39, where Jesus
censures or blames (ἐπετίμησε) the wind and imposes the

---

[1] Cf. Mk. i. 41, viii. 2, Mt. xx. 34, Lk. vii. 13.
[2] Bultmann, *Geschichte*, pp. 224 f.

command of silence on the sea. The form of all the healing narratives answers to that which we find in stories of miraculous cures recorded by secular writers of the period except that, as has been already indicated, Jesus is not like Apollonius of Tyana a θεῖος ἄνθρωπος, a virtuoso in divine science, whose acts point to the *numen* in himself, but is throughout a witness to the God of Israel and to the nearness of His kingdom and righteousness.

We shall therefore be prepared to find upon closer examination of these narratives—and this applies to the nature-miracles as much as to the others—that, despite their similarity in feature to tales of the miraculous current elsewhere, the main factor in the formation of the Christian narratives was the initial, specifically religious impression produced upon the mind of the community by Jesus himself, and that next to this comes the influence of certain Old Testament narratives and of Christian conceptions rooted in the Resurrection-faith and projecting themselves backwards into the earthly life of Jesus. Clearly, wonderful things happened at the hands of Jesus through the intense realism with which he apprehended the nearness and the power of God and with which he helped others to apprehend them. And if his actions in such cases, by the very fact of their transcending the ordinary assumptions of normal everyday experience, demanded for their expression the plastic aids of religious thought and imagination, it is only to be expected that the reporters would avail themselves first of those sources of religious insight which lay nearest to their hands and were most familiar to their minds. Bultmann is not disposed to rate very highly the formative influence of Old Testament language in the case of the miracle-narratives, but it is difficult to think that Old Testament theologoumena such as " He maketh the storm a calm, so that the waves thereof are still " or " He gave them bread from heaven to eat " would not powerfully affect the formation of certain traditions connected with the experiences of the first disciples. As little need we rule out the influence of ideas or of psychical experiences associated with the heavenly presence of the Risen Lord when we are dealing with the form of narratives like the walking on the Lake or the Transfiguration. The free development characterizing all such narratives precludes our recovery of the nature of the original event or experience, but one thing is certain : the evangelical tradition was stamped from the beginning with the sense that the God of Israel was with Jesus, making His sovereign power and glory known. Miracle is not a late importation into the tradition of Jesus, but constitutes the primary stratum. Nor need we suppose with Bultmann that, to satisfy the community's needs, miracle-narratives were dragged in or taken over into the Christian tradition from Jewish and Hellenistic sources.[1] Such derivation of what we have in the Synoptic Gospels is not necessary, and is not even likely.

For, with all the free development of detail in these narratives, it has to be recognized that the miraculous element in the Synoptic tradition as a whole is restricted within comparatively narrow limits. It is plain that there was a check within the community upon the production of new marvels and upon the metamorphosis of non-miraculous into miraculous events. For example, in the freely developed story of the healing of the epileptic boy in Mark, we read (Mk. ix. 26) that " the boy became like one dead, so that the many said, ' he is dead.' " If there was an ungoverned tendency to the miraculous in the tradition, it is difficult to explain how a story with such features escaped being turned into a record of an actual raising from the dead. Plainly, it was not a case of the Church being in absolute control of the tradition. We see that at many points the tradition was in control of the Church. And this restraint may have owed not a little to the fact that the early Christian thought of the revelation of God in Jesus was not centered exclusively in the works of Jesus, though these were wrought in God, but depended also on his teaching which at not a few points declares itself against any extravagant emphasis on ' signs.'

The Parables of Jesus as Signs

Before we pass on to the teaching or even attempt a summary appreciation of the primitive gospel of the signs of Jesus, it will be well to glance briefly at those of his parables which the tradition has placed in a special class by themselves through the giving to them more or less explicitly of a reference to the Kingdom of God. That such parables were felt to be signs or intimations of the Messianic salvation is demonstrated by the fact that, to judge from Mark iv. 10-12 and the Synoptic parallels, the meaning of these pictorial narratives continued to exercise the mind of the Christian community as a mystery lying beyond the reach of the ordinary understanding. " Behold, the sower went forth to sow " (Mk. iv. 3). " The kingdom of God is as if a man should cast the

---

[1] *Geschichte*, p. 246.

seed upon the ground " (Mk. iv. 26). " How are we to compare
the kingdom of God ? . . . As to a grain of mustard seed " (Mk.
iv. 30). " The kingdom of heaven is like leaven " (Mt. xiii.
33). " The kingdom of heaven is like treasure hid in a field "
(Mt. xiii. 44). " The kingdom of heaven is like a net cast into
the sea " (Mt. xiii. 47), and so forth. What is the point of the
kingdom of God being compared to something sown, something
hidden, something working secretly but producing amazing
results ? The tradition itself offers expositions of the Sower
parable (Mk. iv. 14-20) and of the parable of the Wheat and
the Tares (Mt. xiii. 36-43), but these interpretations confine
themselves to the externalities of the stories and do not touch the
fundamental question why the Reign of God, the advent of the
blessed age of salvation, is compared to seed working in the soil
or to treasure hid in a field.

The problem here presented is one to which recent Synoptic
scholarship has felt itself obliged to devote a marked degree of
attention, Bultmann, for example, holding that the original
situation to which many of the parables relate had become
unrecognizable in the course of the tradition, and with this their
point had been lost.[1] Was the parable of the Sower, for instance,
an assurance to the disciples that not all work for God fails, even
if a part seems to do so ? Was it a soliloquy of Jesus with respect
to his own fortunes ? Was it a warning to hearers against in-
attention to the word of salvation ? Or did it teach predestination ? Did the parable of the Seed Growing Secretly mean that
the Reign of God comes swiftly in a season, or that preachers of
repentance, if only they broadcast their summons, need have no
further concern about the consequences ? It is to be noticed
as a point of particular importance that the similitudes of the
Kingdom belong to the class of parables to which no explicit
moral or application is attached in the tradition.

For various reasons the solution of these questions would seem
to lie in regarding these parables as parallel in revelational significance to the acts or works of Jesus already considered in this
chapter. Dr. Rudolf Otto takes the view that the original
narrative source which lay behind Mark (which he calls *St* and
which roughly corresponds to Bussmann's G),[2] after characterizing the redemptive activity of Jesus by the narration of a number
of exorcisms and other wonders, went on directly, as we see by
Mk. iv, to give a series of parables which present Jesus " as the

---

[1] Bultmann, *Geschichte*, pp. 216 f.　　　[2] See above, pp. 22 f.

preacher of a strange marvel, a marvel which grows and works of itself." [1] He thinks that in this source-narrative the parables of the Kingdom stood in immediate sequence to the Beezebul-pericope (Mk. iii. 23-30), and he gives it as his judgement that by the time when Mark was written these parables were no longer understood but were already " clouded by allegorizations." [2] This view, I think, we may accept as highly probable. *Just as Jesus is in his actions the instrument or occasion of the divine power breaking in upon human life for our salvation, so in these parables he is the exponent of the idea of this mystery.* The seed, the thing hidden is the power of God already at work through Jesus for the coming of the Kingdom of the End.

Recently the authors of a fresh and illuminating study of the New Testament revelation have laid particular emphasis upon the parallel in point of " Christological significance " between the miracles and the parables of Jesus. [3] In both cases they find the underlying idea of something manifested in humiliation which is yet to be revealed in glory. And they would even claim an explicitly Messianic sense for the figures of speech employed in the parables, such as the seed, the harvest, and so forth. Thus for the metaphor of the seed they cite such passages as Isa. lv. 10, where the springing of the seed illustrates the promise that God's word will not return to him void but will go on operating success-fully until Israel experiences the joy of the divine world-renewal, and for the figure of the harvest they cite passages like Ps. cxxvi. 5-6. The most interesting perhaps of the Christological analogies suggested by Hoskyns and Davey concerns the " lamp " which figures in such parabolic words as Mk. iv. 21 : " Is the lamp brought in to be put under the bushel ? " Reference is made to Old Testament passages where the word lamp is used of the kingdom or secure future divinely promised to the house of David :

" There will I make the horn of David to bud ; I have ordained a lamp for mine Anointed " (Ps. cxxxii. 17).
" Howbeit, the Lord would not destroy Judah for David his Servant's sake, as he promised him to give unto him a lamp for his children alway " (II Kings viii. 19).

If such ideas underlay the figures of speech which Jesus employed, it must indeed be confessed that the revelational import of the

---

[1] Otto, *The Kingdom of God and the Son of Man*, p. 87.   [2] *Ibid.*, p. 91.
[3] E. Hoskyns and F. N. Davey, *The Riddle of the New Testament*, pp. 168 ff.

parables as signs was greater than the redactors of the tradition have perceived, but in view of the familiar uses of such metaphors as seed and lamp, it is perhaps unwise to press out of them an explicitly Christological sense. It is possible that they possessed this significance on the lips of Jesus, but it is not to be presumed as certain.

THE SIGNS OF JESUS AND THE KINGDOM OF GOD

The above summary will have exhibited the nature of the message of Jesus with regard to the Kingdom of God, at least in certain of its primary aspects. In the tradition of his words there occur such statements as the following : [1]

1. The supernatural Kingdom of God has suddenly lighted (ἔφθασεν) upon men.
2. It exerts itself, or makes way for itself by force (βιάζεται), disrupting the kingdom of evil.
3. It is like seed sown in the ground, or like leaven hidden in a mass of dough.
4. It is in the human midst (ἐντὸς ὑμῶν).
5. It is concealed at present, but will yet be revealed in power (ἐν δυνάμει).

While an understanding of the message of Jesus in its inward aspect awaits conclusions from a fuller study of his teaching, it is plain that in all its external aspects the message of the Kingdom of God has its ground and demonstration in deeds and signs fulfilling themselves at the hands of Jesus. So at least in the tradition which, unless it can be shown that Jesus was metamorphosed from a teacher of righteousness into a wonder-worker, has every claim to be regarded as having a basis in history. Words such as the ἔφθασεν saying, the βιάζεται saying, and the ἐντὸς ὑμῶν saying are not such as could have been readily invented by the community, the less so as the latter does not seem in other ways to have shared the vivid sense of the Eschaton which illumines and inspires these utterances.

The question therefore arises in what relation we may conceive Jesus as religious spirit to have stood to the ' signs ' we have considered and to the ' gospel ' of the Kingdom of God. In its broader aspects this problem has already been raised and provisionally answered. [2] Here only one facet of the question directly

---

[1] See Otto, *The Kingdom of God, etc.*, pp. 97-155.
[2] See above, Chapter I, pp. 14-17.

presents itself. Are we to think that Jesus, beginning with an intense objective apprehension of the nearness of the Kingdom of God, was led on by the very vividness of this apprehension to live the life and to do the deeds which the evangelical tradition portrays, or are we to say that it was an intensely realized inward experience of God that led him both to proclaim the immediate nearness of God's Reign and to see in the effects which accompanied his message and his work the actual breaking-in of that divine order? It has been already pointed out that the analogy of the earlier religious development of Israel, as well as certain features in the language of Jesus himself, suggest that the second of these hypotheses is the more likely to be right. If so, we are now in a position to add a further confirmation. *Jesus in his characteristic words about the Kingdom of God reasons from present events and experiences to the coming of that Kingdom, not vice-versa.* His gospel of the End rests on the certainty of the power of God which is with him in the present.

And shall we not say also that the evidential significance which his acts had for him with relation to the coming of the Kingdom owed something of its vividness and intensity to the nature of these acts, as acts redemptively wrought for the liberation of the souls of men? We see him delivering men from Satan and his power, from sin, derangement, physical suffering, oppression and injustice. Can we think that the prescience with which he saw the Reign of God already dawning did not derive something of its clear and unmistakable assurance from the definitely redemptive character of these works to which the urge of the Spirit of God, the divine Will, impelled him? If so, the message of Jesus, so far from involving a negation of all humanitarian sentiment in religion, had its deep roots in compassion for men, and developed step by step with it. It surely seems just to add that wheresoever man's spirit is liberated from sin, captivity, injustice, and heartbreak, there still are the signs of the Kingdom.

Chapter IV

THE TEACHING OF JESUS. I. THE NOTE OF CRISIS AND FULFILMENT

A FACTOR destined from the beginning to exercise a very profound influence on the Christian conception of the revelation of God in Christ was the possession by the community of a tradition of the teaching of Jesus.

THE DIDACTIC ELEMENT COMES TO THE FRONT : THE Q SOURCE

In the primitive statement of the case for Christianity the tradition of the words of Jesus does not appear to have figured with any prominence. Such a tradition existed—for, apart altogether from the citations of words of Jesus in the first generation by St. Paul, we can hardly suppose that the amassing of the great body of didactic material which took place at the close of that period in the Q source was purely the result of an afterthought. But it existed not so much on the surface of the ordinary kerygma as submerged in the general stream of the Church's life and in the ethos inspiring its practical activities. In the measures, for example, which were taken in the early days to relieve the sufferings of the destitute members of the Church at Jerusalem and to make the Christian 'koinonia' a reality (Acts ii. 44 f., iv. 32, 34 f.), it is impossible not to see a very remarkable demonstration of the spirit inspiring the community through the commandments and the teaching of Jesus. If, on the other hand, the teaching element is not particularly emphasized in the confessional utterances of the primitive period, the fact is not without its natural explanation.

In the first place, the new thing in Christianity was not its ethic, exalted as that was, but its Messianic faith. In the period of Christian origins, which is that which succeeded the Crucifixion, the central issue which was forced to the front as between the Nazarenes and the body of the Jewish community turned, not primarily, if at all, on the doctrines of Jesus, but on the claim that he was the divinely revealed Messiah and that his death on the cross had fulfilled the purpose of God. This had the effect of concentrating the public emphasis upon the divine signs

attending Jesus, above all on the Resurrection and on the phenomena of the Spirit in the Church.   The stream of thought flowed
in an intense but narrow channel, carrying in its flood much that
for the time remained in solution in the sub-conscious rather than
in the conscious region of the Christian mentality.

Secondly, no tradition of the teaching of Jesus, strictly so-
called, was capable either then or later of conveying the whole
substance of the Church's message.   The claim that Jesus was
the Messiah was not simply equivalent to the authority of the
moral and religious principles which he had inculcated, any more
than the prediction of his coming on the clouds of heaven signified
only that these principles would one day be universally acknowledged or that they would be made the ultimate test of life.   The
Messiahship of Jesus and the belief in his coming in glory included, and had as their distinguishing feature an entirely active
sense of things which God was yet to *do* through Jesus, whom
in the meantime " heaven must receive pending the times of
that universal Restoration (ἀποκαταστάσεως) of which God has
spoken by the mouth of all his holy prophets since the world
began " (Acts iii. 21).   Such a hope and message travelled
beyond the range of any mere assent to the teaching of Jesus
whether as a whole or in any of its parts.

All the more remarkable is it that the teaching of Jesus,
existing in solution in the mind of the community, comes definitely
to the surface, and as a great collateral to the affirmation of the
' signs ' attending him, affixes a deeper and ultimately a permanent character to the revelation of God of which Jesus was the
source.   First the gathering up of many scattered traditions of
words of Jesus in the Q source, and then the upthrust of this mass
of didactic material through the strata of the earlier gospel of
' signs ' to a firm place in the revised Synoptic representations of
Matthew and Luke, secured for the historical record of Christianity the inward, spiritual, and reasonable character in which
it was thenceforth to be given to the world (cf. Mt. xxviii. 19-20).

The importance of the teaching-tradition in its bearing on the
primitive emphasis becomes apparent the moment that we
consider the terms of the teaching.   The earliest proclamation,
as we have seen, made a great point of the signs attending Jesus,
but here in the Q-narrative of the Temptation of Jesus in the
wilderness, for instance, we find a *criterion* of the signs which
legitimate Jesus as the Messiah, and this criterion is located not
in anything outward but in the utterly obedient, humble, and

devoted mind of Jesus as the ' Son of God.' The conception of the revelation of God in Jesus here asserts its intrinsic spiritual character. Not all signs have validity for the faith of the Christian community but only those which can be reconciled with perfect trust, obedience, and reverence towards God. So throughout the Q-teaching Jesus as the Messiah-Son of God is presented not only as the object of the divine ' eudokia ' or choice, to whom the signs are granted and with whom the Messianic age comes to fulfilment (Mt. xi. 4-6, Lk. vii. 22-23), but as himself the source and channel of the knowledge of God. The signs are correlative to a commission which has been inwardly given to Jesus, and which rests upon a unique knowledge of the Father's will.

We shall have to consider later the great passage, Mt. xi. 27, Lk. x. 22, in which this conception rises to its climactic expression. It is enough for the present to note that an attitude to Jesus appears here which grounds the Messianic claim and mystery essentially upon the possession by Jesus of the Father's mind, and for this there must have been deep reasons in the general character of the antecedent oral tradition. So also in the ascription to Jesus of words about the Law of Moses such as Lk. xvi. 16, Mt. xi. 12-13, or of words which make demands exceeding the requirements of the Law, or which represent him as the fulfiller of prophecy, a consciousness is revealed on the part of the community which indicates that for it the mind of Jesus is the ultimately all-determinative factor in the Christian conception of the revelation of God. Here in the Q source speaks one who by wisdom as well as by signs is accredited as a greater than Solomon, and who as standing to the Father in the altogether unique relation of ' Son ' transcends Jonah and God's other servants, the prophets.

The Didactic Emphasis in St. Matthew and St. Luke

The incorporation of the Q-material in our Gospels of Matthew and Luke brings with it a certain qualification of the Christological standpoint of Mark, if not an entire displacement of the Markan emphasis. More firmly than Mark, the two later evangelists have drawn around Jesus the mantle of the teacher, the revealer of the deep things of God. It is not, therefore, true to say that the development from Mark to Matthew and Luke—and *per analogiam* the earlier development from Jesus to Mark—represents a transition from a less to a more dogmatic position in

the matter of Christology, unless by Christology we mean something broad enough and inclusive enough to comprise the whole
extent to which Jesus determines the spiritual and ethical relations of our souls to God.   While Matthew and Luke have taken
over from Mark the early emphasis upon signs and wonders, they
have qualified the epiphany-doctrine of Mark by didactic supple-
mentations and revisions which signify the re-entrance into the
picture of the original historical lineaments of Jesus the teacher
of religion.   Or was this act of theirs merely the result of a
growing tendency to ' rabbinize ' the portrait of Jesus ?   That
suggestion has been made, and it will not do to dismiss it im-
patiently as if no colour of verisimilitude could be claimed for it
especially as regards the Gospel of Matthew.   On the other
hand, certain evidences lying very close to us show that the conception of Jesus as teacher of the things of God was primordial
to the Christian consciousness.   To mention only one of these,
the original name—and it is a very honoured name—by which
the followers of Jesus were known to one another was ' mathetai '
or disciples, and though this ancient name went soon out of
ordinary use, being restricted, as time went on, to members of
the earliest generation of Christians such as Mnason the Cypriote
who is styled an ἀρχαῖος μαθητής in Acts xxi. 16, the idea which
the word connoted was not displaced but continued to influence
and determine the pattern of Christian life in later circles.   In
the Epistle to the Ephesians, for example, Christians are addressed
as those who " have learned Christ " (ἐμάθετε τὸν Χριστόν) and
have been taught in him " as the truth is in Jesus " (ἐν αὐτῷ
ἐδιδάχθητε καθώς ἐστιν ἀλήθεια ἐν τῷ Ἰησοῦ, Eph. iv. 21).   Such
evidence is of capital importance.

The emphasis on Jesus as teacher which is so pronounced a
feature of Matthew and Luke as compared with Mark has been
brought about not merely by the massive incorporation in these
Gospels of didactic material drawn from Q and other sources, but
more subtly by the nature of the revision to which Mark has been
more or less consistently subjected in these recensions.   It is to be
noted, for example, that in all but one of the cases in which Mark
employs his favourite term ' gospel ' Matthew has substituted
' gospel of the Kingdom,' and he has done this not so much in
order to underline the ultimate reference of the message of Jesus
as to bring out its essentially ideal character.[1]   Both Matthew

[1] Hoskyns and Davey, *The Riddle of the New Testament*, pp. 106, 110.   The
cases in Matthew are iv. 23, ix. 35, xxiv. 14.   The exception occurs in xxvi. 13.

and Luke, it appears, think of the message of the Kingdom primarily in terms of truths regarding the Kingdom which Jesus revealed. A most striking illustration is the revision-form in which these two later evangelists have presented one of the most challenging words attributed to Jesus in Mark :

Mk. iv. 11	Lk. viii. 10, Mt. xiii. 11
" To you has been given the mystery of the kingdom of God."	" To you has been given *to know* the mysteries of the kingdom of God."

In place of Mark's " mystery," which probably meant for Mark the undifferentiated totality of the religious revelation made in Jesus, Matthew and Luke have set " mysteries," and by making these the content of a divinely communicated " knowledge " they have drawn attention to the many-sided fullness of the *truths* imparted by Jesus with regard to the Kingdom of God. From their standpoint the gospel of the Messiah authenticates itself to our God-awakened nature by its reasonable character, its appeal to thought.

The upthrust of the teaching of Jesus to a place at the heart of the Messianic kerygma was thus an event of far-reaching consequence. *In the form of the incorporation of Q into the Gospels of Matthew and Luke it represents perhaps the most important single incident in the history of Christian literature.* For thereby there was secured for the gospel of the ' signs ' of Jesus and above all for the supreme sign of the Cross the inward and spiritual significance which inhered in the events. A reasonable character is claimed for the message of the Kingdom in that, while it transcends history, it is related to ideals so organic to man's nature as humility, unselfishness, love and service to humanity. There have been times when men have wearied of dogma and of the incrustations which dogma has imposed on the gospel of Jesus, but in such days, when the upper strata of the Christian dogmatic ideas have, so to speak, suffered erosion over wide areas, the underlying core of the teaching of Jesus with its great outcrop or sill in the Sermon on the Mount has remained *in situ*, indestructible and immovable, a permanent witness to the revelation of God in Christ to the mind and heart of humanity.

Yet nowhere in the Christian tradition has this teaching been separated off and presented *per se*, or as not having a directly Messianic significance.

FORM-CRITICISM AND THE TEACHING OF JESUS

It is now necessary, going behind the Q source, to ask what were the motives and principles governing the preservation, interpretation, and formation of the sayings of Jesus from which Q was so largely drawn. Here a very real debt is due to Martin Dibelius, Rudolf Bultmann, and other exponents of Form-Criticism who by their special researches in this field have helped to focus the problem and to define more closely the character of the material.

The sayings of Jesus, as Dibelius points out, were preserved and collected at first not from any interest in them of a biographical kind " as the utterances of a famous man," but for the practical reason that the Christian communities needed them " in order to order their lives according to them." [1] But he also recognizes that the interest of the community in gathering up the logia-tradition was quite distinct from that of Jesus when he spoke the words. Jesus was not giving general rules, prescribing what was to be done on all occasions and in every situation, but was concentrating on the repentance of those whom he was addressing, directing his demands to the precise situation of the moment. " His listeners were to understand the demand as a sign of the coming kingdom of God." On the other hand, when the community gathered and codified the words of Jesus, it was thinking of them not as signs of the coming kingdom of God but as rules for a society in which the kingdom of God was already in a sense actual, and the change in the point of view would inevitably involve some degree of adaptation of the sayings to the requirements of the Church in the world. [2] To the prayer " Thy kingdom come ! " would be mentally supplied the addition " Thy will be done on earth as in heaven."

Nevertheless, the distinction here made must not be exaggerated or pressed too far. There can never have been a time when the words of Jesus most vitally present to the Christian consciousness were not felt to involve it in a sense of crisis, in that the prophetic urge and challenge of the words flung the existing achievements and practice of the Church into deep shadow by the side of the transcendent ideal which they revealed, and so summoned Christians afresh to repentance in the name of the kingdom of heaven. The teaching of Jesus which was with authority proclaimed not the sanctions or title adhering to the

[1] *Gospel Criticism and Christology*, p. 38. [2] *Ibid.*, p. 39.

existing Church and to its life and practice, but, as Prof. C. H.
Dodd says, " an immediate and absolute sovereignty of God in
every sphere of human life," a word of *God* transcending and over-
ruling all human wisdom and attainment.[1] The early Church
must have realized that the sayings of Jesus which it repeated to
itself and which it taught to the world proclaimed a high and
unattained, if not unattainable, measure of life. Sayings such
as " Resist not the evil " and " Love your enemies " were, as
Johannes Weiss observes, not ordinary rules of rational ethics,
and the early Church in holding on to them as principles bound
up with its hope of inheriting the kingdom of God was confessing
" its completely enthusiastic outlook on life." [2] The judgement
upon the existing practice of the Church which was involved in
the consciousness of such standards would by no means be overlooked in the daily concern to find in the sayings of the Master a
' nova lex ' for the regulation of the community.

THE WISDOM-LOGIA OF JESUS AND THE NOTE OF CRISIS

In the light of what has just been said, we shall expect to find
that a note of crisis in the words of Jesus will serve generally as a
distinguishing mark of their originality. The consciousness that
beyond the Church and its life stood the transcendent Kingdom
of God would keep such sayings alive in the mind of the community, and a regard for this fact will predispose us against the
temptation to affix a trite or conventional interpretation to the
mass of aphorisms or parables handed down to us in the tradition.
It is necessary to say this because Bultmann in his elaborate
analysis of the Logia-tradition makes too much, as it seems to me,
of the parallelism between the words of Jesus and the sayings of
an outwardly similar type occurring in Jewish Wisdom or Rabbinical literature.[3] Thus in the treatment of the Wisdom-
utterances of Jesus, to which he devotes the first part of his valuable analysis, numerous sayings which are decidedly patient of
a distinctly personal or Messianic interpretation are regarded as
expressions of general ideas, and are therefore considered by
Bultmann to have been taken over by the community from
popular sources. Bultmann's attitude to the Wisdom-sayings is
not indeed everywhere of this description. Thus, while he notes

---

[1] *History and the Gospel*, p. 124.
[2] *History of Primitive Christianity*, Vol. I, p. 79.
[3] *Geschichte*, pp. 73-113. The Wisdom-logia are listed on pp. 73-84.

that in this type of utterance on the whole " the basic forms of the Old Testament and Jewish ' mashal ' are clearly to be recognized," he qualifies this statement by the admission that among the logia exhibiting the Wisdom ' form ' there are some " which in their expressly religious character leave behind them alike the form and the substance of the proverbial type of piety." [1] He instances the following cases among others :

> " No man, having put his hand to the plough, and looking back, is fit for the kingdom of God " (Lk. ix. 62).
>
> " Whoever shall not receive the kingdom of God as a little child, shall in no wise enter therein " (Mk. x. 15).
>
> " How hardly shall they that have riches enter into the kingdom of God ! " (Mk. x. 23b).
>
> " All things that you pray and ask for, believe that you have received them, and you shall have them " (Mk. xi. 24).
>
> " If you have faith as a grain of mustard seed, you shall say unto this mountain, Remove hence to yonder place, and it shall remove " (Mt. xvii. 20).
>
> Saying about ' eunuchs ' (Mt. xix. 12).

It may be conceded that in respect of outward form there is not one of the above sayings which might not have stood in some Jewish Wisdom writing, yet in the Messianic context of the Christian tradition how incomparably great is their force and point ! In the case of the fifth of the above sayings (Mt. xvii. 20) a Messianic context, as we have already seen, can be regarded as practically certain. [2] But while Bultmann does not contend that any of the above cited words had a currency in the Christian community apart from the situation of religious crisis which Jesus was felt to have created for his followers, in other cases he is not so definite. He is of the opinion that in the tradition and in the Q-document there were numerous logia of the wisdom type which were not authentic words of Jesus and were not originally intended to be understood as such, but which were simply taken over from other sources to minister to the society's need of edification. His point is that the incidental use of proverbial sayings by Jesus would scarcely have left its mark on the tradition, nor are even the Christian modifications of such *meshalim* necessarily to be put down to historical reminiscence of the form in which

---

[1] *Geschichte*, p. 84.
[2] See above, Chapter II, pp. 29-30.

Jesus quoted them.[1] Despite certain exceptions, therefore, Bultmann's conclusions from the form of the Wisdom-logia in the tradition are in the great majority of cases unfavourable to their historicity as words of Jesus, and this position calls for closer scrutiny.

Among words included by Bultmann among " profane m*shalim* " which were " perhaps first made into words of Jesus by the tradition " there occur the following :

1. " There is nothing covered that shall not be revealed ; and hid that shall not be known " (Lk. xii. 2, Mt. x. 26. Cf. Mk. iv. 22).

2. " What does it profit a man to gain the whole world and to forfeit his life ? " (Mk. viii. 36, and parr.).

3. " What should a man give in exchange for his life ? " (Mk. viii. 37, and parr.).

4. " Man (literally, the Son of Man) has not where to lay his head " (Mt. viii. 20, Lk. ix. 58).

5. " Is the lamp brought to be put under the bushel ? etc." (Mk. iv. 21, and parr.).

6. " Every one that exalts himself shall be humbled, and he that humbles himself shall be exalted " (Lk. xiv. 11, Mt. xxiii. 12. Cf. Lk. xviii. 14).

Bultmann's procedure here is to stress the proverbial form of the sayings, and to conclude that general truths of popular currency were adopted by the Church and yoked to Christian purposes. It is to the Church's preaching that we are listening, not to that of Jesus. " If Mk. viii. 36," he writes, " happened to stand in the Book of Proverbs or in Sirach, nobody would mistake its sense. Mk. viii. 37, conjoined to it by association of ideas, is a proverb . . . to which there are parallels in Oriental literature." [2] So also he thinks that the saying (No. 4 above), " Man has not where to lay his head," was possibly a popular saying which was first given a relation to the person of Jesus in the Hellenistic Church.[3]

But if it is conceivable that the above words, or some of them, came into the evangelical tradition in this roundabout way, it is certainly as conceivable and vastly more probable that they originated as words of Jesus spoken in the context of his historical mission and with direct relation to the crisis which that mission treated for his followers. The explanation which Bultmann gives

[1] Bultmann, *Geschichte*, pp. 105-106. [2] *Ibid.*, p. 101.
[3] *Ibid.*, p. 102.

of No. 4 seems to me extremely improbable. No such generaliza-
tion regarding ' man ' was likely to belong to popular philosophy
nor, if it had a place there, to establish itself in the Christian
tradition apart from the pathos of its peculiar relevance to the
situation of Jesus. On the other hand, the formulation of the
word by Jesus, either directly with reference to his own fortunes
or indirectly with allusion to some doctrine of the self-abnegation
or suffering which the apocalyptic ' Son of Man ' was to endure,
is intelligible.[1] The attribution of the logion to the Hellenistic
Church is, therefore, unnecessary. Again, as regards No. 1 of
the above sayings, what proof have we that the word about
things now " hidden " which will later be " revealed " was not
first spoken by Jesus with precise reference to the situation
created by his work in which he saw the powers of the kingdom
of the End to be already active, though not yet in a manner which
was fully visible to ordinary eyes ? [2] As to No. 5, the saying
about the " lamp," while a precisely Christological sense is not
perhaps to be forced on the metaphor, it remains that the word
is patient of a specific application to the mission of Jesus, and
possibly originated with exclusive reference to that mission.[3] The
same is even clearer in the case of No. 6, " Every one who exalts
himself shall be humbled, and he who humbles himself shall be
exalted ($\dot{v}\psi\omega\theta\eta\sigma\epsilon\tau\alpha\iota$)." In Isa. liii. 13 it is said of the Servant
of Yahweh : " My servant . . . shall be exalted (LXX $\delta \pi\alpha\hat{\iota}s$
μov . . . $\dot{v}\psi\omega\theta\eta\sigma\epsilon\tau\alpha\iota$)," a reference to God honouring the lowly
Servant. What proof have we that Jesus did not first give
currency to this saying, proverb-like as it is, with the Messianic
figure of the Servant in his mind ? In other words, *all these
sayings which seem by their form to express general truths may have
originated as words of Jesus having definite and precise relation to the
circle of crisis in the centre of which he was conscious of standing.* Even
more does this seem to hold true of the remaining pair of sayings,
Nos. 2 and 3. These words undoubtedly have parallels in other
literatures, but their currency in the Christian tradition may owe
everything to the fact that Jesus stamped them as his own by the
relation he gave them to the mission of the Son of Man to suffer
and only through suffering to attain to his exaltation. Our conclusion, therefore, is that the Wisdom-logia in the tradition, even
those of an apparently general type, are charged with real or

---

[1] See above, Chapter I, pp. 7-11, and Appendix D.
[2] See above, Chapter III, pp. 46-49.
[3] *Ibid.*, pp. 48 f.

potential critical and Messianic significance to a greater extent than the theory under consideration has allowed.

THE ETHICAL IDEAL IN RELATION TO THE LAST THINGS

The Form-Critic to whose analysis of the Logia such constant reference has been made in these pages is prepared to allow the authenticity of three types of sayings traditionally ascribed to Jesus. These are (1) sayings exhibiting a strong concentration on the last things, (2) sayings expressive of intense earnestness in calling men to repentance, (3) sayings demanding total newness of life. In the first group are words of so apparently general a form as those referring to the strong man's house being invaded (Mk. iii. 27) or to a divided kingdom (Satan's) collapsing (Mk. iii. 24-26). To the second group belong the words about losing or winning life (Mk. viii. 35, etc.), putting the hand to the plough (Lk. ix. 62), leaving the dead to bury their dead (Lk. ix. 60), entering in by the strait gate (Mt. vii. 13), the difficulty of rich men entering into the kingdom of God (Mk. x. 23b), etc. In the third group are placed the words about the childlike mind (Mk. x. 15), humility (Lk. xiv. 11, etc.), non-retaliation (Mt. v. 39b-41), love to enemies (Mt. v. 44-48), and other similar words. In sayings like these, which have no longer the pure form of the generalized logion, but which transcend popular wisdom and piety without displaying specifically rabbinical or apocalyptic mannerisms, we are to find, if anywhere, the genuine mind of Jesus.[1]

It comes to this, that what is here proposed for recognition as the authentic stamp of the teaching of Jesus is the intense religious realism of his outlook, above all in the matter of God's sovereign will and demand, and this criterion is to be admitted, so far as it goes. If Jesus had preached a merely familiar doctrine of the kingdom of God, there would have been no religious crisis and no historical rise of Christianity. The Jewish people had had a sufficiency of such doctrine before. But because Jesus not only proclaimed the kingdom of God as a glorious event of the future, but laid the arrest and the power of it upon spirit and conscience in the present, bringing it into direct practical and converting relation to men's lives, he opened a new era in spiritual history. He created a religious crisis, indeed the supreme religious crisis for mankind. Hence it is right to find in the energy of his

[1] *Geschichte*, p. 110.

summons to repentance and to total newness of spirit a sure mark
of his authentic teaching, though here we would also need to
recognize that the repentance to which Jesus called and to which
he awakened men was conditioned primarily by the grace of God
to the sinful which he put in the forefront of his message.[1]   In Q,
for example, his teaching opened with Beatitudes, with the offer
of the Kingdom of God to the penitent and humble.   Among
words which occur as the central or nuclear element in pronouncement-stories or elsewhere in the tradition are such as the
following :

" Son, thy sins are forgiven " (Mk. ii. 5*b* and parr.).
" I tell thee, her sins, which are many, are forgiven " (Lk. vii. 47).
" I came not to call the righteous, but sinners " (Mk. ii. 17).
" To-day salvation came to this house, inasmuch as he too is a
son of Abraham " (Lk. xix. 9).
" All sins shall be forgiven to the sons of men, and the blas-
phemies with which they shall blaspheme " (Mk. iii. 28).

It is apparent that for Jesus God's will, God's absolute ought-to-
be, God's kingdom included His saving grace as well as His
will to righteousness.

" I have never understood," wrote Karl Holl, " how anyone
could doubt that Jesus taught a new idea of God as compared with
the Old Testament. . . . In the Psalms of Solomon it is only the
righteous man who is called ' son of God.' Jesus, however,
addresses himself not to the righteous but to sinners. Judaism of
itself was quite unable to take this forward step. . . . To affirm
that God could stand specially near to a heinous sinner was impossible."

" It is all the more astonishing that on the basis of such a conception of God, which seemed to dissolve all morality, Jesus nevertheless
built up an ethic, and the most exacting ethic conceivable at that.
. . . The meaning is clear : pardoning grace overcomes, because
at the same time it encourages and humbles. It creates an inner
affection, a feeling of gratitude which must find expression, and
for which the highest is not too much to do. . . . From this follows
the most splendid feature of the ethic of Jesus, namely, the natural-
ness, the spontaneous character of the action, which he supposes
even in things most difficult and self-denying. . . . God takes the
initiative : with His forgiveness He creates something quite new,
out of which arises at once a real, close, and warm relationship to

[1] See Karl Holl, *Urchristentum und Religionsgeschichte* (Eng. trans. by N. V.
Hope, pp. 17-23) ;   Maurice Goguel, *Life of Jesus*, pp. 559-562 ; and A. von
Harnack, *Sayings of Jesus*, pp. 201-203.

God, and with it at the same time a morality which ventures to take even God Himself as its model." [1]

There is a further relation between the message of the Kingdom which Jesus announces and the repentance and righteousness to which he calls. It is given in the character of the Kingdom itself, and is stated by Rudolf Otto when he says :

"Holiness and righteousness—to be ' justified,' to be ' sanctified ' —are not possible in the present, earthly, fleshly, worldly existence, or in an existence and situation of an earthly kind. Rather do they require the wondrous new creation—the condition of being ' reborn,' ' renewed,' ' transfigured '—as the ontological presupposition of their possibility." [2]

For Jesus the immediacy and the realism with which the Kingdom of God is apprehended carries with it the high tension of the summons to newness of life. The realization of the hope of righteousness is in sight. Hence the high confiden with which Jesus makes the most absolute demands upon his followers. It is a confidence in God.

"Jesus, looking upon them, saith : With men it is impossible, but not with God ; for all things are possible with God " (Mk. x. 27).

Hence also the note of crisis running through and through his teaching. The revelational significance of his ethical teaching is not something which has been imported into it by the Messianic Church but which inheres in its character and substance.

PROPHETIC AND APOCALYPTIC UTTERANCES OF JESUS. THE NOTE OF CRISIS ACCENTUATED

Before we can turn, however, to the ethical substance of the teaching of Jesus and its bearing upon the Christian conception of the revelation of God in him, a topic which is reserved for Chapter V, it is necessary—partly in order to complete our survey of the logia of Jesus, and partly to prepare the way for the question of his Messianic consciousness, which will follow in Chapter VI—to take up two other classes of sayings which Bultmann has segregated respectively as prophetic and apocalyptic utterances, and personal deliverances making use of the formula " I came " and other similar expressions. In these sayings the note of crisis which has been remarked in the Wisdom-logia rises to a high pitch of clearness, for what is here stressed is

---

[1] *Urchristentum und Religionsgeschichte*, Eng. trans., pp. 17-23.
[2] *The Kingdom of God and the Son of Man*, p. 49.

essentially the fulfilment or transcendence by Jesus of the Old
Testament predictions regarding the age of salvation. The
revelational interest here is not in the content of the words so
much as in the situation to which the words point or in the
personal consciousness of Jesus of which they are the manifestation. Form-Criticism tends to regard these utterances, at least
in so far as they seem to involve a Messianic claim for Jesus, as
formulations of the post-resurrection Church, but this is a judgement which in many cases is grounded on doctrinaire ideas of
' form ' rather than on strict evaluations of objective probability,
and which needs therefore to be carefully scrutinized. We take
first a number of examples of the prophetic or apocalyptic class
of logia :

1. Mt. xi. 5 f., Lk. vii. 22 (The blind receive their sight, etc.).
2. Mt. xiii. 16 f., Lk. x. 23 f. (Blessed are your eyes and ears,
   etc.).
3. Mt. xi. 21-24, Lk. x. 13-15 (Judgement on the Galilean
   cities).
4. Mt. xii. 41-42, Lk. xi. 31-32 (A greater than Jonah, a
   greater than Solomon is here).
5. Lk. xi. 49-51, Mt. xxiii. 34-36 (The divine wisdom and
   this generation).
6. Mt. xxiii. 37-39, Lk. xiii. 34-35 (O Jerusalem, Jerusalem).
7. Mk. viii. 12, cf. Mt. xii. 39 f., Lk. xi. 29 f. (No sign to this
   generation, or no sign but that of Jonah).
8. Lk. xvii. 20 f. (The Kingdom is in your midst).
9. Lk. xii. 54-56 (The signs of the time).
10. Mt. viii. 8-12, Lk. xiii. 28-29 (They shall come from the
    east and the west, etc.).
11. Mt. x. 32 f., Lk. xii. 8 f., Mk. viii. 38 and parr. (Confessing
    Jesus).
12. Mt. xi. 6, Lk. vii. 23 (Blessed is he who shall not be
    offended in me).
13. Mt. x. 23 (You shall not have gone over the cities of
    Israel till the Son of Man shall have come).
14. Mt. xxiv. 37-41, Lk. xvii. 26-27 (The judgement involved
    in the swiftness of the Son of Man's coming).
15. Mk. xiii. 33-37, Mt. xxiv. 43-44, Lk. xii. 35-38, Lk. xii.
    42 f., Lk. xxi. 34-36 (The call to watchfulness).
16. Lk. xvii. 23-24, Mt. xxiv. 26-27 (Suddenness of the Son
    of Man's coming).

17. Mk. xiii. 30 and parr. Cf. Mk. ix. 1 and parr. (This generation shall see the Parousia).
18. Mk. xiii. 2 and parr., Mk. xiv. 58, Mt. xxvi. 61, Jn. ii. 19. Cf. Acts vi. 14 (The passing away of the temple).
19. Mk. ix. 12-13 and parr. (Elias has come).
20. Mt. xxv. 31-46 (The final Judgement by the Son of Man).

It will be observed that a considerable proportion of the above sayings, viz. Nos. 1-10, have for background the phenomena of the 'signs' of Jesus as discussed in the preceding chapter, and do not require to be handled afresh. Their revelational interest is in the claim that with the work of Jesus the divine purpose for Israel has entered on its fulfilment or *Malkuth* phase.

"For all the prophets and the law prophesied until John" (Mt. xi. 13, Lk. xvi. 16).

But now the Kingdom of God presses in, and men of determined purpose lay impatient hands upon it. Hence also the vividness with which in most of the remaining sayings—Nos. 7, 11, 13, 14, 15, 16, 17, 19, 20—the coming of the Son of Man is foreshadowed. *The coming of the Son of Man stands in very close relation to the situation in which according to these words Jesus finds himself.* With regard to this whole section of the teaching of Jesus it will be enough at the present stage to make the following general comments :

1. If the situation created by the exorcisms and other 'mighty works' of Jesus marked for him the inbreaking of the kingdom of heaven into the world's life, there appears no reason why the majority, if not all, of the above sayings should not, rightly understood, be held to rest on authentic oracles of Jesus.

2. It is argued that in such of the above sayings as Nos. 1, 2, 4, 8, in which the Messianic age is implied to be dawning, and also in Nos. 5 and 6, the claim to fulfil prophecy or to transcend earlier revelation is made not with reference to the person of Jesus, but merely to his message or his works. In such words as

Mt. xi. 6, Lk. vii. 23, "Blessed is he who shall find no offence in me,"
Lk. xii. 8, Mt. x. 32, "Whosoever shall confess me before men him shall the Son of Man (Mt. him shall I) confess, etc.,"
Mt. xii. 41-42, Lk. xi. 31-32, "A greater than Jonah," "a greater than Solomon is here,"

it is averred that Jesus was thinking only of the testimony which he had borne to God. But even if this should be admitted as a correct account of what was intended to be understood at the

5

place and time at which Jesus uttered the words, the crisis or revelation value of the sayings is not thereby exhausted and disposed of. *The person of Jesus is inevitably drawn into the circle of crisis created by the signs or works, and the question must arise sooner or later for his hearers, as for himself, in what relation he stands to the coming Messiah.* We see this process completing itself in the tradition in the case of No. 5 of the above sayings. In the Q text of this word, to judge from Lk. xi. 49-51, Jesus quoted a Jewish wisdom-writing *à propos* of his indictment of the scribes. In Mt. xxiii. 34 f. the words have become the words of Jesus himself. The divine revelation implied in the situation has drawn its significance over the person of the central figure.

3. It is contended by Bultmann that in the original form of most of the Son of Man sayings a distinction was clearly implied between the person of Jesus and that of the heavenly Son of Man. In defence of this view appeal is made to such of the above sayings as Nos. 7, 11, 13, 14, 16, 17, 20. There appears, indeed, no absolute reason why Jesus should not in these and other utterances belonging to his public teaching have spoken of the coming of the Son of Man with the same objectivity with which he spoke of the coming of the Kingdom of God. The Son of Man from heaven would be the final sign to that generation. The Son of Man would honour those who had acknowledged the mission and message of Jesus. The Son of Man would pronounce the reward or punishment of men and nations. Only on the assumption that Jesus' message of the Kingdom *started* from the assurance that he was the Messiah would this possibility have to be excluded. But even if Jesus did speak objectively of the Son of Man and his coming, it is clear that in the historical context in which the words were uttered these words would become charged with a significance going altogether beyond their formal terms. If Jesus saw the kingdom of God breaking through into history in the signs attending him, he cannot but have been occupied with the question in what relation his own work stood to the predicted coming of the Son of Man. The idea, then, that the formal distinction between himself and the Son of Man was maintained to the end is contrary to the probabilities of the case. *If Jesus saw the kingdom of God to be foreshadowed in his work, he cannot but, sooner or later, have thought of the Son of Man as fore-shadowed in himself.*

4. If we hold to the realism with which Jesus confronted his actual situation, we can explain also such other prophetic utter-

ances as we find in Nos. 18 and 19 of the above list. The " Elias
is already come " of Mk. ix. 13 has indeed been set down to the
theological debates of the early Christian community.[1] But is
there any reason why Jesus, if he pronounced his own work to be
the sign of the advent of the age of salvation, should not have
seen the fulfilment of past revelation in the events of contemporary history and declared that in John the Baptist the precursor
of the End, the herald of the Son of Man, had come ? As regards
No. 18, the saying about the dissolution of the temple, the question
is complicated for us by the difficulty of recovering the original
terms of the prediction. In the form in which it appears in Mk.
xiii. 2—apart from Codex D, the Old Latin, and Cyprian, which
have a different text—the prediction represents but one aspect of
the approaching doom which Jesus may well have announced
as the consequence of the nation's blindness to the call of God at
the supreme crisis of history. But if some different form of the
logion, implied in one or other of the various traditions which we
find in Acts vi. 14, Jn. ii. 19, Mk. xiv. 58, should have to be taken
as the historical starting-point, if in other words Jesus said, " I
will rear the new temple," it would follow that the witness of
Jesus to the coming events of the Messianic age had already
passed over into the explicit disclosure of himself as the Messiah,
and in that case the saying would have to be assigned to the final
stage of his self-revelation. At this point, therefore, we may turn
to the personal group of sayings in which Jesus speaks expressly
of his own mission and destiny.

THE PERSON OF JESUS IN THE CIRCLE OF CRISIS

As instances of personal sayings making use of the formula
" I came " or the like, we may take the following : [2]

1. " I did not come to call the righteous but sinners "
   (Mk. ii. 17).
2. " I came to cast fire on earth, etc." (Lk. xii. 49).
3. " I did not come to cast peace on earth but a sword "
   (Mt. x. 34. Cf. Lk. xii. 51).
4. " I did not come to annul (the law or the prophets) but
   to fulfil " (Mt. v. 17).
5. " The Son of Man came to seek and to save that which
   was lost " (Lk. xix. 10).

[1] Bultmann, *Geschichte*, p. 131. [2] *Ibid.*, pp. 161-179.

6. " The Son of Man came not to be ministered to, but . . . to give his life as a ransom for many " (Mk. x. 45, etc.).

7. " Whoever shall receive me, receives not me but him who sent me " (Mk. ix. 37. Cf. Mt. x. 40, Lk. x. 16).

8. " I saw Satan as lightning fallen from heaven " (Lk. x. 18).

9. " Lo, I have given you the power to tread on serpents and scorpions, etc." (Lk. x. 19).

10. " I make disposition to you, as my Father made disposition to me, of a kingdom, that you may eat and drink, etc." (Lk. xxii. 28-30. Cf. Mt. xix. 28).

11. " All things have been delivered unto me by my Father " (Mt. xi. 25-26, Lk. x. 21).

12. " No one knows the Son except the Father, etc." (Mt. xi. 27, Lk. x. 22).

13. " Come unto me . . . and I will give you rest, etc." (Mt. xi. 28-30).

14. " Where two or three are gathered together in my name, there am I in the midst of them " (Mt. xviii. 20).

In his criticism of this personal group of sayings Bultmann acknowledges that there can be no à priori objection to the idea that Jesus declared himself at times on the subject of his coming, for this could be done without any abandonment of the " prophetic " level of consciousness which alone counts with Bultmann as historical. In point of fact, this limitation is not observed in the actual character of the traditional sayings of the " I came " type, and formal as well as material grounds exist, he thinks, for attributing them en masse to the community rather than to Jesus. For one thing, the " I came " formula indicates of itself that the life and mission of Jesus are now seen in the retrospect, and therefore the words—even in such otherwise unobjectionable cases as Nos. 1 and 2 of the above sayings, or in Mt. xv. 24, " I was not sent except to the lost sheep of the house of Israel "—are words of the post-resurrection Church. Here we have a typical illustration of the Form-critical method. As regards the ' Son of Man ' utterances included in the group, of which there are examples in Nos. 5 and 6, there exists the additional objection that for the prophetic consciousness of Jesus and for the faith of the primitive Church the Son of Man counted always as " the coming one," not as one who had " come," and therefore the

sayings are pronounced to be late, and, as Bultmann thinks,
Hellenistic productions. The only escape from this position
would be to suppose that Jesus, if he spoke the words, was alluding
to the Son of Man of some semi-Gnostic speculation or mystery,
who appears *on earth* seeking the lost souls of men and suffering
in order to effect their release, a theory which Bultmann dis-
favours. Finally, as regards sayings of the type exemplified in
Nos. 8-14, Bultmann's general judgement is that it is the Risen
Lord, speaking through his prophets in the Church, who is the
source of these assurances, just as it is the Risen Lord who declares
in Mt. xxviii. 18-20, " All power is given to me in heaven and on
earth . . . and lo, I am with you all the days till the consummation
of the age." Indeed these sayings, according to Bultmann, do
not in any way essentially differ from the Logia of Jesus found in
the Oxyrhynchus papyri and in the apocryphal Gospels. The
' form ' is the same.[1]

As an example of the rejection of these sayings on material as
well as formal grounds the treatment accorded to saying No. 2
in the above list is noteworthy.

> " I came to cast fire on earth, and how I would it were already
> lit ! But I have a baptism to be baptized with, and how constrained
> I am till it has been accomplished ! " (Lk. xii. 49-50).

If any saying in the tradition has *prima facie* the claim to be an
authentic dominical utterance, it is this enigmatic and oracular
allusion to the meaning of Jesus' work and fortunes. It is not the
kind of trite and conventional saying which the later community
would invent, any more than is Mt. xi. 12, the word about the
kingdom of heaven suffering violence. But when the saying is
brought to the exacting test of exegesis, Bultmann would say that
every confidence in it as a genuine word of Jesus disappears.[2]
For what is the ' baptism ' in verse 50. Is it the martyr-death of
Jesus ? Then, like Mk. x. 38, the word is a *vaticinium ex eventu*.
But is verse 49 any more genuine ? The ' fire ' cannot be the
purifying process of repentance which Jesus had come to inaugurate, for the cry, " How I would it were already kindled ! "
must refer to something not yet in progress. Does it refer, then,
to the Spirit which was to descend from heaven ? In that case,
the word is a production of the Pentecostal Church. Or does
the word reflect the expectation made popular by some ' Son of
Man ' myth that the heavenly Messenger after anguish on earth

---

[1] *Geschichte*, pp. 175 f.   [2] *Ibid.*, p. 168.

is to bring about a world-judgement which as fire will consume the earth ? In that case, too, the word will not be a word of Jesus, but a fragment or citation from the myth. In every case the word reveals itself as a post-resurrection formation. To all this it may be replied that the cry, " How I would it were already lit ! " does not necessarily imply that a light had not already been set to the fire in question. The purifying process of repentance might have already begun, and Jesus still desire to see it thoroughly going, just as the kingdom of God is declared to be already in the midst, and yet Jesus looks forward to its coming one day with power (Mk. ix. 1).

The general attitude to the " personal " sayings illustrated in the preceding pages calls for certain criticisms.

1. If Jesus saw the kingdom of God already manifesting its presence and power in the world around him, it becomes inept to impose on him the strict canons of the prophetic type of consciousness, and to require that a saying in order to be passed as historical must conform to these rules. No prophet speaks of himself as coming or having come in the sense in which Jesus does.[1] Yet no word of Jesus has better title to be regarded as historical than that which throws " the law and the prophets " into the past (Mt. xi. 12-13, Lk. xvi. 16a). Why should not Jesus, as in Nos. 1-4 of the above sayings, speak of his mission with the reflective consciousness that it marked a new and final era in divine-human relations ?

2. As regards Son of Man utterances belonging to this class, the possibility exists that in sayings Nos. 5 and 6 in the above list and indeed in an indefinite number of other similar sayings, the locution ' Son of Man ' has simply replaced an original ' I ' of Jesus, so that these sayings fall into the same category as Nos. 1-4. At the same time, the alternative possibility must be kept in mind that Jesus, whether with or, as is more likely, without any suggestion from contemporary Son of Man mysticism, had come to interpret the destiny of the heavenly Son of Man as fulfilling itself in terms of the suffering and sacrifice of the ' Servant ' of Isa. liii,[2] in which case the *style* of these utterances is no argument against their historicity.

3. It can be granted that post-resurrection mysticism has left traces and products of itself in the sayings-tradition, and that No. 14 of the above words, in which the presence of Jesus among his followers is defined in terms of universal, all-pervading spirit,

---

[1] Bultmann, *Geschichte*, p. 168.   [2] See later, Chapter VII.

is best explained in that way. But to suppose that such utterances as Nos. 8-9 can only have originated as revelations to the post-resurrection community is to ignore the place which *ecstasy* may have had at great moments in the consciousness of Jesus. As a matter of fact, these two sayings are sufficiently grounded in the reflective consciousness of Jesus with regard to his exorcisms. In these acts Satan's power was already seen to be overthrown and his demons to be trodden under foot. There is no need, therefore, to postulate a post-resurrection standpoint either here or in the case of saying No. 10, which will be considered in a later chapter.

THE FATHER AND THE SON. A STUDY OF MATTHEW XI. 25-30, LUKE X. 21-22.

There remain the sayings in the great passage, Mt. xi. 25-30 (Nos. 11, 12, 13), which with the parallels to the first two in Lk. x. 21-22 may be said to represent the climax of the self-revelational logia of Jesus in the tradition. In point of form and substance the Q part of the passage (Sayings 11-12) so resembles the oracles characteristic of the Fourth Gospel that it is customary to describe it as a 'Johannine' ingredient in the Synoptic tradition, and a considerable controversy has arisen around the question of the origin, primitive form, and Christological significance of the sayings. The best-known modern critical discussion of the passage is still perhaps that of von Harnack,[1] but more recently Form-Criticism, following in the wake of Norden's penetrating study of the religious style of this and similar utterances,[2] has taken up the question afresh and produced, apart from the critical estimates of Dibelius[3] and Bultmann,[4] a special monograph on the subject by a Swedish scholar, T. Arvedson.[5]

It is the merit of Harnack's contribution that, over against a criticism which would relegate these great Q logia to a secondary place as originating in a Christian hymn or incantation, he considers the possibility that in its original form the passage expressed " conceptions which fit in with the genuine sphere of thought " of Jesus.[6] On the strength of certain features in the

---

[1] *The Sayings of Jesus*, pp. 272-310. [2] *Agnostos Theos*, pp. 277-308.
[3] *From Tradition to Gospel*, pp. 279-283.
[4] *Die Geschichte der Synoptischen Tradition*, pp. 171-172.
[5] *Das Mysterium Christi* (Uppsala, 1937).
[6] *The Sayings of Jesus*, p. 218.

second-century Patristic tradition of the passage, Harnack convinces himself that in the original text of Luke, and therefore in Q, what now appears in the form of Mt. xi. 27, Lk. x. 22 stood as follows :

πάντα μοι παρεδόθη ὑπὸ τοῦ πατρός, καὶ οὐδεὶς ἔγνω τὸν πατέρα εἰ μὴ ὁ υἱὸς καὶ ᾧ ἐὰν βούληται ὁ υἱὸς ἀποκαλύψαι.

"Everything (i.e. all knowledge) has been delivered to me by my Father, and no one has known the Father except the Son, and he to whom the Son wills to make the revelation."

Here the clause which stands first in our texts of Matthew and Luke : "No one knows the Son except the Father" is missing. It is considered to have been absent from the original text of Luke and from Q.[1] Harnack thinks it probable that it was first inserted by the writer of Matthew, who also changed the aorist tense of the verb (ἔγνω) into the present tense (γινώσκει).[2] The subsequent assimilation of the text of Luke to that of Matthew was not, however, accomplished without leaving traces of the original in manuscripts known to second-century and later Fathers. Hence the difference of their text from ours. On this showing the original logion stated a claim of Jesus to have received, and to communicate to men through his teaching the true knowledge of God, and admits of being understood in a manner which, Harnack thinks, is in keeping with the actualities of the historical situation of Jesus. "The concrete situation in which Jesus found himself limited the sphere of the significance of the utterance both for himself and for his hearers."[3] The claim to special knowledge of God does not, Harnack considers, exceed the claim which is made elsewhere in the word about blessed eyes and ears in Mt. xiii. 16 f. or in the declaration in Mt. xii. 41-42 that a greater than Jonah and Solomon is present.[4]

In the present passage, however, the special knowledge which makes the teaching of Jesus a revelation of God is expressly grounded upon the filiality of his consciousness in relation to God, and this is a unique relation. Jesus knows himself as the Chosen One, the Beloved, the 'Son' of the Father.[5] The saying, therefore, is definitely Messianic in form, and as such it will fall

---

[1] *The Sayings of Jesus*, pp. 292-295.

[2] *Ibid.*, p. 294. On the whole question of the text, on the original form of which scholars are by no means agreed, see besides Harnack, Dr. B. S. Easton's discussion of the passage in his *Gospel According to St. Luke* (1926), and Dr. A. E. J. Rawlinson's *New Testament Doctrine of the Christ* (1926), pp. 251-264.

[3] *The Sayings of Jesus*, p. 298.   [4] *Ibid.*, p. 220.   [5] *Ibid.*, p. 300.

to be considered at the proper place.[1] Enough meantime that
the logion in its primitive form stands, in Harnack's judgement,
in sufficiently close relation to the concrete actuality of the situation of Jesus to be defensible as an historical utterance and as
furnishing a valuable clue to his mind and personality.

Similar is the position taken by Harnack with regard to the
sequel, the great " Come unto Me " utterance in Mt. xi. 28-30.
As this saying does not stand in Luke, it cannot be proved to have
been drawn from Q, but it has an inward affinity with the Q
logia with which it is conjoined, and Harnack sees no convincing
reason for deriving it from any later tradition.[2] It is indeed an
arguable sign of primary tradition that the ' yoke ' of Jesus is
declared to be easy and his burden to be light. The later community did not confess the commandments of Jesus to be so easy
a matter unless in the one passage I Jn. v. 3. The saying, therefore, has its origin in the enthusiasm of Jesus, who called the
burdened to himself as another Jesus, the son of Sirach, called
his contemporaries to submit to the yoke of Wisdom (Ecclus. li),
using language which our logion in its present form seems distinctly to reflect. The echoes of Ecclesiasticus in the passage
exactly resemble those of Isa. l. 6-8 in Mt. v. 39-40, and reference
may be made to the discussion of that parallel at an earlier point
in the present work.[3]

Ecclus. 51	Mt. 11
(1) " I will give thanks (ἐξομολογήσομαι) to thee, Lord (κύριε), King . . ."	(25) " I give thanks (ἐξομολογοῦμαι) to thee, Father, Lord (κύριε) . . ."
(23) " Draw near to me (πρός με) . . ."	(28) " Hither to me (πρός με) . . ."
(26) " Place your neck under the yoke (ζυγόν), and let your soul (ἡ ψυχὴ ὑμῶν) receive instruction . . ."	(29) " Take my yoke (ζυγόν) upon you, and learn from me . . ."
(27) " For I laboured but a little, and found for myself much rest (ἀνάπαυσιν)."	" and you will find rest (ἀνάπαυσιν) for your souls (ταῖς ψυχαῖς ὑμῶν), for my yoke is easy, etc."

The meaning is that because Jesus is the revealer of God in his
teaching he holds the secret of life for all who turn to him. Unlike

---

[1] See later, Chapter VI, pp. 108-109. [2] *The Sayings of Jesus*, p. 307.
[3] See above, Chapter II, pp. 30-32.

the son of Sirach, however, he has not *learned* the secret of rest, but possesses it in himself.

That the sayings in Mt. xi. 27-30 and Lk. x. 22 have undergone considerable elaboration, both in form and in substance, is scarcely to be doubted, but Harnack's contention that genuine words of Jesus expressive of a more than prophetic consciousness of bringing to men the knowledge of the Father form the underlying basis is reasonable in itself, and accords with the reality of the historical situation in which, as we see by other proofs, Jesus believed himself to stand. The only question is, Is Harnack right in his reconstruction of the original text of Mt. xi. 27, Lk. x. 22 ? The textual phenomena which serve him as ground for cutting out the primary clause referring to the Father's knowledge of the *Son* are exceedingly slight, and admit of other explanations, even mechanical ones. Moreover, it is possible, and indeed intrinsically probable, that the historical event or crisis which the thanksgiving of Jesus signalized had to do with the disclosure to the disciples of the secret of his Messiahship. In that case the asseveration that " No one knew the Son except the Father," or words to that effect, would be integral to the situation.[1] God had ' recognized ' Jesus by revealing him as the elect Son, a destiny which had been foreshadowed in the signs attending him and in the ' exousia ' of his doctrine, but had not been made known until now. With this qualification it can be acknowledged that Harnack's interpretation by its emphasis on the essentially revelational character of our Lord's teaching affords a more convincing explanation of the source and origin of these logia than do the more modern theories sponsored by the school of Form-Criticism.

For the latter the logia in question are almost entirely " community productions," being proved such by their form. According to Dibelius a mythological idea of Jesus and his gospel has here penetrated into the Q tradition.[2] It is visible in the emphasis placed upon ' gnosis ' in the passage, in the high concentration of attention upon the person of Jesus as hierophant or revealer, and in the conception of salvation as ' rest.' Such features indicate that the true *Sitz im Leben* of these oracles lies outside the historical teaching of Jesus, and indeed outside the bounds of primitive Judean Christianity. " This combination of

[1] See in particular Dr. B. S. Easton's discussion of the passage in his *Gospel According to St. Luke*.

[2] *From Tradition to Gospel*, p. 279.

self-recommendation and of the preaching of conversion is the typical mark of the divine or semi-divine herald of revelation in Hellenistic religion, i.e. of a mythological person." [1] Dibelius would therefore assign the logia to Church circles which had transposed the stern message of Jesus with regard to repentance and judgement-to-come into a redemption-mystery revelation. [2] Bultmann, in turn, thinks that the passage is a conglomerate of ideas borrowed by the post-resurrection community or created within its pale. Mt. xi. 25-26, indeed, might be a word of Jesus, but it falls outside of the ordinary framework of the tradition, and is probably derived from a late Jewish writing. Mt. xi. 27 is a specifically " Hellenistic " word of revelation, which resembles Mt. xxviii. 18, and like that passage it may have been originally delivered as a word of the Risen Lord. Mt. xi. 28-30 has as a whole the stamp of a Wisdom-utterance, which has its true affinities, not as Dibelius thinks in Hellenistic conversion-religion, but in teaching like that of Ecclus. li. 23 ff. and xxiv. 19 ff., and Bultmann would derive it from a Jewish Wisdom-book. [3] It is interesting here to see how widely the Form-Critics differ. Finally, Arvedson regards the whole passage as a product of the liturgical worship of certain mystical circles within Christianity. [4] The influence of Mowinckel's work on the Psalms is apparent in his idea that the cultus-context of the logia was a mystery-celebration having for its subject the Enthronement of Christ.

In answer to these theories which find in the *form* or style of religious utterances a sure clue to their origin and provenance, two things need to be said. (1) It is possible to draw the line of division between Jewish and Hellenistic Christianity too sharply, or more sharply than our actual knowledge warrants. We do not know to what extent mystical ideas had found a place in late Jewish circles so as to form a part of the heritage of Jesus. [5] (2) Form may be bestowed or imposed on words or traditions which have originated in some quite other milieu than that which finally stamps them. Thus it is possible to hold that Form-Criticism has something to say for itself as regards the *final* shape of the logia which have been here under review, and at the same time to hold with Harnack that these logia originated on the lips of Jesus and reveal his authentic claim to offer men in his teaching a saving knowledge of God.

---

[1] *From Tradition to Gospel*, p. 281.   [2] *Ibid.*, p. 282.
[3] *Geschichte*, pp. 171-172.   [4] *Das Mysterium Christi*, pp. 229 f.
[5] This is a point which is strongly urged by Rudolf Otto.

It is not necessary to add anything further *à propos* of modern views of the passage except to notice that Rudolf Otto, who finds the key to much of the teaching of Jesus in the influence of the Enoch-literature upon his thought, avers that the logia in question, gnostic as they have been pronounced to be, were not impossible on the lips of one " who believed the prediction of Enoch to be fulfilled in himself." [1]   He cites I Enoch xxxvii. 4 :

> " Such wisdom has never been given by the Lord of Spirits as I have received according to my insight, according to the good pleasure of the Lord of Spirits, by whom the lot of eternal life has been given to me." [2]

It would, however, be unwise to make much of this supposed dependence of the mind of Jesus on the Enoch-literature.   In Otto's book the theory has been pushed to an inordinate length.

In this Chapter the main topic which has engaged us has been the fulfilment-significance of the teaching of Jesus.   But this teaching claims not merely to mark the consummation of prophecy but to possess an absolute character.   In other words, its revelation-value lies not in its historical context alone, in which it stands related to a moment of religious crisis, but in its intrinsic content.   To that aspect of it we have now to pass on.

[1] *The Kingdom of God and the Son of Man*, pp. 235-236.
[2] R. H. Charles's translation.

CHAPTER V

THE TEACHING OF JESUS. II. ITS CHARACTER AS RELIGIOUS AND ETHICAL ABSOLUTE

THE nature of the teaching of Jesus as embodying a religious and ethical absolute has received incidental attention at certain stages in the preceding argument, but some fuller treatment of the subject must now be undertaken.

OBJECTIVE CHARACTER OF THE Q RECENSION

As the authority with which Jesus taught was recognized in the early community, it was natural that there should be a desire to present the terms of his teaching objectively and with as close an approach to system as the nature of the material permitted. It is as thus abstracted and objectified that we have now to consider it, recognizing that words of Jesus first spoken to men in situations of crisis created by the near approach of the kingdom of God possess a value and significance which are not limited by consideration of the temporal and historical circumstances under which they were originally delivered.

That this was felt from the earliest days is shown by the circulation in the tradition, as far back as we can trace it, of 'situation-less' words of Jesus, of which it can be said without any hesitation that they originated not as general truths or precepts but as particular pronouncements made to individuals at decisive moments and under a given set of circumstances. Some of these moments are still illustrated for us in 'pronouncement-stories' of the type of Mt. viii. 19-22, Lk. ix. 57-62, where the word, "Leave the dead to bury their dead," is issued not as a general command, but in a definite context, and indeed it is very probable that many of the detached logia which came to be embodied in the Q source were first transmitted in pronouncement-stories. These pronouncement-stories were subsequently broken up or lost, leaving the logia as their *debris*. It is no contradiction of this position that we see the contrary process also taking place in the tradition, and words of Jesus forming fresh contexts and becoming the nuclei of new pronouncement-stories. We find probable instances of the latter process in the narrative settings

77

provided for quite a number of words of Jesus in St. Luke's Gospel, and there are unquestionable instances of it in the text of Codex Bezæ and other manuscripts and in non-canonical literature. The truth is that both processes worked side by side in the early tradition. What primarily concerns us here is that *from a very early time a mass of words of Jesus had become detached from their original roots and were free to form ideal or didactic unities in the mind of the community.*

Thus when the Q redaction of the teaching came into existence, it represented already the result of an advanced process of abstraction and systematization. Words of Jesus originally spoken in concrete situations and to stamp the significance for individuals or groups of individuals of the near approach of the last judgement and the Reign of God were here assembled apart from their contexts and presented as truths of general application. Not that this signified in any real way an abstraction of this body of truth from *Jesus*, or the will to replace the gospel of God's intervention in him by the authority attaching to a system of ideas. For, firstly, much of the Q matter, consisting as it did of exhortations, warnings, predictions and the like, had a character which could not but keep alive a sense of the religious crisis forming the background of the sayings ; and, secondly, many Q sections such as the Temptation-narrative or the answer of Jesus to the messengers of John were inextricably bound up with the ' signs ' of Jesus. The Q source therefore pointed forward not to an independent future, but to such an ultimate re-integration into the Church's gospel as has taken place in Matthew and in Luke. Nevertheless, a body of truth has here come together which is capable of being looked at by itself, as possessing a self-evidencing character, and as constituting a revelation of God apart from the circumstances of historical crisis in which the constituent elements had their origin.

In other words, *the Q document is a manifesto that the teaching of Jesus has an absolute as well as a crisis and fulfilment significance, and this claim is re-asserted in the Gospels of Matthew and Luke, into which the Q matter has passed.*

THE SERMON ON THE MOUNT. I. ITS CHARACTER AND CONTEXT

The Q source already contained a sequence of teaching which began with Beatitudes, passed on to formulate the law of love as the central commandment of Jesus, and ended with warnings and with a parable about building houses on rock and on sand. This structure is preserved for us with comparative simplicity in Lk. vi. 20-49. The same sequence, but in fuller outline, with more art and fashioning, and with great accretions of material from other parts of Q and from other sources, appears again in Mt. v-vii in what we call the 'Sermon on the Mount.' Here, more than in Q, the words of Jesus have been detached from their living situations and worked into a system on the strength of their own internal coherency. Here, more than in Q, *the substance of the teaching of Jesus has been capitalized or funded, so to speak, so as to bear interest of itself as an objective summation of the Christian doctrine of righteousness*. Here, more than in Q, the absolute character of the revelation of truth in Jesus is affirmed. It is indeed also true that in Matthew, as compared with Q, the Sermon is fitted more closely and definitely into the framework of the signs and of the power attending Jesus,[1] and is more articulately expressed as personal voice, deliverance, and revelation of the Son of Man.[2] It comes in as only an episode in a larger history, and therefore as presenting but one facet of a revelation which shines also in the works of Jesus, in his death and resurrection, and in his coming again to judge the world. Nevertheless, the terms of the teaching are so set down as to speak for themselves and to challenge and engage attention by their intrinsic quality of spiritual and ethical truth, all the more so because the teaching in question claims to transcend the 'righteousness' inculcated in the religion of Israel.

THE SERMON ON THE MOUNT. II. GRACE IN THE TEACHING OF JESUS

The Sermon in our Gospels, as in the source, opens with 'Beatitudes.' The kingdom of heaven is promised to the poor, the sorrowful, the hungry, the persecuted—clear evidence that the religious and ethical absolute of Jesus is set in a context of grace. What is it that has made these spirits poor, sorrowful, and a-hungered after righteousness? Is it divine predestination, or is it human experience of life, or is it the working of God's word on the heart that accounts for this spiritual receptivity? Such

---

[1] Cf. Mt. iv. 23-25, viii. 1-ix. 34, vii. 28-29.
[2] The formula " I say unto you " occurs fourteen times in the Mt.-Sermon.

questions are not reflected upon in the context any more than they are reflected upon in Isa. lxi. The likeliest explanation is, I consider, the third mentioned. Jesus trusted that the divine Word, when presented to the souls of men, would produce the appropriate spiritual reaction, and so fulfil the redeeming purpose of God. As it is by the divine Word that we truly live, as we have fullness of life only as God speaks to us, every vital reaction of the religious spirit is to be taken to a source in God. Here clearly, as the forefront position of the Beatitudes indicates, it is in grace that the Christian revelation begins, and it is on grace that it rests—a point which must not be overlooked in the construing of any part of the Mt.-Sermon. God *wills* that the kingdom of heaven and its righteousness shall be given to men, and He accomplishes this purpose by the very token that the first effect of the radical apprehension of the final good is to reduce the soul to a consciousness of its own unqualifiable poverty, heart-ache, and need.

Even in Mark, where the theme of the preaching of Jesus, like that of the Baptist, appears as ' metanoia ' or repentance, the repentance is presented as the concomitant or obverse of faith in the ' evangelion,' the good news that " the time is fulfilled, and the kingdom of God has drawn near " (Mk. i. 14-15).[1] But in Q and in the Sermon on the Mount the prevenience of grace is more articulately expressed, and Harnack would stress this as a primary historical feature of the representation. " How, indeed, are we to conceive of Jesus' preaching of repentance ? It could not have consisted simply of the repetition of the word ' Repent ! ' It must have pictured in glowing colours the blessedness of conversion and of the new life. And this is just what we find in the Sermon on the Mount." [2] Certainly it is not by excoriating sin so much as by showing us the absolute nature of goodness, above all in its form as love, that the Jesus of the tradition leads us to repentance.

As a matter of fact, not the Beatitudes only, but the whole Sermon on the Mount stands in a very close relation to the glowing redemption-programme of Isa. lxi. This is a point which has not, so far as I am aware, been noticed by critics or commentators, and I take the opportunity to set out the parallelism.

[1] Cf. Goguel, *Life of Jesus*, pp. 313-316.
[2] Harnack, *Sayings of Jesus*, p. 203.

Isa. lxi

Mt. v-vii

(1-3) The commission of the anointed prophet or Servant is to proclaim good news (LXX, εὐαγγελίσασθαι) to the poor, the mourners, etc., and to comfort all who mourn.

(v. 3-4) Jesus pronounces blessings on the poor, the mourners, etc., and assures the mourners that they will be comforted.

(6) "You shall be named the priests of the Lord : men shall call you the ministers of our God."

(v. 13-14) "You are the salt of the earth . . . You are the light of the world, etc." (Spoken to disciples as the prophets of the new era.)

(3b) "That they might be called trees of righteousness, the planting of the Lord."

(vii. 17-20) "Every good tree brings forth good fruit . . . Therefore by their fruits you shall know them."

(8) "I the Lord love judgement" (LXX, δικαιοσύνην).

(v. 20) "Except your righteousness exceeds, etc." (vi. 33) "Seek first his kingdom and his righteousness."

(9) "Their seed shall be known among the nations (LXX, ἐν τοῖς ἔθνεσιν) . . . that they are the seed which the Lord hath blessed."

(v. 45, 47) "That you may be sons of your Father who is in heaven. . . . If you salute your brethren only, what do you more than others ? Do not even the Gentiles (οἱ ἐθνικοί) do as much as that ? "

(11b) "The Lord will cause righteousness . . . to spring forth (LXX, ἀνατελεῖ) before all the nations."

(v. 45) "Your Father makes his sun to rise (ἀνατέλλει) . . . on the just and on the unjust, etc."

The verbal coincidences may be slight, but it is difficult to think that they originated by accident. *Was the original discourse, memoranda of which the Q tradition preserved, a commentary by Jesus on the prophetic vision of redemption, pointing the moral for his disciples as heirs of the promises of grace ?* In that case we should have an interesting proof of what is otherwise probable enough in itself, that Matthew has preserved the Q sermon in fuller detail and with more of its original colouring than has Luke, whose reproduction in vi. 20-49 lacks some of the Isaianic touches. We should also have reason to think that the Q sermon and the other sermon which Luke's special L source ascribed to Jesus at Nazareth (Lk. iv. 16-21) were possibly variants of the same original. Finally, we should have impressive additional

6

evidence that the primitive material of the tradition was more deeply impregnated with Old Testament prophetic ideas than some of the later redactors recognized.[1]

THE SERMON ON THE MOUNT. III. JESUS AND THE JEWISH LAW AND ORDINANCES

The foundation of the teaching of Jesus in grace being once recognized, we are in a position to come face to face with its absolute content in the demand of righteousness. In the Q sermon the absolute content formulates itself at once in the principle of love, a love extending even to enemies, and requiring the ruthless abandonment of all ordinary considerations of prudence and self-interest (Lk. vi. 27-36). In the Mt.-Sermon this supreme principle of love comes as the climax of a series of demands developed antithetically with reference to the current legal understanding of the divine commandments, and requiring whole-hearted sincerity, purity, truth, and unselfishness, as well as love in return for hatred. To what extent this antithetical presentation of the teaching of Jesus was suggested by the pre-existing tradition in Q or other sources drawn upon by the evangelist, to what extent it reflects the evangelist's own architectonic freedom of exposition and arrangement, is a question which is not easily answered. The form in which the Lk.-Sermon introduces the love-commandment, viz. "But I say unto you my hearers, love your enemies" (Lk. vi. 27), looks like the relic of an antithetical setting in Q, which the writer of Matthew has taken occasion to develop. In any case, it is the purpose of the Mt.-Sermon to show that Jesus, so far from abrogating the law and the prophets, came to 'fulfil' them by putting an absolute construction on the righteous demand of God and by calling His followers to be "perfect even as your heavenly Father is perfect." The perfection in question stands in particular relation to the love of God to sinners (Mt. v. 48). Here, then, *in the formulation of an absolute ethic of love the teaching of Jesus develops a supreme intrinsic revelational significance.*

Certainly it is on a plane above the Law that the Sermon makes Jesus stand when (1) over against the partial and relative notions of a Judaism which, with all its stress on the Law, had never, as Rudolf Bultmann rightly observes,[2] learned to think

---

[1] Cf. what has been said above, Chapter II, pp. 29-32, and Chapter III, pp. 48-49.

[2] *Jesus and the Word*, pp. 147 f.

radically of either righteousness or sin, of either the will of God or the actual moral condition of itself, Jesus sets up his ideal of absolute obedience, and (2) above every other principle governing duty he exalts love, a love like that of God Himself, extending even to sinners and enemies.

1. The Jewish religion of the Torah received and interpreted the Law as not only a definition of the nature of duty, but a circumscription of its province. A stipulated measure of obedience was demanded which, if it were rendered, left men in a position to consider themselves as for the rest their own : such a construction, at any rate, was open to the legalist mind. In this way the Law of God tended in certain quarters to become a sheltering roof between the souls of men and the searching light of God, and the same held true in essence of the apocalyptic programme of the last events. This interposed itself between the average Jew and any radical realization of what the kingdom of God, the divine salvation, meant. The pronouncements of apocalyptic preachers that the End was near did not minister always to repentance and spiritual sincerity, but often only to fantasy and to self-congratulation : blessed was he who should eat bread in the kingdom of God ! Duty, from the legal standpoint, was measurable, ponderable, practicable : the reward was definable, calculable, unquestionable. The effect of the pronouncement of Jesus is that every fancied security of this kind is at once swept away. Men are brought face to face with God's infinite and immediate claim to sovereignty : " This night is thy life required of thee ! " In other words, the ethic of Jesus is *existential*. It demands a man's total life for God.

2. While the religion of the Torah had given a place to the conception of love, it was not a place by which love could become the inspiration of religion over the whole sphere of its activity. Rabbinical Judaism at a later period distinguished between duties exactly regulated by precept, such as keeping the Sabbath and refraining from forbidden foods, and other duties not so regulated but left to conscience or, as the Rabbis phrased it, ' committed to the heart ' (*masur-la-leb*).[1] To the latter class belong the duties of charity and kindness to others. It does not appear, however, that this recognition of obligation lying beyond all statutory definition led to serious modification of the essential moralism of Pharisaic religion, much less to the paradoxical inversion of all customary ideas of duty in the principle of loving

[1] See G. F. Moore, *Judaism*, Vol. II, pp. 82 f.

enemies. *What the teaching of Jesus here does is to elevate the ' un-measured ' element in ethic to pre-eminence, to give love the control, and to extend it to the entire domain of human relations.* The result is—and here we see the real relation in which the teaching of Jesus stands to Judaism as observance of the Law—that it is no longer possible for the life of religion truly conceived, that is to say, for the life of religion as a fully restored relationship between the soul and God, to come down again to the old moralistic level at which love has to divide the field with an indefinite number of other imperatives. The Law is transcended by the fact that it is now grasped in its perfect norm.

Before passing on to questions connected with the origin of this supreme formulation of duty, and with the bearing of its absolute on our life, occasion may be taken to note that the same radicalism with which the ethical part of religion is defined in Mt. v is used in Mt. vi and vii to bring out the true character of the divine-human relation at other points. In vi. 1-10 the nature of the soul's approach to God, particularly in prayer, is the theme, and absolute sincerity is demanded as the essential spirit of worship.

"Thou, when thou prayest, enter into thine inner chamber, and having shut thy door, pray to thy Father who is in the secret place, and thy Father who seeth in secret shall recompense thee. . . . If you forgive men their trespasses, your heavenly Father will also forgive you, etc."

In vi. 19-34 the disciple's attitude to earthly goods and values is considered, and absolute trust in God for all needful things is required.

"No man can serve two masters : for either he will hate the one, and love the other, or else he will hold to one, and despise the other. You cannot serve God and mammon. Therefore I say to you, Be not anxious for your life. . . . But seek first his kingdom and his righteousness."

Finally, in vii. 13-27 the soul is confronted with the ultimate issues of life.

"Enter in by the narrow gate : for wide is the gate and broad the way that leads to destruction. . . . For narrow is the gate and constricted the way that leads to life, and few are they who find it. . . . Every one who hears these words of mine and does them shall be likened to a wise man who built his house upon the rock, etc."

Nothing could be more unlike either the prudential counsels of the Wisdom-literature or the moralistic assumptions of Pharisaic observance than this absoluteness of the religious call of Jesus. The ethic involved, as Prof. C. H. Dodd says, stands for the unattainable, which yet we are bound to strive to attain. " For to receive the kingdom of God is to place ourselves under this absolute obligation." [1] Though we may find in rabbinical literature and in the heathen moralists many parallels to the precepts of Jesus, nowhere do we find the same rigour either in the formulation or in the application. In the realism, therefore, with which the sovereignty or kingdom of God is brought home to men, we find the sign of the revelation of God in the teaching of Jesus.

THE SERMON ON THE MOUNT. IV. THE ETHICAL ABSOLUTE IN RELATION TO THE GOSPEL

It is at this point that certain urgent questions arise as to the real connection between this demand of righteousness and the ' gospel ' of Jesus, and between the ethical absolute of his teaching and our existence in a world of relativities. To some extent these questions have been already touched on,[2] but a more thorough investigation of the subject must now be undertaken. It will be convenient to take the aspects of the problem *seriatim*.

1. It has been observed, *à propos* of the Beatitudes, that the religious and ethical absolute of Jesus is set in a context of grace. We have also seen that the immediacy and the realism with which the kingdom of God was apprehended by Jesus carried with it the high tension of his summons to newness of life. *With the near approach of the kingdom the realization of the hope of righteousness had come into view.* Jesus does not make use of the term ' grace,' as St. Paul does, but in his message of God's immediate will to establish His kingdom we have its equivalent. If God purposes now to bestow His kingdom on the poor and the penitent, it means that He will also satisfy them with righteousness (Mt. v. 6). But if it is for God to bring about this consummation, it is for men on their side to seek it (Mt. vi. 33). The Lord God will cause righteousness to spring forth before all the nations (Isa. lxi. 11) : but, as Jesus interprets this righteousness, it is something which permits no divided loyalties on man's side, no faltering

---

[1] *History and the Gospel*, pp. 126-127.
[2] See above, Chapter IV, pp. 61-63.

purpose. It is impossible not to see in this that Jesus thinks of human nature not in its empirical actuality but as taken up and engaged by the divine redeeming purpose, so as to become the field of that purpose. Jesus cannot have known less about human nature than St. Paul does in Romans vii, but he looks at it in the light of the divine power and love now breaking from the skies. The powers of the kingdom of God are already at work in the world. The seed of the new life is cast into the ground. In passionate prolepsis Jesus also sees the righteousness of God in all its purity and perfection realizing itself among men. Nevertheless, because it is ethic, man must will and seek it. And that he may will and seek it, Jesus holds it up in all its truth.

This at any rate is one side of the matter. The prophets of the Old Testament, indicting the nation's sin, had projected the hope of righteousness or justification into the future, so that it had become a mark of the kingdom of God. As such, Jesus now announces it, and announces it with the assurance that, when God's word is presented to man, it cannot fail of its fulfilment.

2. The prophetic teaching of the Old Testament had stressed the inwardness of pure religion, and had looked forward to the interiorizing of the Law of God as a mark of the ' new covenant ' (Jer. xxxi. 33-34, Ezek. xxxvi. 26-27). This is associated in Jeremiah with the knowledge of God and with the forgiveness of sins, and in Ezekiel with the gift of a new heart and a new spirit. If the absolute ethic of the Sermon on the Mount is grounded in the revelation of the true knowledge of God, may we not also say that the confidence of Jesus in its fulfilment is implicitly supported by the prophetic intimations regarding the renewal of mankind which is to come with the new order ?

It will be necessary to return to other aspects of this question later. Meantime, the whole historical context of the Sermon and its significance as pronouncement of the *Messiah* have to be kept in mind, for they locate both demand and fulfilment within the sphere of grace.

3. How did Jesus come to formulate the supreme principle of the will of God as love ? In this he goes beyond the prophets. It is true that on the path by which the ethic of Mt. v. winds upwards to its highest point prophetic ideals keep company with it almost to the end. The prophetic principle of the inward law goes together with everything that Jesus says about the third, sixth, seventh, and ninth commandments. *However difficult or even impossible it may be from the empirical human standpoint to attain*

to such a standard of obedience, it is all written in the prophets. There is prophetic precedent even for the great principle of non-retaliation, which forms the penultimate stage in the ascension of thought to the final principle.

" I say unto you, Resist not him that is evil : but whoever smites thee on thy right cheek, turn to him the other also."

Compare with this the Servant-passage in Isa. l. 6-8 :

" I gave my back to the smiters, and my cheeks to them that plucked off the hair : I hid not my face from shame and spitting. For the Lord God will help me ; therefore have I not been confounded. . . . . He is near that justifieth me."

The Lord God will help me ! It may be seen here how the ethic of Jesus is oriented. In the LXX text of Isaiah the points of connection with the requirement of Jesus are, as has been noticed above, even more numerous than appears in our English version,[1] nor can there be any doubt that Jesus was basing this penultimate commandment on the principle revealed by the Servant who fulfils his redeeming task by bearing men's iniquities. This is a point of cardinal importance. Jesus does not envisage the fulfilment of the ideal of righteousness except in the sequence of the divine redeeming purpose and in association with the spirit manifested by the Lord's Servant. Yet not even the Servant is said to suffer and to die in *love* to men. This, however, is the interpretation which Jesus puts upon his work, and at this supreme point Jesus stands alone.

" I say unto you, Love your enemies, and pray for them that persecute you ; that you may become sons of your Father who is in heaven."

Love, as here presented, is the highest thing that men are taught of God, and what Jesus is formulating is not an abstract ideal of righteousness *per se*, but the life to which men are called in response to the redeeming love of God and as sons of God, sharers of His spirit.

4. The Q teaching, as we have seen, locates the authority and source of the Christian revelation in the perfect determination of Jesus by the mind of the Father in heaven, and with this agrees the form as well as the substance of the love-commandment when

[1] See above, Chapter II, pp. 30-32.

it adds as motive " that you may become the sons of your Father who is in heaven." In recent years, through the urge to subordinate everything in the teaching of Jesus to the apocalyptic idea of the immediate world-end which he announced, there has arisen a tendency to think of the whole content of the doctrine of Jesus as if it were deducible by dialectical process from the challenge to our minds of One who as perfect in Himself, or as absolutely sovereign, or—to use an over-worked modern expression —as " wholly other " in relation to His world, confronts us with His judgement. But is this actually in accord with the substance of the teaching of Jesus ? Would any one say, for example, that the divine amnesty, the pardoning mercy of God to sinners, is dialectically deducible from the absolute sovereign claim with which God as the all-holy One confronts us ? or that it was by such a process of thought that the prophet Hosea in the Old Testament divined it, and not through the impressions wrought upon his tender human affection by heart-breaking contact with the sinful and the fallen ?

When, therefore, we speak of Jesus as having the mind of the Father and as asking of men a love like that of the Father, we should hesitate before separating either this insight or this imperative from the actualities of his human situation, from the impression wrought upon him by the pitifulness and wreckage, the guilt and sorrow, the pathos and tragedy of the lives of men. Dr. Rudolf Bultmann has written very brilliantly and suggestively on the Biblical ethic in its profound difference from Greek and modern naturalistic or humanistic ethic,[1] but when following up his dialectical method he seems to make the love which Jesus commands primarily another expression for that total negation of the self and its claims which results from the radical confrontation of our souls by God, one cannot but demur. We cannot read the Gospels without encountering on every page the evidence that pity for man in the tragic situation wrought by sin was a factor giving shape and content to Jesus' thought of the nature of divine-human relations. " Should not this woman, a daughter of Abraham, whom Satan has bound, see !, for eighteen years, be set free from this impediment on the Sabbath day " (Lk. xiii. 16). Such sentiments are not peculiar to the Lukan version of the tradition. " He said to them, ' Is it lawful to do good on the Sabbath, or to do evil ? to save a man, or to kill him ? ' And looking round on them with anger, distressed inwardly at their

---

[1] In his book, *Jesus and the Word.*

hardness of heart, he says to the man, ' Stretch out thy hand '
. . . and his hand was restored " (Mk. iii. 4-5).

The ethic of Jesus is not, indeed, to be called humanistic in a
formal sense. Its first principle is not man, but God. Where,
for example, Jesus takes issue with the religious leaders of his
time over the heavy burdens which they laid on men, his protest
is an affirmation, as C. H. Dodd says,[1] not of " the natural
freedom of the spirit of man against hampering circumstance and
regulation " but of " an immediate and absolute sovereignty of
God over every sphere of human life." Nevertheless, it would
surely seem that the strength and purity of the human sympathy
of Jesus was a factor which contributed to the emphasis with
which he affirmed the love of God to the unthankful and the evil.
What had been made known within the covenant relation through
the divine patience with a sinful and refractory Israel is here
extended to God's relation towards all mankind. We can only
explain this extension as the result of Jesus' own encounter with
humanity. *His theology is not a deduction from the pure idea of God
in His transcendence but starts rather from the historical conception of God
as in redeeming fellowship with man.* From this point of view it may
be considered that certain theoretical emphases and tendencies in
recent theology stand in need of some correction. They are too
narrow to do justice to the fullness of the Christian revelation.

It appears, then, if the results of the argument up to this
point are to be summarized, that the ethical absolute involved in
the teaching of Jesus requires for its understanding that we look
at it in the light of his thought regarding both God's gracious will
and man's predicament. What now of its relation to human
possibilities ?

THE SERMON ON THE MOUNT. V. THE ABSOLUTE OF JESUS IN
RELATION TO OUR EXISTENCE IN THE WORLD

What is the bearing of the absolute of Jesus on us as we are
placed in the world ?   We have seen that Jesus looked at humanity
in all its brokenness from the standpoint of the divine will to
redeem it, and how, faced by contradictions in experience which
showed how hard it was for men to enter into the kingdom of
God, he still fell back on the power of God to which all things
were possible. It is now to be noticed that the context in which
this assurance of divine power is given makes it plain—and the

---

[1] *History and the Gospel*, pp. 123 f.

early tradition must certainly have appreciated the point—that, in order to know this power of God, a man must break with the existing order of the world and with its interests and values : " Sell whatsoever thou hast, and give to the poor, and thou shalt have treasure in heaven, and come, follow me " (Mk. x. 21, 27). What are the issues which here confront us ? On the one hand, it is certainly an ethic of crisis which Jesus announces. The kingdom of God is at the door. Its powers are already at work. The seed of the new life is cast into the ground. It remains for all serious spirits, by extraordinary measures if need be, to enter into and possess the new realm of life. And Jesus trusts the power of God to make such accomplishment possible. On the other hand, a serious difficulty presents itself. *The realm into which men enter in response to the summons of Jesus is the kingdom of God, but if this kingdom is at present only incipient and not yet manifested ' in power ' (Mk. ix. 1), it would seem to follow that the ethic of the kingdom is realizable only in part and not yet in its absoluteness.*

It is now necessary to look more closely into the exact nature of this limitation as it presents itself in its various aspects.

1. The sphere of life by reference to which the ethic of Jesus is defined is the transcendent kingdom of God as announced and revealed in the present. This kingdom makes its demands, and offers its specific blessedness. But from this kingdom the present world with its complex of duties and relationships, rooted in the existing political, social, and economic orders, is not differentiated as an independent realm of obligation. There is an incidental admission of secular obligation in matters like the state conscription of labour (Mt. v. 41), and the payment of tribute to Cæsar (Mk. xii. 17), and this admission is important. But in point of fact the obedience which is here enjoined betrays no further interest in the present world than to claim it as sphere of operations for the law of the kingdom of heaven.

The existing world is not, as such, in the focus of the teaching of Jesus. It is to the disciple of the kingdom of heaven, not to the ordinary man in the world that Jesus says : " Whoever shall impress your service for a single mile, go with him two " (Mt. v. 41).

2. While the law of the kingdom of heaven thus directly claims the obedience of the individual living in the world, the ideal which it sets up is one which points beyond the range of anything fully accomplishable under the conditions of the present life. To be perfectly pure, sincere, truthful, unselfish, loving and

trustful admits of no other fulfilment here than that of continually pointing and urging us onwards from the lower to the higher, and from the better to the best. Even if we should give all our goods to feed the poor and turn our backs on the world, the position would not be essentially altered. The absolute of Jesus in this matter is relative to the kingdom of God in its ' power,' not to the kingdom of God as it here intersects the orbit of our mundane existence.

3. The ethic of Jesus is, nevertheless, organic to our life under the present order, and it is vastly more important to stress this organic-ness of the principle than to concern ourselves with the impossible ulterior reaches of its application.

On the one hand, (a) we have to distinguish, both as regards the outward and the inward realms of life, between the absolute as *knowledge* of the good, and the absolute as norm of practical achievement. As to the first of these aspects, the primary religious necessity of life is to know, not what is possible or practicable for us in our present state, but what is *the Will of God*, and clearly the making plain of this—not primarily as a point to be established in face of a defective Jewish moralism, but for its own essential sake— was the motive which inspired Jesus at every step in his teaching.

To bring us to the knowledge of God—to cause us to see His will not shadowed or deflected, but as it really is ! Jesus was speaking to men who thought they knew the will of God, for had they not the Law, and did not the Law say, or was it not at least understood to say that " Thou shalt love thy neighbour, and hate thine enemy ? " Over against this obscuration of the truth Jesus sets the Will of God in all its radiance and white-winged purity. And though the revelation of it humbles us to the dust, exposing the hollowness of our moralism, reducing our complacency to shreds and patches, and bringing us under a boundless sense of sin, this is only what we must expect if we are ever to know God. Only in the searching light of this exposure can we know the radical nature of any truly religious experience—penitence, grace, the forgiveness of sins, hope, blessedness, life. At this point, to which we shall return in Chapter VIII, the absolute of Jesus has entire revelance to our present existence.

On the other hand, (b) the principle is stated not for con-templation only, but for action : and here it must be recognized that, while no other principle of conduct, private or public, can be acknowledged by Christians as defining for us the Will of God, the absolute of Jesus as a law of practice remains related to the moral potentialities of the situation. It is in the present world that, as ethic of the kingdom of God, the teaching of Jesus is meant to be applied, and, as ethic of love, it represents the sublimation of a principle which is already most cohesive, strong, and fruitful in the existing life of society. It is necessary to stress this organic-ness of the Christian absolute to existence in the world, because in the family, in human friendships, in social and economic relationships, as well as in the Church, forces are at work which, without the Christian ideal, would not attain to their full norm and significance. These are spheres in which the ideal of unselfish life, as taught by Christ, connects itself with the structure and necessities of the social order and finds an almost boundless field for its operation. The real difficulty concerns the higher reaches of the principle where the ideal points clearly beyond the limit of what is attainable by the individual spirit, or what is practicable for organized society within the structure of its function. As regards the personal requirement of perfect purity, sincerity, unselfishness, love and trustfulness, this is manifest. The approach to the supreme pattern of Christian life must for ever be asymptotic : the best life will be short of the highest, and the shadow of sin will certainly cleave to everything that can be accomplished even in the effort to do the will of Christ. The Christian response can represent at best only a beginning of the great repentance towards God to which we are summoned. On the other hand, only an absolute ideal can rightly inaugurate and sustain that repentance, or supply a norm by which society can be judged in respect of the direction of its aims.

Less simple in their bearing on the question are those particular expressions of the absolute which, like the requirements of non-resistance to aggression, giving to all who ask, abjuring worldly cares and interests, seem to set up not indeed an impossible, but an anarchic ideal of conduct. It may, however, save us from much misconception to observe that the commandments in question have the intention of revealing what perfect trust in God and love to man really mean with regard to the spirit of our actions, from which it would follow that the right understanding and fulfilment of the principles may not be disjoined from a clear-eyed vision of the character of the situations in which we are called to act. Here it will not be possible to dismiss from consideration the divine sanctions attaching to orders of life which, though they do not embody the ideals of the kingdom of heaven, make nevertheless their own claim upon our respect as the instruments of public justice, good government, and the defence of the weak against the strong. The New Testament recognizes that such divine sanctions pertain to the civil authority in the discharge of its appropriate moral functions (Rom. xiii. 1-7, I Pet. ii. 13-17). The trust and love towards God which Jesus requires of his followers will not, therefore, easily construe themselves in terms which, for the sake of the things of the spirit, would abandon the ordinary obligations of citizenship, or which alternatively would press upon the State ideals of action, such as non-resistance to armed aggression, which under given circumstances would overthrow the foundations of law and order, and defeat the good which the State exists to serve. It would seem, therefore, at this point that it is not Christian to press the Christian absolute, understood in its true character as love, upon orders of life which stand outside of the powers of the kingdom of God. As the ethic of a spiritual life revealed by Jesus Christ, the Christian ideal binds all who have been brought by him to see God, and as such it will determine the spirit of their citizenship in the State and their whole life in the world. In this manner Christianity will ultimately affect the State's conception of its functions. But so long as the kingdom of God only intersects our mundane existence, and does not fill the whole sphere of it, there will be limits to what can be demanded of the State in its name, and to what can be set up as definition of social duty. What the Christian ethic does here is not to provide a law for society, but to create a tension in its midst which cannot but have transforming results. The Kingdom of Heaven is as leaven. Thus indirectly, not directly, politics and law, the social and the economic ordering of life, and the principles governing our international relations all come at last under the sign of the kingdom which Jesus revealed.[1]

[1] Further consideration of the revelation of God in the teaching of Jesus is reserved for Chapter VIII.

CHAPTER VI

THE MESSIANIC CATEGORIES IN THE TRADITION

THE conception of the revelation of God in Jesus which at the simplest level of Christian preaching turned principally upon the signs attending him, and at a later stage finds a solid basis for itself in the truth of his teaching, involves from the beginning certain presuppositions regarding his person.

Strictly speaking, there is not within the frontiers of the Synoptic tradition any presentation of the person of Jesus which does not keep throughout to his *functional* significance as Messiah, Son of God, and Son of Man. According to Dr. Martin Dibelius there is not such a presentation anywhere in the New Testament. " The faith of the early Christians," writes this theologian, " was centred not in what Christ was, but rather in what he had done for mankind. The New Testament contains practically nothing about the person of Jesus Christ in his ontological significance, nothing apart from his relations with mankind." [1]

HISTORY AND CHRISTOLOGY IN THE GOSPELS

It has been an ordinary assumption of much modern historical criticism of the Gospels that the life of Jesus has been overlaid by an incrustation of dogmatic Christology, and that if this accreted matter were stripped away, we should be left with a pure residuum of history. How untenable this position is has been shown by the results of a closer approach to the ancient material which forms the underlying substance of the Synoptic tradition. *There is no smallest unit of this tradition which is not instinct with Christological significance.* And this is because the motive which from the start led to the preservation of historical material in the tradition was a Christological motive. The primitive Christian mind, as Dibelius shows, had no interest in the deeds or words of Jesus which was not also an interest in the salvation which he had brought to men. [2] When it turned back to the events of the past or tried to put into words the teaching which it had received, it instinctively thought of the final religious

---

[1] *Gospel Criticism and Christology*, pp. 86 f.   [2] *Ibid.*, pp. 28-29.

purpose which all these events and utterances served. Therefore if in the tradition we find such incidents recorded as that
Jesus at Nazareth " could do no mighty work " because of the
prevailing unbelief (Mk. vi. 5), or that he repelled the man who
addressed him as " Good Master " with the disconcerting rejoinder, " Why dost thou call me good ?   None is good save one,
and he is God " (Mk. x. 18), we would need to be on our guard
against imagining that these are escapes of ' history ' from the
enmeshing web of ' dogma,' or that here a non-Christological
tradition has preserved itself. In actual fact the former statement may have no other point than to serve as a warning against
unbelief on the part of Christians generally, while the other may
be construed in the same sense as Lk. vi. 46 : " Why do you call
me Lord, Lord, and not do the things which I say ? "   Christology
is not really here in question.

How closely, on the other hand, the Christological motive
within the Synoptic tradition kept company with history is shown
by the character of the Christology itself.   Here there is no attempt
to import what did not blend with a definite conception of the
character and spirit of Jesus. For proof we need only refer to
the narrative of the Temptation of Jesus or to such a pronouncement-story as Lk. ix. 51-55. " The New Testament writers,"
says Prof. C. H. Dodd, " for all their anxiety to discover fulfilments of prophecy and all their ingenuity in doing so do not
attempt to exploit the whole corpus of Messianic prediction." [1]
What is here said of the New Testament as a whole applies with
particular force to the Synoptic tradition which in claiming that
Jesus fulfilled the Scriptures makes no use of the conception of
mighty king, warrior, and judge so characteristic of Jewish
Messianism both in its national-historical and in its apocalyptic-
transcendental forms. On the other hand, this same tradition
lays a very decided emphasis on the features of Jesus which
correspond to the lowly and self-effacing character of the Isaianic
Servant of God. The obvious inference is that here, as the writer
just quoted says, " a true historical memory determined the use
of prophecy by the Church." The Messianic idea of early
Christianity is no mere product of theological idealism. It has
resulted from " the impact of historical fact " on the ideas
belonging to a traditional doctrine of the last things, as the
result of which these ideas have been drastically recast. [2] If the
Synoptic Christology were the unfolding of a myth, or if it were

---

[1] *History and the Gospel*, p. 61.   [2] *Ibid.*, p. 63.

the precipitate of the Church's inward and mystical experience in pseudo-historical form, we should have expected it to be at once more consistent and more outspoken in its terms, and to be less hampered by regard for the kind of facts with which in the tradition it is found to be involved.

For hampered and embarrassed the Synoptic Christology undoubtedly is. The tradition itself indicates that Jesus was reticent and ambiguous on the subject of his person and claims. He never revealed himself to his Galilean audiences on this particular subject. At the close of the Galilean ministry,

> "He asked his disciples . . . Who do men say that I am? And they told him, saying, John the Baptist : and others, Elias : but others, One of the prophets " (Mk. viii. 27 f.).

He discouraged even his disciples from speaking publicly of his Messiahship (Mk. viii. 30), and at his trial there was no agreement among his accusers as to the precise charge on which he might be arraigned (Mk. xiv. 55-60). His words about the Son of Man were almost everywhere equivocal. It has been argued that some or all of these features in the tradition are the result of the Church's projecting its fully developed Messianic idea back upon a pre-Messianic stage or phase in the work and teaching of Jesus. Formally this may to some extent be right. We do not see through to the origins of the mind regarding God and man which we call the ' Messianic consciousness ' of Jesus, nor do we know when or where it first found expression. All we know for certain is that at some stage in his ministry Jesus stood self-disclosed as the Messiah or Son of Man to be. The Synoptic tradition, therefore, is at points embarrassed to some extent by the character of the material it has to utilize and interpret. Yet in its general Christological instinct it is right. *For whether with or without the open claim to be the Messiah, the personality of Jesus plainly stood from the beginning of his mission within the circle of crisis marked by his signs and by his teaching about God*, so that the projecting back of the Messianic idea upon the whole history was not altogether against the grain of the facts. We may speak, however, of a stage or phase of the self-expression of Jesus in which the Messianic claim was held in reserve or was implicit rather than overt. What is the significance of this fact in relation to the total unfolding of the mind of Jesus and to the final position which he occupies in the faith of his followers and in the New Testament records ?

Anticipating for the moment the results of fuller inquiry, we may, I think, express its significance thus. The Messianic idea of early Christianity, as we have seen, bears every sign of being the result of " the impact of historical fact " upon a traditional doctrine of the last things. Tracing this to its cause, we may say that what the Messianic terminology has really done is to set a final and definitive stamp upon the extraordinary sense of mission to Israel which inspired Jesus and bore him onwards. Or, to put the same thing in other words, *the Messianic thought of Israel was the reagent or medium which in the mind of Jesus and of his Church brought out the true colour and significance of the revelation from God of which Jesus knew himself to be the bearer.*

JESUS AND HIS EXTRAORDINARY SENSE OF MISSION

We start here from a point where we are standing on sure historical foundations. Jesus came into Galilee preaching and saying : " The time is fulfilled, and the kingdom of God has come near. Repent " (Mk. i. 14 f.). That this summary of Mark records the actual starting-point, outlook, and motive of the public work of Jesus admits of no reasonable doubt. For the evangelist and for the tradition it means, of course, that in Jesus the *Messiah* has stepped on to the stage. The reason why the kingdom has come near is that the royal ' Son ' of the Second Psalm, the Chosen of God, has appeared (Mk. i. 11). But even if we ought not to read this connection of ideas into the mind of Jesus himself, but should regard his vision of the nearness or instancy of the kingdom as springing simply from the intensity of his consciousness of God's redeeming purpose, it still remains that the distinctive and arresting feature of his work was not simply the realism with which he proclaimed the advent of the kingdom and its meaning for mankind, but the completeness with which he identified himself with the bringing about of the conversion of his people, the ingathering and restoration to God of the lost sheep of the house of Israel. This is the phase of consciousness marked by his words about the signs attending him, and by the parables of the kingdom. We may speak of it as characterized in the tradition, if not by an explicit Messianic claim on the part of Jesus, at least by the distinctest conviction that his mission created a supreme crisis in the religious history of his nation. To this stage belong most of the sayings considered above in Chapters III-IV, of which the gist may be summarized as follows. They ascribe to Jesus—

7

1. The belief that a crisis is at hand for the nation, that the kingdom of God has suddenly appeared (ἔφθασεν) or is forcing its way in (βιάζεται) or is present in the midst (ἐντὸς ὑμῶν).[1]

2. The conviction that prophecy is being fulfilled in his words and deeds, and that he is the bearer of a higher revelation than any given in the past : something greater than Jonah or than Solomon has appeared.[2]

3. The claim not merely to supersede the tradition of the elders, but to set his own interpretations upon the commandments of the Torah (ἐγὼ δὲ λέγω ὑμῖν) and to offer these not as matters of opinion but as authoritative declarations of the will of God.

4. The consciousness of performing his mighty works by divine inspiration (ἐν πνεύματι θεοῦ), so that to indict him as a sorcerer is to blaspheme against the Holy Spirit.

5. The sense of authority not only to summon men to follow him, but to pronounce their salvation conditional upon their acceptance of what he reveals.

Such claims are not easily resolved into *placita* of the Christian community, but embody themselves in words which, as we have seen, have every title to be considered original utterances of Jesus.

The Messianic Concepts of Judaism

It is not necessary to dwell further on what Rudolf Otto calls " Jesus' consciousness of mission regarded apart from its Messianic dress." [3] What we have now to consider is the form or forms in which the mind of Jesus, bearing this extraordinary sense of mission, came to an articulate Messianic self-expression, and what drew it to these forms. Here the tradition is of a character to help us. As we have seen, it does not utilize the whole vocabulary of Messianic prediction, but concentrates in one way or another on three main concepts : Son of God, Servant of the Lord, and Son of Man. As will be shown in detail elsewhere, these concepts, however distinct and separate in origin, do not in Biblical or Jewish thought signify alternative or mutually exclusive notions of the agent of the divine salvation but rather embody successive historical phases of the one idea.[4] A certain common pattern of thought appears throughout, turning upon the ideas of exaltation

---

[1] See above, Chapter III, pp. 49-50, and IV, pp. 66-71.
[2] See above, Chapter IV, pp. 63-67.
[3] *The Kingdom of God and the Son of Man*, p. 162.
[4] See later, Appendix C.

and divine gift. An illustration is afforded by the following passages :

Ps. ii. 6-8 (LXX). This represents the Davidic prince, the prototype of Israel's Messiah, as saying : " I was appointed king by Him over Zion his holy mountain. . . . The Lord said to me, ' My Son art thou . . . I will give to thee (δώσω) the nations (τὰ ἔθνη) as thy inheritance (τὴν κληρονομίαν σου) and the bounds of the earth as thy possession,' etc."

Isa. lii. 13, liii. 9, 12 (LXX). This says of the Servant of Yahweh : " My Servant shall understand and shall be exalted . . . and I will give (δώσω) the wicked for his grave. . . . For this reason he shall be the inheritor (κληρονομήσει) of many and shall divide the spoils of the strong, etc."

Dan. vii. 13-14 (LXX). Here it is recorded as part of Daniel's vision : " Lo, on the clouds of heaven there came one as a son of man . . . and there was given to him (ἐδόθη) authority, and all the nations (τὰ ἔθνη) of the earth . . . and all glory doing him service."

Apart from this common pattern of thought, it will be seen that all three figures are invested with the same attributes of wisdom, judgement, righteousness, and the possession of the Spirit of God. All three are ' a light to the Gentiles,' all three are associated with a ' covenant ' which God makes with His people, all three receive the homage of ' kings ' and raise the mighty from their seats. The evidence is too abundant to be presented here, but it will be found set out in the above-mentioned Appendix.[1] There it will appear by many signs that *functions first attributed to the Davidic prince in the prophets and in the Psalms reappear in a form transfigured or infiltrated with suffering in the person of the Servant and finally are invested with every circumstance of apocalyptic glory and splendour in the figure of the supernatural Son of Man.* It would appear that Israel's inextinguishable hope of the salvation of God had laid hold of each of these Saviour conceptions in turn and pressed them into its service. In this manner there was given to prophets and to apocalyptic mystics a language and a plastic ideology by which to work out their thought of the coming redemption.

It has been necessary to stress this community of type and identity of function in the three great conceptions of the Messiah because there has been a tendency in certain quarters to over-emphasize their disparate origins and on the strength of this

[1] Appendix C.

disparateness of origin to argue that Jesus, when he came to concentrate his vision of the future primarily upon the coming and the exaltation of the Son of Man, was *ipso facto* rejecting the Old Testament and Jewish idea of the Messiah in favour of a mystery conception of other provenance. This is substantially the thesis advanced in recent books by A. F. von Gall [1] and Jean Héring. [2] According to von Gall the Son of Man and the Messiah had originally nothing to do with each other, but were first united in a single conception by the primitive Jewish-Christian Church. "Jesus," says this writer, "who held himself for the pre-existent ' Son of Man ' and therewith for the Son of God, unconditionally rejected the Jewish national hope of the Messiah. . . . It was the original Jewish-Christian community which made him into the Messiah, because it was antipathetic to the Iranian ' Son of Man ' belief." [3] Certainly Jesus rejected the nationalistic aspect of the Jewish Messianic belief, but to make this equivalent to saying that he attached himself to a non-Jewish doctrine of redemption is greatly to overstrain the evidence, and is to be rejected. I cannot discover any reliable proof that the Iranian ' Urmensch ' or First-Man belief anywhere developed a real redemptive significance in association with the last things except in Jewish and Christian circles or under their influence. [4] Von Gall's attempt to establish a proof seems to me to involve incredible assumptions.

It may be added that in later Rabbinical literature, as well as in Christianity, we find evidences of an interest in correlating the Biblical ideas of Son of God, Servant of the Lord, and Son of Man. Thus a Midrash on Psalm ii, in commenting on the words of verse 7 : " I will tell of a decree : the Lord has said to me : Thou art my Son," makes the following statement :

> " This is recorded in a decree of the Torah and in a decree of the Prophets and in a decree of the Writings. It is written in a decree of the Torah : ' My first-born Son is Israel ' (Exod. iv. 22). And it is written in a decree of the Prophets : ' Behold, my Servant will deal wisely ' (Isa. lii. 13) and . . . ' Behold my Servant whom I uphold, my Elect in whom my soul has pleasure ' (Isa. xlii. 1). And it is written in a decree of the Writings : ' Word of Yahweh to

[1] *ΒΑΣΙΛΕΙΑ ΤΟΥ ΘΕΟΥ* (1926).

[2] *Le Royaume de Dieu et Sa Venue* (1937).

[3] Von Gall, p. viii. It will be noticed that this view is the exact opposite of Bousset's in *Kyrios Christos*, Chapter I.

[4] See above, Chapter I, pp. 7-11, and Appendix D.

my lord : Sit thou at my right hand ' (Ps. cx. 1) ; it is further written : ' Yahweh has said to me : thou art my Son ' (Ps. ii. 7), and another Scripture passage says : ' Behold, there came with the clouds of heaven one like a Son of Man ' " (Dan. vii. 13).[1]

Billerbeck thus explains the passage : " The first decree relates to Israel, the third to the Messiah, in the case of the second it remains uncertain whether Israel or the Messiah was understood by the Servant of Yahweh." We have seen elsewhere, however, that the Jewish Targum explicitly identifies the Servant with the Messiah, though not in point of the suffering and death ascribed to him in Isa. liii.

THE APPROACH OF JESUS TO THE MESSIANIC INTERPRETATION OF HIS DESTINY

We may assume, then, that what Scripture and tradition offered to the minds of men in the age of Jesus was not a number of alternative or disparate conceptions of the coming Redeemer, but a general conception, the product of a lengthy historical development, into which traits derived from the prophetic royal ' Son,' the Isaianic ' Servant,' and the apocalyptic ' Man,' as well as other features had variously entered. It is important to keep this fact in mind at any approach to the terms of the Synoptic doctrine of Christ. The occurrence together in the record of concepts like Christ, Son of God, and Son of Man by no means necessarily indicates confusion of thought or conflation of discrepant traditions. On the contrary it may be regarded as a point in favour of the tradition that it attributes to Jesus a great breadth and inclusiveness of outlook upon the religious history of his people in the past, and a rich appreciation of what prophets and righteous men in one way or another had felt as they projected their thoughts forward upon the symbol of the coming salvation. This is at least a tenable position.

Before, however, a beginning can be made with the study of the Synoptic presentation in detail, it will be well to allude to one special feature of the tradition. The facet of the Messianic concept which is most prominent in our records of the teaching of Jesus is that of the Son of Man or Heavenly Man who represents the final or apocalyptic projection of the Jewish idea. If the tradition here reflects the emphasis of Jesus—and of this, I think,

[1] The passage is taken from Strack-Billerbeck, Bd. III, pp. 18 f.

there can be little question—it means that the Messianic consciousness of Jesus came to an ultimate point in the question of
his relation to the Son of Man, and reasons of a very definite
kind can be assigned for the explanation of this fact.

In the first place, it was in the ' Son of Man ' form that the
Messianic concept was most closely associated with the transcendent kingdom of God which Jesus preached.

> " I saw in the night visions, and behold, there came with the
> clouds of heaven one like a son of man, and he came even to the
> Ancient of days, and they brought him near before Him.
>
> " And there was given him dominion, and glory, and a kingdom,
> that all the peoples, nations, and languages should serve him : his
> dominion is an everlasting dominion, which shall not pass away "
> (Dan. vii. 13-14).

In apocalyptic circles, as the section of I Enoch known as the
Similitudes makes plain, the symbolic figure in this passage of
Daniel had become invested with the full personality and attributes of a pre-existent heavenly Messiah combining certain strong
features of the ancient Davidic prince with functions belonging
to the prophetic Servant of the Lord.[1]   The concept of the Son
of Man had thus an inclusiveness, finality, and ultra-national
range and transcendence belonging to none of the earlier forms
of the Messianic idea.   In the second place, this concept with its
wider and more heavenly horizon lent itself to purer religious
uses than the more nationalistic forms of the Jewish idea, and
when Jesus saw himself confronted by national rejection in its
extremest form, this aspect of the hope of Israel cannot but have
drawn his thoughts towards it.   In the third place, as Jesus
believed the supernatural Reign of God to be foreshadowed and
anticipated in his own exorcisms and mighty works, the question
of the relation in which his activities and fortunes stood to the
coming of the Son of Man could not but press for an answer.[2]
But if here we discover the situation in which, as I believe, the
mind of Jesus regarding his vocation was brought to a Messianic
determination and point, this is far from saying that we have
reached a full explanation of his Messianic consciousness.

For, admitting that the close correlation of the Son of Man
conception with the divine kingdom of the future made the
coming of the Son of Man the ultimate determinant or standard
of reference for Jesus' understanding of his own commission and

[1] See Appendix C.   [2] See above, Chapter IV, pp. 65-66.

destiny, we have still to ask what accounted for the passion and the realism with which he took up and preached the theme of the kingdom of God. And if for an answer to this question we are driven back upon depths of religious insight underlying his message of the last things, may it not be that in those depths there was room for a more varied and flexible expression of the nature of his religious function than the single concept of the Son of Man redeemer suggested? The Synoptic tradition, at any rate, makes it plain that he expressed himself at times in terms of such other Messianic ideas as the Son of God and the Servant of the Lord, and that his interest in the Son of Man himself had a broader basis than is given in the mere correlation of that figure with the future Reign of God. This feature of the tradition is one of great interest and importance for our understanding of the revelation of God in Jesus.

'Son of God'

We take first the Synoptic usage of the title 'Son of God.'

1. In the form in which it first comes before us in St. Mark and the other Synoptists, the designation Son of God connects historically with the Second Psalm and with the halo of religious significance surrounding the person of the Davidic prince in Israel. Whatever ideas of a mythological kind explain the ascription of divine origin or sonship to kings in the ancient East, the motive which procured a sanction for such language with reference to the king of Israel was grounded not in mythology but in the prophetic persuasion of Israel's election by the Most High, and of a divine purpose of grace governing her institutions and history. Hence when the Davidic monarchy ceased to exist as a political entity, the sanctity and the religious hopes with which the prophets had invested the royal line in Israel did not lapse but wrapped themselves around the expectation of a 'Messiah' or anointed prince who should afterwards arise. The Son of God conception was thus through Scripture (cf. Ps. ii. 7, lxxxix 27) a Messianic potential. It will not do to say, therefore, that a doctrine of Christ as Son of God could only have arisen in Christianity under purely Hellenistic influences, or that the saying about the Father and the Son in Mt. xi. 27, Lk. x. 22 was impossible in any form for Jesus, as Clemen avers.[1]

---

[1] *Religionsgeschichtliche Erklärung des Neuen Testaments* (2nd ed. 1924), pp. 77 f.

2. As used by Mark and his successors, the title Son of God clearly represents the higher and Christian equivalent of the Jewish term ' Messiah.' This appears plainly by the fact that at the supreme moments of the Baptism and the Transfiguration the voice from heaven, the word of revelation addressed to Jesus or to his followers names him not as the ' Christ,' as Peter does at his confession (Mk. viii. 29), but as ' My Son, the Beloved ' (Mk. i. 11, ix. 7). It is as Son of God accordingly that the demons acclaim Jesus (Mk. iii. 11, v. 7) and that the centurion at the cross acknowledges him (Mk. xv. 39). But that the term, though it is a feature of the Markan doctrine which the latter shares with the Pauline, did not come into the Synoptic tradition purely through Mark or through the influence of the Hellenist Churches is shown by its appearance at high points in the teaching matter derived from what we call the Q source, as for example in the narrative of the Temptation of Jesus (Mt. iv. 3, 6) and in the saying about the Father and the Son (Mt. xi. 27, Lk. x. 22). Bultmann declares against both these passages on the ground that they are ' Hellenistic,' but he does so for the unconvincing reason that the ideas of wonder-working and ' gnosis,' with which the title Son of God is associated in the passages, cannot be proved to be in accord with Jewish Messianic sentiment.[1] This objection ignores the extent to which Palestinian religious thought in the time of Jesus may have been already affected by the infiltration of Greek ideas, and cannot, therefore, be regarded as conclusive.

This does not mean, indeed, that Hellenistic influences did not powerfully reinforce the instinct of Christianity to express the significance of Jesus predominantly in terms of a Son of God doctrine. From the earliest times the Greek mind had been accustomed to interpret all genius and heroic achievement, all superhuman excellence and virtue as manifestations of the divine. One has only to consider the multitude of adjectives compounded with θεός in the Greek classical lexicon to realize the range and the spontaneity of this tendency. In the Hellenistic age the instinct expresses itself in the idea of the divine origin or in that of the apotheosis of the great and good. And that this tendency has invaded the language of the Synoptic tradition itself at a few points may be seen by comparing the above-cited passage, Mk. xv. 39, with a passage of Plutarch to which Bultmann has called attention.[2]

[1] Bultmann, *Geschichte*, p. 275. Cf. pp. 171 f.   [2] *Ibid.*, p. 296, note 1.

Mk. xv. 37-39	Plutarch, *Cleomenes* 39, p. 823c
The centurion at the cross, witnessing the death of Jesus and the rending of the temple veil, exclaims : " Truly this man was a son of God " (ἀληθῶς ὁ ἄνθρωπος οὗτος υἱὸς ἦν θεοῦ).	When Cleomenes was impaled, the report of a portent at the time of his death gave rise to the popular rumour that he was a hero and a son of the gods (ἥρωα τὸν Κλεομένη καὶ θεῶν παῖδα προσαγορεύοντες).

But while the instinct of the Hellenistic mind may thus have contributed to the development of a particular phase of the early Christian doctrine of Christ, this is far from saying that we are to look to that mind for the source of the Son of God confession. With the Second Psalm before us, it is needless to resort to that hypothesis, and in view of certain features in an undoubtedly Palestinian tradition of the teaching of Jesus it is not only needless but unjustified.

3. The emergence of a Son of God Christology on Palestinian soil is a very remarkable phenomenon and one which demands explanation. Since Dalman's book on the *Words of Jesus* forty years ago, it has been usual to recognize that Son of God as a Messianic designation had, despite the Second Psalm, no place in Jewish official usage. In this connection the practice of the Targums as reflecting the ideas of Synagogue-Judaism in the Aramaic-speaking world is especially illuminating. While seeking and finding the ' King Messiah ' everywhere in the Old Testament, the Targumists systematically explain away the substantive force of all the passages which refer to him as ' Son of God.' We select the two outstanding instances of this procedure.

Hebrew Text	Targum
Ps. ii. 7. " Thou art my Son, this day have I begotten thee."	Ps. ii. 7. " Thou art dear to me as a son to a father, innocent as if I had this day created thee."
Ps. lxxxix. 27. " I will also make him my First-born, the highest of the kings of the earth."	Ps. lxxxix. 27. " I will make him to be the first-born among the kings of the house of Judah, the highest over the kings of the earth."

The terms of the paraphrase here indicate a certain ethicizing of the father-son relation in the thought of later Judaism, but even more they signify the reaction of abstract Jewish monotheism against a manner of speech which savoured of mythology in the older prophetic diction, and to this reaction the Jewish polemic against Christianity may have contributed not a little. What is true of the Targums holds of the Rabbinical exegesis of scripture generally. In the Talmud, as Billerbeck shows, the Messiah is named Son of God only when an Old Testament passage, under-stood to be Messianic, makes use of that appellative. The designation never occurs in independence of a Biblical text.[1]

How, then, are we to explain the singular resurgence of the substantive use of this Messianic title in Christianity and, indeed, in Palestinian Christianity? It cannot have been due to the pure influence of scripture working *ab extra*, for the dominant Palestinian exegesis ran counter to the attribution of anything except a general ethical connotation to the expression Son of God. This forces to the front the question *whether we are not to seek in the depths of Jesus' own spirit the source and origin-point of this particular form of the Christian Messianic idea*. We cannot indeed draw special conclusions from the fact that in Mark and in the Sayings-source it is as Son of God that Jesus is first presented to us. In the baptism and temptation narratives, in which the designation plays a part, it is always possible that we have the language of the Church speaking in its own terms. Moreover, it is not possible from the sequence of events in the Gospels to infer the order of ideas in the mind of Jesus. Nevertheless, from a certain stratification of ideas in words and thoughts having a reasonable claim to come to us from Jesus certain inferences may still, I think, be drawn as to the relation in which the Son of God con-fession of Christianity stands to the general structure of his religious consciousness.

The form in which the message of Jesus to his generation was delivered was, as we have seen, the announcement that a future and supernatural event, the advent of the kingdom of God, was at hand, and that men should repent. But from the radical spiritual nature of the repentance which Jesus demanded and from the specific form of the new life to which he called, it is apparent that underneath his emphasis on the nearness of the last things there lay a deeper stratum of conviction, a mind pro-foundly concerned with the holiness of God and with his char-acter as the Father in heaven. It is this conception of God which fills the mind of Jesus in his highest moments of joy, and it is this

---

[1] Strack-Billerbeck, *Kommentar*, Bd. III, p. 20.

conception which is represented as upholding him in his Gethsemane hour.

> " Abba, Father, all things are possible unto Thee. . . . Never-
> theless, not what I will, but what Thou wilt " (Mk. xiv. 36).

The Fatherhood of God, so far from being a commonplace of
religious thought, is indeed of the very substance of the ' mystery '
which Christianity knows itself to have received through Jesus.[1]

> " God sent forth the Spirit of his Son into our hearts, crying,
> Abba, Father " (Gal. iv. 6).
> " You received not the spirit of bondage again unto fear ; but
> you received the spirit of adoption, by which we cry, Abba, Father "
> (Rom. viii. 15).

And that this recognition of God as Father, which the Church
owes to Jesus, was prior in the order of Jesus' thought to his pronouncements regarding the last things seems certified to us by
the structure of such words as " Fear not, little flock, for it is
your Father's good pleasure to give you the kingdom " (Lk. xii.
32).   From this point of view it would seem that in the mind of
Jesus we have the same sequence of ideas as in the prophetic
religion of Israel.[2]   In the Hebrew prophets an intense apprehension of the righteousness and faithfulness of God led to the
casting of their message into the form of the annunciation of a
world-judgement coming and of the Lord being exalted in that
day.   In Jesus, but in purer and more positive form, this process
repeats itself.   His vision of the kingdom projects the intense
inwardness of his spirit's realization of God.

*But if the message of Jesus with regard to the last things thus leads
back to a basis in his realization of God as Father and Lord, may we not
say that similarly the Messianic form which sooner or later comes over
his own consciousness of destiny had its support, if not its origin, in something which, whether it so objectified itself from the start or not, can only
be called the filial quality of his spirit in relation to God?*   We see the
ideal of religious life in his teaching expressing itself in terms of
sonship to God.

> " That you may become the sons of your Father who is in heaven "
> (Mt. v. 45. Cf. Lk. vi. 35).

Is it not possible that the filial determination of his own spirit in
relation to God was a fundamental factor in the process by which

---

[1] Cf. T. W. Manson, *The Teaching of Jesus*, pp. 89-115.
[2] See above, Chapter I, pp. 16-17.

Jesus came to a Messianic understanding of his calling? As deep calls to deep, may not the Messianic salutation of Ps. ii. 7, " Thou art my Son," have come to him as the answer which resolved the mystery of his own extraordinary sense of mission to Israel? *In this way we should reach an explanation of the form of the great utterance recorded in Mt. xi. 27, Lk. x. 22 about the Father's knowledge or recognition of the Son.* Jesus saw prophecy being fulfilled in the signs attending his earthly work. Would he not also find the psalms and the prophets speaking to his spirit with the directness of a personal revelation? The possibility exists at this point that not the Church merely but Jesus saw his calling marked out for particular definition by aid of the Messiah-Son of God conception.

It is indeed only a possibility which is here contended for. The form under which the Messianic consciousness of Jesus characteristically expresses itself is, as we have seen, given by another term, ' Son of Man.' [1] But if it is remembered that in the tradition this Son of Man also appears as the Son of the Father in heaven—compare Mk. viii. 38, " Whosoever shall be ashamed of me and of my words in this adulterous and sinful generation, the Son of Man also shall be ashamed of him, when he comes in the glory of his Father with the holy angels "—it is seen that the deeply filial communion of Jesus with God was not out of relation to his choice of the more apocalyptic title. In any case it would be arbitrary to declare that Jesus never could have employed the kind of language about himself which underlies the saying in Mt. xi. 27, Lk. x. 22. As we have seen, this saying has been seriously called in question on the ground that it reflects the language not of Jesus but of Christian theology and worship.[2] In discussing this view, however, we discovered no real ground for disputing Harnack's contention that genuine words of Jesus expressive of a more than prophetic consciousness of bringing to men the knowledge of the Father may well have formed the underlying basis of the tradition at this point. The claim is not out of accord with the reality of the historical situation in which, as we see by other proofs, Jesus believed himself to stand. He was conscious of bringing to men a revelation of transcendent importance (Mt. xii. 41-42, Lk. xi. 31-32), and therefore of enjoying a unique confidence of God. The saying may, therefore, authentically reveal the mind of Jesus at some moment of crisis such as the disclosure of his Messiahship to the disciples (Mk. viii. 29),

[1] See above, pp. 101-103.   [2] Above, Chapter IV, pp. 71-76.

an episode " which is not likely to have passed without leaving some trace in Q." [1] Be that as it may, the emphasis of Jesus on the Fatherhood of God is of supreme interest as revealing the fundamental character of his personal religious consciousness. By the side of this it is a question of minor importance whether he employed the expression Son of God in an explicitly *Messianic* sense, but there is no conclusive reason against his having done so on occasion.

It is a tenable position, accordingly, that, to quote the words of Harnack, " Jesus' consciousness of Sonship must have preceded in time his consciousness of Messiahship, must indeed have formed a stepping-stone to the latter." Harnack adds that " the consciousness of divine Sonship and Messiahship could not have existed together from the beginning ; for the consciousness of Messiahship never meant anything else for Jesus than a consciousness of what he was about to become," [2] and he points for confirmation of this to the fact that in Mark and in the Q source alike the Messianic claim of Jesus does not become articulate before the closing phase of his ministry, and then only under the imagery of the coming of the Son of Man. This may well be right. What it means, however, is that *the Messiahship of Jesus comes as the final seal or imprint upon that sense of revealing the Father which had carried him into all his work for men.*

The only alternative to this view would be to suppose that Jesus, starting with the conviction of a Messianic call, went on to interpret that vocation in terms of a Son's love, trust, and obedience. This is not impossible, but it makes against this interpretation, on the whole, that it not only leaves the origin of the Messianic consciousness of Jesus unexplained, but it inverts the order of things which we find in the prophetic religion of Israel and which we find also in the structure of the thought of Jesus himself. Jesus, as we have seen above, is revealed at great moments as pointing from present signs to future certainties, [3] and therefore it is more reasonable to think of him as coming to the Messianic conception of his destiny from pre-existing experience of filial communion with God than *vice versa*.

[1] T. W. Manson, *The Teaching of Jesus*, p. 110.
[2] *The Sayings of Jesus*, p. 245, note 2.
[3] See above, Chapter III, pp. 49-50.

'SERVANT OF THE LORD'

If a profound sense of engagement to bring his nation to the knowledge of the heavenly Father formed the basic consciousness from which Jesus came to the understanding of himself as Messiah-Son of God, the same explanation will underlie his use for the purposes of self-expression of the concepts Servant of the Lord and Son of Man. In Biblical and Jewish belief the ideas Son of God, Servant of the Lord, and Son of Man, however separate they may have been in origin, had come to signify only variant phases of the one Messianic idea, and approaches to an actual synthesis of the features of all three had already taken place in I Enoch.[1] Nevertheless, as the Jewish Messianic idea in that book, as elsewhere, presents other facets, which are not reflected in the Synoptic doctrine of Christ, it is natural to suppose that the mind of Jesus, more than any other factor, accounts for the special emphases in the Christian tradition. We have sought to explain in this way the rise of a Son of God doctrine of Christ in the Christian Church, and the question now presents itself whether the important place taken by the Servant and the Son of Man in the language of the Christian tradition does not go back similarly to the attraction which the Messianic idea under these particular forms exercised over the mind of Jesus.

In the Synoptic presentation of Jesus the conception of the Servant appears from the start in the closest connection with that of the Son of God, and as constituting along with it the initial revelational aspect under which Jesus enters on his work. The voice which calls him at his Baptism combines the "Thou art my Son" of the Second Psalm with an addition recalling the terms in which the Servant is introduced in Isa. xlii. 1 (Mk. i. 11). As we can scarcely think of the evangelist himself as conflating these two texts for the occasion, the presumption is that it was instinctive or traditional in the community to think of Jesus the Messiah as at the same time the Servant in whom the Lord had pleasure. In the Gospel of Matthew the correlation of the two conceptions is open and explicit. The avoidance by Jesus of publicity causes the evangelist to pause in his narrative and to comment that here a prophecy of Isaiah was fulfilled (Mt. xii. 17-21. Cf. viii. 17).

"Behold, my Servant (ὁ παῖς μου) whom I have chosen, my Beloved (ὁ ἀγαπητός μου) in whom my soul has pleasure, . . . he shall not strive, nor cry aloud" (Isa. xlii. 1-3).

[1] See above, 98-101, and Appendix C.

But this is language of the evangelist and of the Church.   In the sayings of Jesus himself, however, it is made clear that the spirit, the example, the obedience, and the self-renunciation of the Isaianic Servant possessed a high significance for him, and exercised a profoundly formative influence on his interpretation of his work and destiny.

It is to be noted, however, that nowhere in the tradition of the dominical teaching is the Servant the *subject* of any pronouncement of Jesus about his personal vocation or fortunes, though he is often, so to speak, the predicate.   That is to say, Jesus never speaks of himself directly as ‘ the Servant,’ nor does he employ the title indirectly, as he sometimes does the expressions ‘ the Son ’ or ‘ the Son of Man,’ in allusions to himself.   Thus he nowhere says “ The Servant of the Lord came to seek and to save that which was lost,” or even “ The Servant of the Lord came not to be ministered unto, but to minister and to give his life as a ransom for many.”   He says : “ The Son of Man came to seek and to save that which was lost ” (Lk. xix. 10), “ The Son of Man came not to be ministered unto, but to minister, and to give his life as a ransom for many ” (Mk. x. 45), “ I am among you as one who serves ” (Lk. xxii. 27).   In every case the Servant supplies the predicate.   That is to say, he furnishes the example or standard for the task or destiny which the Messiah is to accomplish.   He who is called to be the Messiah-Son of God sees the way marked out for him by the practice of the Servant, and teaches also that only through the humiliation and self-sacrifice of the Servant is the glory of the Son of Man to be attained.   It may be said that we are here altogether dependent on tradition for the words of Jesus, and that the transmission of the tradition was exposed to risks of accident.   That may well be, but such a consideration hardly prevails against the fact that, while we have a profusion of Son of Man sayings in the tradition, Jesus never once *designates* himself as the Servant or speaks in his name.   For this there must have been reasons, and they are perhaps not far to seek.   Either (1) the name Servant, though used in Deutero-Isaiah to designate a genuinely Messianic figure, was too general in itself to convey a sense of the authority with which Jesus acted and spoke, or (2), as is perhaps more likely, the Son of Man symbol had come by the latter half of the ministry of Jesus to absorb for him all other aspects of the Messianic idea. This latter reason, if admitted, would explain not only the absence of the Servant title in the tradition of the sayings of Jesus but the very restricted usage of the other Messianic title, Son of God.

All the more remarkable is it that Jesus finds in the Isaianic Servant the pattern and the method which he is to follow for the execution of his peculiar task. The Servant's duty supplies, in fact, the middle term between his filial consciousness towards God and his perception of his ultimate destiny as the Son of Man. The recognition of the Servant comes to expression along two principal lines of thought, the line of ethic, and the line of sacrifice.

Along the second of these lines Jesus taught—and this, according to the Markan representation constitutes the very heart of the Christian mystery—that *the glorification of the Son of Man, the supreme event to which apocalyptic Messianic expectation was directed, could only come about through the endurance of the sufferings predicated of the Servant in Isa. liii.*

" How does it stand written with regard to the Son of Man ? That he should suffer much, and be rejected " (Mk. ix. 12).

" He began to teach them that the Son of Man must suffer much, and be rejected . . . and be killed, and . . . rise again " (Mk. viii. 31. Cf. ix. 31, x. 33-34).

" The Son of Man came . . . to give his life as a ransom for many " (Mk. x. 45).

Here we have to some extent a language formulated by the Church, but I see no reason for doubting that the doctrine which it embodies goes back to Jesus and to a great intuition born of his experience of suffering. As this connection of ideas involves, however, the conception of his Passion, it may be deferred for fuller treatment in Chapter VII.

As to the other line, the line of ethic, it is apparent that Jesus regarded the Servant as affording a supreme example of righteousness in his humility, his patient acceptance of reproaches, his steadfastness, his perfect trust in God. His own life as reflected in the evangelical tradition is in every way a transparent of the Servant's, and only the impression wrought by his historical image on the minds of his original followers is sufficient to account for this result. But even more decisive as a proof of the influence exercised by the conception of the Servant on the mind of Jesus is the great word on non-resistance in the Sermon on the Mount (Mt. v. 39-40). This passage has already been discussed in some detail, and need not be re-handled.[1] It has the interest of showing

[1] See above, Chapter II, pp. 30-32, and V, p. 87.

us that the teaching of Jesus on righteousness was dyed in the grain with reminiscence of the Servant. The evangelist has perhaps touched up the colouring of the original saying of Jesus, but that is all.

'SON OF MAN'

The course of the preceding argument has at various points brought to the front the concept of the ' Son of Man,' and has opened up a series of questions connected with the origin, history, and significance of this remarkable designation. It has been noticed that the figure of the Son of Man presented itself to Jesus objectively through its close association with the future supernatural Reign of God, and that more than the other forms of the Messianic concept it served as the final determinant of his sense of personal destiny.[1]

Now, however, the question has to be raised *whether the Son of Man concept did not appeal to Jesus for other reasons besides this objective givenness, and whether in taking it over from the apocalyptic tradition of his people he did not attach to it a quite special significance, the reflex of his own spiritual and ethical intuitions.* This is a question which has a most intimate bearing on the nature of the revelation of God in Jesus, and which as such needs to be pondered. The answer, however, can only come by a more thorough analysis of the Synoptic material than has yet been undertaken. The general evidence may be presented as follows :

1. It has been observed above that in the Markan and Q traditions the title Messiah or Christ is at significant points replaced by the higher Christian equivalent ' Son of God.' It has now to be noticed that over still wider areas of the tradition and *in words of Jesus himself* another title is substituted, viz. ' Son of Man ' or *barnasha*, which is the ordinary Aramaic equivalent for man. A possible instance of this substitution may lurk under the Greek text of the narrative of the Temptation, where in answer to the tempter's " If thou art the Son of God " Jesus is reported as making use of a word from Deuteronomy relating to man : " Man shall not live by bread alone " (Deut. viii. 3). I find that the Targum of Onkelos on this passage uses *'enash* for man, but that that of Jonathan has the more customary *barnasha*. It is just possible, therefore, that in the Aramaic original of the Temptation narrative Satan's suggestion about the Messiah turning stones into bread was countered by a statement making

[1] See above, Chapter IV, pp. 65-66, and VI, pp. 98-103.

8

use of the term *barnasha* and capable, therefore, of being understood as a reference to the *Son of Man*.

" The Son of Man shall not live by bread alone."

Be that as it may, we have indisputable evidence elsewhere of the form Son of Man being substituted in sayings of Jesus for other Messianic expressions. In Mk. viii. 29-31, for example, St. Peter confesses Jesus as the ' Christ,' and Jesus immediately goes on to announce the sufferings of the ' Son of Man.' Again in Mk. xiv. 61-62 the high priest asks Jesus : " Art thou the Christ, the Son of the Blessed ? " and Jesus answers : " I am, and you shall see the Son of Man sitting at the right hand of power, and coming with the clouds of heaven." Thus at high points in the narrative the tradition suggests that in the thoughts of Jesus regarding his vocation and destiny all other forms of the Messianic idea were superseded by that of the Son of Man, and with this goes the fact that in the tradition most of the allusions, direct or indirect, which Jesus makes to his work or to his fortunes are in the form of Son of Man sayings.

2. It is characteristic of the tradition in all our sources (Mark, the Q document, the M source of Matthew, and the L source of Luke) that the term Son of Man occurs only on the lips of Jesus. This is a strong argument for holding that it was a mark of his own language, not of the language of his Church. Bousset, indeed, in *Kyrios Christos*, takes the opposite view, but Bousset's case can hardly be defended. On the other hand, one or two qualifications need here to be made.

(*a*) Not all sayings in the tradition which make use of the term Son of Man need to have been originally uttered in that form. For example, the Q word which in Mt. x. 32 has the form : " Everyone who shall confess me before men, I will confess him, etc.," appears in Lk. xii. 8 as " Everyone who shall confess me before men, the Son of Man will confess him, etc." The saying in Mk. ix. 1 : " Shall not taste of death, till they see the kingdom of God come with power," is reproduced in Mt. xvi. 28 in the form : " Shall not taste of death, till they see the Son of Man coming in his kingdom." The question in Mk. viii. 27 : " Who do men say that I am ? " reappears in Mt. xvi. 13 as " Who do men say that the Son of Man is ? " The tendency to work in references to the Son of Man is obvious in the last two of the three instances, and possibly accounts for the form of Lk. xii. 28 as well. What was a conspicuous feature of the style of

Jesus is thus found extending itself to words which were not, to begin with, cast in that mould.

(b) Not all original words of Jesus making allusion to the Son of Man were intended to have reference to *himself*. He may at a certain stage or for a definite reason have spoken of the Son of Man with as entire an objectivity as he spoke of the kingdom of God. On the other hand, the formal distinction of himself from the Son of Man, which appears in these sayings, cannot be carried all the way. Just as Jesus saw in his exorcisms and other mighty works a sign that the kingdom of God had come upon men (Mt. xii. 28, Lk. xi. 20), and spoke of it as being in the midst (Lk. xvii. 21), so he came to see the advent of the Son of Man to be signified or foreshadowed in his own historical fortunes.

> " The kingdom of God," writes Rudolf Otto, " throws its shadow forward into the present ; it is not yet here in power, but is already here in secret. Likewise the Son of Man is not yet here in his power, but is already here before his power . . . as the one who some day will be the Son of Man in his power." [1]

3. The Son of Man sayings in the tradition come under three main categories :

(1) There are the sayings which speak of the Son of Man as *coming in glory* with the clouds, as sitting upon the throne of his glory, and as judging the world. Examples of these sayings have been already before us, and it has been seen that, while in certain cases the allusions may have been purely objective, there comes a point, marked probably by the first announcement of the sufferings of the Son of Man, when all distinction of a formal kind between the Son of Man and Jesus disappears. Jesus, in language derived from Dan. vii, expresses his final assurance of his Messiahship and vindication by God. There are scholars who hold that such sayings are not authentic utterances of Jesus but formulations of the Church's faith attributed to him. We know, however, that Jesus stood revealed as the Messiah before his death, and that it was as Son of Man that the Messiah was most present to his thought. Moreover, such a prediction as Mk. xiv. 62 is not easily regarded as a product of the Church's mind. Some definite basis in the actual self-revelation of Jesus was necessary before the Church could have committed him, as he stood before the Sanhedrin, to the unfulfilled prediction :

> " I am : and you shall see the Son of Man sitting at the right hand of power, and coming with the clouds of heaven."

[1] *The Kingdom of God and the Son of Man*, p. 161.

(2) There are the sayings, of which Mk. viii. 31, ix. 31, x. 33-34, x. 45, and xiv. 21 are examples, which speak of the necessity of the *suffering, rejection, death, and exaltation* of the Son of Man. Much of the detail in such sayings has clearly been conformed to the character of the events of the Passion history. But unless we are prepared to say that what was later called " the offence of the Cross " had no place at all in Jesus' thought of divine-human relations, the possibility that the general substance of these words had a basis in authentic oracles of Jesus is not to be ruled out. The sufferings of Jesus are predicted in the form of a dogma relating to the Son of Man. But this dogma is not only not derivable from Jewish apolyptic tradition but stands in extreme paradoxical relation to it. That the Son of Man enters on his heavenly glory through humiliation and self-sacrifice was an idea which despite Isa. liii had not entered into the Messianic calculations of Judaism.

(3) There are the sayings in which, according to the tradition, Jesus speaks of his *present activities and experiences* as those of the Son of Man. It may be that in a few of these cases, such as Mk. ii. 10, " The Son of Man has authority on earth to forgive sins," or Mk. ii. 28, " The Son of Man is Lord of the Sabbath," the voice of the Church is to be discerned rather than the voice of Jesus. The sayings are official statements about the Church's Lord. They are fragments of early Christian preaching. The one is a part of the accreted matter which Form-Criticism considers to have been overlaid on the pronouncement-story of the paralytic, and the other, Mk. ii. 28, may have had a similar origin.[1] Greater is the difficulty presented by such sayings as the following, which have been transmitted through the Q source :

" The Son of Man has not where to lay his head " (Mt. viii. 20 Lk. ix. 58).

" The Son of Man came eating and drinking " (Mt. xi. 19, Lk. vii. 34).

" Whosoever shall speak a word against the Son of Man, it will be forgiven him " (Mt. xii. 32, Lk. xii. 10).

These sayings differ in one very important point from those which have appeared under the category of the Son of Man's suffering and death. In the latter the element of suffering appears as a dogmatic presupposition of the glory of this celestial figure, therefore as a stage through which Jesus must yet pass in order to be

[1] See above, Chapter III, pp. 40-42.

revealed as the Son of Man. On the other hand, in the sayings now before us, the manifestation of the Son of Man is related not to the future but to the present life of Jesus, and this feature requires explanation.

The sayings have been interpreted, first, as " I " words which have been assimilated to the Son of Man type of utterance. This view has a certain plausibility, for the oracular form of the genuine Son of Man sayings tended to become a pattern for all self-utterances of Jesus. In the second place, they have been regarded as special examples of the prolepsis by which the coming of the Son of Man is anticipated in the fortunes of Jesus. This, too, is possible, though so convinced an advocate of the prolepsis idea as Rudolf Otto does not favour it in the present case but regards the sayings as originally " I " words. A third explanation, which takes the sayings in question to have been objective allusions by Jesus to the Heavenly Man of some esoteric doctrine, who descends to earth and shares the human lot before being restored again to his heavenly status, makes too many assumptions to be convincing. We have no knowledge that any developments of Son of Man belief such as this theory assumes had taken place within Judaism or, for that part, anywhere else in the time of Jesus. But here, while not ruling out the formal propriety of one or other of the two first explanations, we come face to face with a question which can no longer be ignored. *Is it not possible that the great expansion of Son of Man doctrine according to which the Son of Man's exaltation (Dan. vii. 13-14) is from a human life of suffering on earth originated first in the mind of Jesus himself?*

On this view the ultimate basis of the self-recognition of Jesus as the Son of Man is to be found not in any special developments of Jewish apocalyptic tradition, whether in Enoch or elsewhere, nor in any supposed Son of Man myth current in that age, but in the depths of a religious spirit which, grasping that the true nature of all glory and service, especially of all redemptive service, is revealed in suffering and sacrifice, applied this conception to the coming of the Son of Man. In the actual analysis this would be equivalent to saying that Jesus perceived the last consequences of the Messianic synthesis of lowly Servant and glorious Son of Man, thus accepting what Judaism in its retrospect upon its own prophetic history had refused to see or failed to grasp. On this view it is ' the man of sorrows,' the man who identifies himself with his sinful nation to the extent of making its guilt and tragedy his own (Isa. liii), who is raised to glory as the Redeemer-Man (Dan. vii. 13-14). The Son of Man is thus revealed in his solidarity with men, as their friend, helper, benefactor, vicarious substitute, and intercessor : so he becomes their Saviour. We know that this conception existed in New Testament Christianity. It speaks of Jesus Christ as one who,

> " Found in fashion as a man (ὡς ἄνθρωπος), humbled himself, becoming obedient unto death, even the death of the cross. Wherefore also God highly exalted him " (Phil. ii. 8 f.).

Have we any right to say that such an expansion of ideas could have arisen only after the crucifixion, and that it was not possible for Jesus in the days of his flesh ? To take this attitude may conceivably be to beg the whole question of Christian origins.

It has been seen with what selective insight Jesus at a great moment drew to himself the Messianic concept of the Son of God, thus charging a pre-existing style of words with new and passionate religious significance. Would it be strange if among the causes which led him to place his whole personal work and fortunes under the final sign of the Son of Man (Mt. xxiv. 30) the element of his deep compassion for men played a part ; *if among the attractions which this Messiology had for him was the fact that it gave back to him something of his own sense of oneness with the poor and the unfriended, the sinful and the ostracized among his people whom he came to save?* Let it be remembered that the symbol in Dan. vii. 13 was weighted from the start with a deeply human pathos. The figure as conceived in Daniel is indeed that of a heavenly being resembling an angel : but the fact that he is deliberately contrasted in his human *likeness* with the bestial forms which symbolize the world-empires throws on the human element in the picture a greater fullness of ethical meaning than belonged to any mythological ' First Man ' after whose image the Danielic concept is sometimes supposed to have been fashioned. Let it be remembered also that man and son of man were ideas to which the religion of Israel in the past had lent a deeply ethical connotation, as we see by the Psalms and by the prophet Ezekiel. Let it be remembered, finally, that humanity is a feature which the Davidic Messiah, the Isaianic Servant, and the apocalyptic Son of Man all share.

> " Behold, a king shall reign in righteousness, and a man shall be as an hiding place from the wind " (Isa. xxxii. 1-2).
> " A man of sorrows, and acquainted with grief " (Isa. liii. 3).
> " One like a son of man " (Dan. vii. 13).

It is true that in the first of these three passages the Hebrew word *'ish* is held by many scholars to mean only " each one " (of the princes mentioned in verse *1a*). But opinion is by no means unanimous on the point, and the LXX renders the word by ὁ ἄνθρωπος, as parallel with βασιλεύς in verse 1.

If the human element which was thus always present in the Messianic vision is kept in view, it will no longer seem impossible that Jesus should have come to see the sign of the Son of Man covering the whole measure of his historical experience.

These perhaps are theorems, but if any particular proof is needed that Jesus interpreted the Son of Man prediction in terms reflecting his own human passion, it may be found in the great parable of the judgement of the Son of Man which is recorded in Mt. xxv. 31-46. As it stands, this parable relates to the judgement to be exercised upon the ' nations ' or Gentile world, and those to whom the righteous show and the unrighteous deny compassion are the ' brethren ' or disciples of Christ. But we know enough of the evangelist's methods and tendencies to render it extremely likely that in the original form of the parable the judgement of the Son of Man bore not on the Gentiles but on all men without distinction, and the mercy which is singled out for reward was mercy to the strangers and the naked, the sick and the oppressed among all mankind. And there in the end we may perhaps leave the matter.

" When the Son of Man shall come in his glory, and all the angels with him,
Then shall he sit on the throne of his glory. . . ."

" Then the king shall say to those on his right hand, Come ye blessed of my Father, inherit the kingdom prepared for you. . . .

For I was an-hungered, and you gave me meat :
I was thirsty, and you gave me drink :
I was a stranger, and you took me in : naked, and you clothed me :
I was sick, and you visited me ;
I was in prison, and you came unto me."

NOTE ON A THEORY OF RUDOLF OTTO

In the above survey no notice has been taken of the theory of Dr. Rudolf Otto that the Son of Man Christology of Jesus was decisively influenced by I Enoch, and in particular by Chapters lxx-lxxi of that book.[1] In these chapters we read of Enoch's

[1] *The Kingdom of God and the Son of Man*, pp. 201-210.

personal translation to heaven, and of his recognition there as the Son of Man. Otto's thesis is that this idea of a powerful preacher of righteousness and of the coming judgement being hailed in heaven as the Son of Man provided the mould and determined the outlines of Jesus' final interpretation of his calling.[1] Otto will not say indeed that the consciousness of mission which inspired Jesus originated in pre-existing notions of this kind, but he holds that Jesus was led, as time went on, to clothe his consciousness in the form of these ideas. But Enoch lxx-lxxi is a very obscure and precarious foundation on which to build such a theory. The date of these chapters is uncertain. They may be a late insertion into I Enoch, and possibly anti-Christian in their origin and intention. In other ways also Otto's idea makes too many assumptions to be convincing. The terms in which the Synoptic Jesus speaks of his exaltation and coming again recall the language of Daniel, but not at all that of Enoch. And where in the Gospels do we hear echoes of the peculiar Enochian style —' Lord of Spirits,' ' Head of Days,' ' the Son of Man who has righteousness ' ? For these reasons Otto's book, though deeply suggestive in other respects, does not seem to me to assist our understanding at this particular point.

[1] *The Kingdom of God and the Son of Man*, p. 213.

CHAPTER VII

THE PASSION AND DEATH OF THE MESSIAH

THE death of Jesus on the Cross made a permanent impression on
the early Christian mind, and became the factor which above all
others was destined to determine its conception not only of the
Messianic salvation but of God's entire revelation of Himself to a
sinful world. It took time to bring out the whole immensity of
this determination, but from the first days of the Church the
event on Calvary by the very fact of its having befallen one who
had stood self-disclosed as the predestined Messiah could not but
raise profound questions for the Christian community and could
not but become a focal point through which sooner or later all
lines of thought connecting God and man had to be drawn.
First apologetic necessity, then a deepening of religious and
theological insight prescribed that this event should be regarded
not as a mere contingency, as merely one of a series of episodes
forming the earthly history of Jesus, but as the climax of the
revelation, as the supreme sign under which the whole manifestation of God in Jesus had henceforth to stand. What was at first
a blinding darkness to the followers of Jesus became in time the
very fountain of their seeing. From saying that Jesus was the
Messiah despite the event of the Cross they came to say that he
was the Messiah in virtue of that event.

The Christian doctrine of salvation thus starts from an historical fact, but would this fact have acquired the centrality which
it possessed for early Christian thought if rays of light proceeding
from the mind of Jesus himself had not converged upon it, catching
it in their beam, and imparting to it as thus illumined a supreme
revelational significance ?

THE DEATH OF JESUS IN THE PRIMITIVE TRADITION

From the prediction attributed to Jesus on the night of his
betrayal : " All of you shall be offended : for it is written, I will
smite the shepherd, and the sheep shall be scattered " (Mk. xiv.
27), it may be inferred that the first effect of the arrest of Jesus on
his disciples was to break up their ranks and to scatter them. But
the dispersal was only for the moment. Johannes Weiss, who

recognizes in the prediction the reflection of " a hard fact which the old tradition could not altogether make away with—though Luke and John have suppressed it—namely, that the disciples wandered and fell away," [1] limits the significance of the fact to a temporary collapse of morale which did not carry with it any abjuration of faith on the part of the disciples or any actual flight to Galilee. As a matter of fact the brethren, even on Mark's showing, were still in Jerusalem on the days following the crucifixion, and it is surely more likely that the phenomena of the resurrection-visions, whatever their precise nature may have been, presuppose an attitude of expectant faith on the part of the beholders rather than of despair. But while the outward effects which the seizure and crucifixion of Jesus had on his adherents should not be exaggerated, the moral consequences produced by the collapse of their inherited Messianic ideas were nothing less than fundamental. The resurrection-experiences which indicate the stress of the disciples' passion for re-assurance of faith indicate also the transformed character of the faith to which they now come. Out of the old national Messianic idea the conception of a transfigured heavenly Messiah is born (Acts i. 6-7). The kingdom of Christ draws apart from the kingdoms of the world, and between the followers of the Nazarene and the rest of mankind stands the stark and irreducible fact that the Jewish nation and the imperial power of Rome had adjudged Jesus a criminal and condemned him to die. This fact, when faith returned firmly to its proper basis in the unshakable religious certainties of which Jesus had been the centre, inevitably inaugurated a new world of spiritual values, a new conception of divine glory and love.

A real sense of that ' offence of the Cross ' which St. Paul later brings to unforgettable expression in the words : " Never be it mine to boast except in the cross of our Lord Jesus Christ, through which the world has been crucified to me, and I to the world " (Gal. vi. 14), must have been present to the minds of Christians from the start as they reflected upon their position as followers of the Nazarene, sharers with him of reproach and shame at the hands of an alienated nation.

The question arises, however, whether, apart from this external significance of the cross as a sign planted between the Christian community and the world, there did not exist from the beginning the elements of a deeper and more inward under-

[1] *History of Primitive Christianity*, Vol. I, p. 17.

standing of the mystery of the Messiah's death. It was not possible to detach that event from the will of God, from what an early discourse of St. Peter in Acts calls " the deliberate purpose and foreknowledge of God " (Acts ii. 23), nor from the revelation of that will as made known in the character and mind of Jesus. It would seem, however, from the evidence of Acts that the early preaching largely limited itself to the stressing of the divine necessity of the event and to the citing of Old Testament prophecies in which the will of God had come to light. There is a lively sense that the Jewish nation had sinned against the divine manifestation made in Jesus by which he was indicated as the predestined Messiah (Acts ii. 22 f., iii. 14 f., etc.), that a crisis in religious history had been reached, and that the necessity of a final breach with the existing evil order had been declared (Acts ii. 40).

For the evidence of a more inward appreciation of the meaning of the Messiah's death on the part of the primitive Church we have, however, to look away from Acts to St. Paul. We know from one very revealing passage in the latter's epistles that already in pre-Pauline Christianity the death of Jesus had been given a relation to the fact of *sin*. For, writes the Apostle,

" I delivered unto you, first of all, that which I also received, namely, that Christ died for our sins according to the scriptures " (I Cor. xv. 3).

The most natural interpretation of ' received ' ($\pi\alpha\rho\acute{\epsilon}\lambda\alpha\beta o\nu$) in this context is that St. Paul owed the knowledge in question not to any vision or supernatural communication made to himself personally but to the tradition current in the Church when he entered it, and since the death of Jesus *qua* historical fact was known to him without any instruction from that quarter, the thing which he ' received ' must have been the particular interpretation of that death as for our sins ($\acute{\upsilon}\pi\grave{\epsilon}\rho$ $\tau\hat{\omega}\nu$ $\acute{\alpha}\mu\alpha\rho\tau\iota\hat{\omega}\nu$ $\acute{\eta}\mu\hat{\omega}\nu$). How much, then, is implied in the expression ' for our sins ' ? If the preposition is given its usual sense, some kind of *causal* connection between our sins and the death of Christ is asserted as an article of the primitive Christian belief, but no further light is shed on the exact nature of the relation. The natural suggestion of the phrase, however, is that the death of Christ was construed as a *sacrifice*.[1]

The causal link between the death of Christ and our sins is

---

[1] See Dr. Vincent Taylor's *Jesus and His Sacrifice*, a work with which I feel very deeply in agreement.

further described in this primitive formula as ' according to the Scriptures.' Does this mean that the primitive theology derived its understanding of the death of Jesus entirely from suggestions offered in Holy Scripture, as for example in Isa. liii, or did it start from some ground within the historical teaching of Jesus ? In the one case the Church began with the uninterpreted fact of the death of Jesus and found a meaning for it in Scripture ; in the other case it started from an accepted association between that death and our sins and found that nexus of ideas corroborated by Scripture. The second interpretation is not only preferable in point of strength but is the only one compatible with a tradition which gives the whole revelation of God in Jesus a relation to the fact of sin. But of this later. Meantime, it may be noted that an attempt has here or there been made to give the phrase ' according to the Scriptures ' another reference than to the Old Testament. Thus it has been suggested that written narratives of the Passion-story were already in circulation in the pre-Pauline Church.[1] The existence of such records would explain why the Q document when it appeared did not contain an account of the Passion or of the teaching of Jesus about it. But there is no supporting evidence for Christian ' writings ' at so early a time. Again it has been conjectured that the allusion may have been to lost apocryphal books which taught that the Heavenly Man or Son of Man was to be slain in order to effect the redemption of the souls of men from the powers of evil. We know nothing, however, of such books, nor does anything which we do know of contemporary apocalyptic notions of the Messiah's way of dealing with sinners encourage the belief that the doctrine in question was known. In any case the phrase ' according to the Scriptures ' had too fixed a sense to be used of any non-Biblical writings. The meaning, therefore, of the First Corinthians passage would seem to be that the primitive Christian community taught as an article of faith that " Christ died for our sins," and supported this belief by calling the evidence of Holy Scripture, above all of Isa. liii.

" He was wounded for our transgressions, he was bruised for our iniquities :
    " The chastisement of our peace was upon him, and with his stripes we are healed. . . .
    " The Lord has laid on him the iniquity of us all." [2]

---

[1] W. Bussmann, *Synoptische Studien*, Bd. III, pp. 184-191.
[2] Cf. also Ps. xxii and lxxxix, 38-52.

The Nature of the Synoptic Evidence

It is rightly emphasized by the authors of a suggestive modern work on the New Testament that, when apostles or evangelists declare historical events to be fulfilments of a divine purpose, what they mean is not simply that the events in question are patient of such dogmatic interpretation, but that they demand it.[1] In other words, the revelational significance of Christian history is not a mere epiphenomenon, an interpretation which has settled on the events *ab extra*, but inheres in the very nature of the events. The principle may be applied to any great word of the New Testament, such as Rom. v. 8, " God proves his own love towards us in that, while we were still sinners, Christ died for us," or II Cor. v. 19, " God was in Christ reconciling the world unto himself." The New Testament doctrines of Christ and salvation are not merely illustrated in the New Testament facts, but they have their origin in those facts. The death of Jesus, for example, did not illustrate a love of God in which Christians otherwise believed. It was the event by which they came to know the love of God. The bread and wine in the Eucharist were not symbols in which Christians could find the thought that the self-giving of Christ was sacrificial. They were symbols which Christ chose to reveal and to convey the power of that sacrifice. Obviously for the justification of this principle we are thrown back ultimately upon the mind and teaching of Jesus. Did he face death in the spirit not of a social reformer or prophet of righteousness accepting martyrdom for the sake of his cause, but of one who was conscious of giving his life as a ' ransom-price ' for the salvation of the many, and of instituting by his death a ' covenant ' between their souls and God ? The issue at this point cannot be disguised. It is in the last analysis the question whether the Christian doctrine of redemption originated in human sensibilities of a spiritual order which found in the drama of Calvary an event round which they could fling their desires and hopes, or whether it is rooted in the objective teaching of Jesus and in the will and purpose with which he set his face steadfastly towards Jerusalem.

It should here be borne in mind, on the one hand, that *if Jesus throughout his work was conscious of standing in a circle of crisis, in which the powers of the world to come were seen to be breaking in all around him, he cannot when the prospect of death cast its shadow upon the*

---

[1] Hoskyns and Davey, *The Riddle of the New Testament*, p. 69.

*scene have thought of that event in purely natural terms or in dissociation
from the purpose and power of God which were working with him.* Such
a synthesis of ideas seems at any rate to leap from the heart of
the striking saying recorded by St. Luke which has surely the
aspect of an authentic utterance of Jesus :

> " I came to cast fire on earth, and how I would it were already
> kindled !
> " But I have a baptism with which to be baptized, and how
> oppressed I am till it is brought to pass " (Lk. xii. 49-50).[1]

To say [2] that if the ' baptism ' here is an allusion to martyrdom
the saying must be an *ex post facto* creation of the post-resurrection
Church is quite indefensible. He who received from Herod
Antipas the warning reported in Lk. xiii. 31-33 and spoke or
quoted the Q word about Jerusalem slaying the prophets and
stoning the messengers of God cannot have excluded a martyr-
death from the conditions under which his work would be
' perfected.' Indeed it may well be asked with a modern theologian whether in the Judaism of Maccabean and post-Maccabean
times the conceptions of prophet and martyr for God had not
become definitely one,[3] and whether it is not from the standpoint
of this identification that we should make our initial approach to
the mind of Jesus both as regards his own calling and as regards
the calling of his followers. The basis of Christianity indeed is
not merely prophetic, yet on its supra-prophetic or Messianic
level the essential features of the prophetic ideal would be conserved, and indeed brought to supreme affirmation. From this
point of view the affirmations in the tradition that Jesus predicted suffering and death as his portion or ' cup ' can no longer
be regarded as historically impossible. If the Messianic consciousness of Jesus bears signs of representing the prophetic
consciousness of Israel at its highest or absolute tension, then the
claim

> (*a*) to drink the ' cup ' of suffering (Mk. x. 38, etc.),
> (*b*) to undergo a ' baptism ' of blood (Mk. x. 38, Lk. xii. 50),
> (*c*) to give his life a ' ransom ' for many (Mk. x. 45, etc.),
> (*d*) to call his disciples to suffering (Mk. viii. 34-37, etc.),

can in no way be regarded as contrary to the internal probabilities
of his situation.

[1] See above, Chapter IV, pp. 69-70.   [2] With Bultmann.
[3] O. Michel, *Prophet und Märtyrer* (1932).

And that vicarious and atoning significance was predicable of such martyrdom is shown by the evidence of IV Macc. vi. 28-29 and xvii. 22 to which we shall come later.

On the other hand, the view that the Christian doctrine of redemption originated purely in human spiritual sensibilities wrapping themselves around the mystery-drama of the death of Jesus and finding there the certitudes which men longed for, of forgiveness, mercy, peace with God, and victory over the world, is not one that can be carried through to the end. Quite clearly, the followers of Jesus from the beginning found in the death of the Cross a supreme assurance of these things, and to this Cross their faith, lifting from every other ground, transfers itself. *But how, if the death of Jesus had not been presented to them in a certain objective light, could they have found in it the pledge of the forgiveness of their sins, of the acceptance of their souls with God, and of the hope of salvation?* The Christians of Jerusalem were not devotees of mystery-religions who had brought with them an *à priori* pattern of ideas suited to the explication of the mystery of the death and exaltation of Jesus. They were fervent Jewish apocalyptists who saw history predominantly under the sign of the End and were conscious of a certain fearful judgement awaiting the world.

> " Behold, he comes with the clouds ; and every eye shall see him, and they who pierced him : and all the tribes of the earth shall mourn for him."

Why did the company of Jesus feel themselves exempted from this doom, from which, if they only had their own religious sensibilities to support them, they could in no wise have escaped ? Why did not Christian life from the beginning shape itself as a never-ending lamentation for the death of the slain Messiah, as once women in Jerusalem mourned for Tammuz ? Was it not because Jesus had loved sinners and sought to save them ? In that case the hope and confidence of the first Christians went back to an objective ground in Jesus, and if Jesus loved and sought to save sinners, was it not possible that he might even have said that he died to save them ?

As a matter of fact, the Synoptic tradition states with deliberate intention that Jesus predicted his death at the hands of men not as an irrelevant contingency nor as an unexplained mystery but as a definite necessity appertaining to the exaltation of the Son of Man, and that he invested this necessity with a redemptive significance.

THE MYSTERY OF THE SON OF MAN

The analysis of the Son of Man logia undertaken at an earlier stage showed the existence of a group of sayings taking the form of dogmatic predictions of the suffering and death of the Son of Man. They occur with deliberate reiteration in the second half of Mark, and there their meaning clearly is that the Messiahship of Jesus, hitherto a mystery announced only by supernatural voices and divine signs, is now to be understood as fulfilling itself historically in the acceptance of humiliation, pain, and death at the hands of men. Behind the dogmatic rigidity of the Markan exposition we see the definite features of a tradition according to which Jesus rejected all forms of the Messianic office which were not compatible with the conception of sacrifice, and we may well believe with Maurice Goguel that it was the clear prospect of this course of suffering and rejection that led Jesus to the final identification of the Messiah's career with his own.

> "Through the idea that his sufferings were necessary for the coming of the kingdom of God," writes Goguel, "Jesus was led beyond the sense of a simple prophetic vocation, and to regard himself, no longer simply as the herald of the kingdom of God, but as the one who was to realize it himself, who, after having been humiliated and rejected, would appear as the glorious Son of Man. Thus this Messianic consciousness of Jesus appears as the triumph of faith over experience. . . . This is why, as the human outlook became darker, this consciousness increased in force and certainty." [1]

In the order of Mark the new teaching, the mystery proper of Jesus Messiah, begins at viii. 31, following upon Peter's confession, "Thou art the Christ," in viii. 29. At viii. 27 the public work of Jesus in Galilee is over, for it was in all probability before this time that he had received notice from Herod Antipas warning him to quit his dominions (Lk. xiii. 31-33), and had resolved upon the journey to Jerusalem. It is at this point, face to face with the rejection and death now shadowing him, that the Messianic claim of Jesus touches ground, so to speak, in history.

1. "He began to teach them that the Son of Man must suffer many things, and be rejected by the elders and chief priests and scribes and be killed, and after three days rise again" (Mk. viii. 31, etc.).
2. "He taught his disciples, and said unto them, The Son of Man is delivered into the hands of men, and they shall kill him, and after he is killed, he shall rise the third day" (Mk. ix. 31).

[1] *Life of Jesus*, pp. 390 ff.

3. " We go up to Jerusalem, and the Son of Man shall be delivered
to the chief priests and to the scribes ; and they shall condemn
him to death, and shall deliver him to the Gentiles ; and they
shall mock him, and shall scourge him, and shall spit upon him,
and shall kill him ; and the third day he shall rise again "
(Mk. x. 33-34).

4. " How is it written with regard to the Son of Man ? That he
must suffer many things, and be set at nought " (Mk. ix. 12).

5. " So shall also the Son of Man be in his day. But first he must
suffer many things, and be rejected by this generation " (Lk.
xvii. 24-25).

6. " Truly the Son of Man goes, as it has been determined " (Lk.
xxii. 22).

7. " The Son of Man came not to be ministered unto, but to
minister, and to give his life as a ransom for many " (Mk. x. 45).

A glance at the above statements will show that the details of
the predictions have in several cases been supplied from the
Passion-history. We may therefore leave out of account the
formal precision of sayings like Nos. 1 and 3. On the other
hand, No. 2, and still more Nos. 4 and 5, are comparatively free
of such *ex post facto* features, and No. 4 has the rugged and irreducible form of an original oracle. And when from the details
we pass to the general structure of the sayings we see the whole
tradition to be governed by the very definite idea that the sufferings of Jesus were disclosed not under the form of a mere historical certainty awaiting himself but rather under the form of
a dogmatic necessity appertaining to the Son of Man.

The pattern of thought which here comes to light deserves
more than a superficial notice. It was not necessary for Jesus to
explain the necessity of his suffering in the form of a disclosure
concerning the Son of Man. On one occasion he brings it under
the head of what a prophet may expect.

" See, I cast out demons and work healings to-day and to-morrow,
and the third day I am done ($\tau\epsilon\lambda\epsilon\iota o\hat{\upsilon}\mu\alpha\iota$). Only I must keep
travelling to-day, and to-morrow and the next day after, for it
cannot be ($o\mathring{\upsilon}\kappa \ \mathring{\epsilon}\nu\delta\acute{\epsilon}\chi\epsilon\tau\alpha\iota$) that a prophet perish outside of
Jerusalem " (Lk. xiii. 32-33).

In Lk. xii. 50 he can say : " I have a baptism with which to be
baptized," and in Mk. x. 38 he speaks of " my cup," " my
baptism." On the other hand, it is characteristic of the block of
Son of Man predictions now under consideration that never once
in any of the Synoptic parallels is the Son of Man form dropped

9

and an " I " form substituted as in the other groups of Son of Man sayings, and this is significant. At this point, says Otto, " the tradition is as hard as diamonds, and identical in form in all the records." [1] The natural inference is that the underlying tradition had acquired so definite a stamp at this point as to secure the preservation of the style against variation. Jesus on some great occasion, or more probably on a series of occasions, had announced to his followers a mystery concerning the Son of Man : the Son of Man could only attain his triumph through suffering, and the paradox had made an indelible impression on their minds. There, so far as his open teaching is concerned, Jesus leaves the matter, but he goes forward himself under the sign of the Son of Man to face the last issues of life. The relation of the Son of Man's destiny to his own has by this time become one of complete identification.

The Son of Man who appears before the Ancient of Days to receive an everlasting kingdom for the people of God (Dan. vii. 13 ff.) is one who is lifted up from suffering to glory. He is indeed the Servant of whose mysterious fate the great prophet of the Exile wrote. This sufferer for God had been promised empire (Isa. liii. 12) ; his sacrifice was to bring an age of expansion and blessedness (Isa. liv), in which the sure mercies covenanted to David would be realized (Isa. lv. 3).

In this manner, thinks Goguel, " the sacrifice which Jesus accepted out of fidelity to his vocation reinforced the sense of the vocation itself." [2]

" To him acceptance of suffering was an act of that obedience to God which summed up his whole conception of religion. At the same time, however, Jesus believed in the absolute wisdom of God, and . . . he had the assurance that his sufferings formed part of the plan which God, in his infinite wisdom, had designed for the establishment of his kingdom."

But when this scholar asserts that the resolution of Jesus was taken without knowing, and even without trying to imagine in what way his obedience would serve the redemptive purpose of the divine wisdom, is he not unwarrantably limiting the probabilities of the situation ? Apart altogether from the relation in which Jesus had stood to sinners, had he not Isa. liii before him, and did not Isa. liii contain the words : " When thou shalt make his soul

[1] *The Kingdom of God and the Son of Man*, p. 235.
[2] *Life of Jesus*, pp. 391 ff.

an *'asham*, a trespass-offering, . . . the pleasure of the Lord shall prosper in his hand " ?

THE LIFE OF JESUS A RANSOM

On the way to Jerusalem Jesus rebuked the presumptuous request of the sons of Zebedee, and is then said to have declared that service and self-sacrifice alone were the way to glory, and to have confirmed this statement by a word about the Son of Man.

" The Son of Man did not come to be served, but to serve (διακον-ῆσαι) and to give his life (δοῦναι τὴν ψυχὴν αὐτοῦ) as a ransom for many (ἀντὶ πολλῶν) " (Mk. x. 45).

What is here predicated of the Son of Man recalls the Sufferer of Isa. liii at three points : he ' serves,' he ' gives his life ' as an offering, his offering is ' for many.' The Greek aorist tenses indicate that the allusion is not to a lifelong sacrifice but to one definitive act of self-surrender. The saying differs formally from the other Son of Man sayings which have just been considered in the important point that, whereas these others predict what the Son of Man is fated to suffer, this states what he has ' come ' to do, and therefore it falls under the axe of Dr. Bultmann.[1] The Son of Man here means Jesus on earth—that is enough to pre-judice Dr. Bultmann against the historicity of the logion—and the claim is that he fulfils his vocation by accepting the sacrificial function of the Servant of the Lord who gives his life " in com-pensation for the sins of the people, interposing for them as their substitute." [2]

The authenticity of few words in the Synoptic tradition has been more hotly contested than that of this word about Jesus giving his life as a ' ransom.' It has been pronounced on formal grounds a piece of post-resurrection theology, a dogma of the community which has been transferred to the lips of Jesus. By way of proof appeal is made to the simple and non-soteriological parallel to the saying in Lk. xxii. 27 : " I am in your midst as one who serves." In the latter passage, it is argued, Jesus functions as the Servant of God in his humility, but without the suggestion that his self-abnegation has a redemptive or atoning significance. It is even contended that the Markan saying is a Paulinism. To all this it may be answered,—

[1] See above, Chapter IV, pp. 67-71.
[2] Brown, Briggs, and Driver, *Hebrew Lexicon*, p. 80.

(1) that, even if the *form* of the word should have to be recognized as bearing the stamp of the post-resurrection period, a thing which is by no means certain, it does not follow that the idea which has been expressed in this form does not go back to Jesus ;

(2) that, as the parallel in Lk. xxii. 27 occurs in the context of the Last Supper narrative, it is by no means certain that the 'service' which Jesus renders in the midst of his followers had not a sacrificial or soteriological significance in the tradition followed by the evangelist ;

(3) that, if the Lukan word did not originally belong to the context of the Last Supper, there is no reason why Jesus, who on one occasion cites the Servant as an example of humility, should not on another occasion have emphasized the redemptive and atoning character of his sacrifice ;

(4) that the word *lutron*, though not elsewhere ascribed to Jesus, is not Pauline, but is characteristic of early Greek-speaking Christianity in general, and rests on the usage of the Septuagint where it is employed to render a host of Hebrew expressions.[1]

While none of these considerations proves that Jesus uttered the words of Mk. x. 45, they help to clear away the objections brought against the idea of his having done so. It is not in our power to prove the authenticity of *any* word which tradition has ascribed to Jesus, but if criticism is able to show that it was not historically impossible for him to have spoken this or that particular word or to have held this or that particular idea, it will have discharged a no mean part of its function. As regards the Ransom word certain important considerations help us to a more positive assessment of the probabilities with regard to its genuineness.

1. The Old Testament religion contains the thought that the sinner's soul is forfeit, that he is unable to ransom it himself, and that no one else can ransom it for him. Thus one of the Psalms, speaking of the proud possessors of wealth, declares unequivocally :

"None can by any means redeem his brother, nor give to God a ransom (Hebr. *kopher*, LXX ἐξίλασμα) for him.

For the redemption (Hebr. *pidhyon*, LXX τὴν τιμὴν τῆς λυτρώσεως) of their soul is costly, and must be let alone for ever.

That he should still live alway, that he should not see corruption " (Ps. xlix. 7-9).

The reference here is to physical dissolution, but in later days the redemption of the soul acquired a vaster range of significance. Death was the wages of sin.

---

[1] See Hatch and Redpath, *Concordance to the Septuagint, s.v.* λύτρον.

" Wherefore do not hope to live, ye sinners, but ye shall depart and die : for ye know no ransom : for ye are prepared for the day of the great judgement, for the day of tribulation and of great shame for your spirits " (I Enoch xcviii. 10).

The death spoken of here refers, as Dr. Charles says, " not only to the loss of the life temporal but also to the life eternal."

2. The great prophetic vision in Isa. liii contemplates a trespass-offering (Hebr. 'asham, LXX περὶ ἁμαρτίας) being made by the soul of the Messianic Servant, and the guilt for which the offering is made is the iniquity of the nation of Israel (Isa. liii. 6). What neither Moses nor David was accounted worthy to do, namely, to take upon himself the guilt of his people (Exod. xxxii. 31 f., II Sam. xxiv. 17), the Servant of the Lord is destined to achieve by his self-sacrifice.

3. Late Judaism, as we see by the Hellenistic work IV Maccabees, had come to affix a redemptive and atoning value to the martyr-sufferings of the righteous. Thus the Maccabean martyr Eleazar in delivering himself to the torments of fire for the sake of the Law, when he might prudently have saved his life, prays to God—

" Be merciful to thy people, accepting our punishment on their behalf. Make my blood a purification for them, and take my life as a substitute for their life (ἀντίψυχον αὐτῶν) " (IV Macc. vi. 28 f.).

Later the writer says of the Jewish martyrs—

" They have become as it were a substitute (ἀντίψυχον) for the sin of the nation, and through the blood of these pious ones and their propitiatory death (τοῦ ἱλαστηρίου θανάτου αὐτῶν) the divine providence preserved Israel which before was evilly treated " (IV Macc. xvii. 21-22).

In view of these facts, it will not do to pronounce it impossible or unlikely that Jesus, who saw his work and teaching to be fraught with critical significance for his nation, should think of his sacrifice in terms of an 'asham for many, as completing and consummating the work—the conversion and redemption of the many—which he had sought by his life to effect. As Dr. Rudolf Otto looks at the matter, the primary word in the religious calling of Israel, namely, " Ye shall be holy, for I am holy," came to be interpreted in the sense that " Only he can be holy whom God sanctifies," and this understanding was completed in Israel in Isa. liii. The deepest of all religious ideas was thus born not among Greeks, Indians, or Iranians, but in Jewish souls,[1] and it gave to Jesus the final means of interpreting his historical destiny.

THE INSTITUTION OF THE LORD'S SUPPER

Three narratives representing or incorporating independent accounts of the origin of the Lord's Supper have come down to us in the early Christian tradition.

I. The Pauline Narrative in I Cor. xi. 23-26 :

(23) "For I received from the Lord that which also I delivered unto you, that the Lord Jesus in the night in which he was betrayed took bread ; (24) and when he had given thanks, he broke it, and said : *This is my body which is for you : this do in remembrance of me.* (25) In like manner also the cup, after supper, saying : *This cup is the new covenant in my blood : this do, as oft as ye drink it, in remembrance of me.* (26) For as often as ye eat this bread, and drink the cup, ye proclaim the Lord's death, till he come."

With this account is to be associated Lk. xxii. 19*b*-20, which section of the Lukan narrative is for the most part verbally identical with I Cor. xi. 24*b*-25.

II. The Markan Narrative (Mk. xiv. 22-25) :

(22) "And as they were eating, he took bread, and when he had blessed, he broke it, and gave to them, and said : *Take ye : this is my body.* (23) And he took a cup, and when he had given thanks, he gave it to them ; and they all drank of it. (24) And he said unto them : *This is my blood of the covenant, which is shed for many.* (25) *Verily, I say unto you, I will no more drink of the fruit of the vine, until that day when I drink it new in the kingdom of God.*"

With this is to be taken the account in Mt. xxvi. 26-29, which is a reproduction of Mark with slight modifications. After " take ye " in verse 22 of Mark, Matthew inserts " eat ye." After " he gave it to them " in verse 23 of Mark, Matthew writes, " saying, Drink ye all of it " in place of Mark's " and they all drank of it." After Mark's " which is shed for many " in verse 24, Matthew adds " unto remission of sins."

III. The Lukan Narrative. This appears in various textual forms, of which a conspectus may now be given.

A. In the Uncial Codices אB A C W, in all other Greek Codices except D, and in most versions appears a long form of text containing Lk. xxii. 15-20, which is as follows :

---

[1] *The Kingdom of God and the Son of Man*, p. 261.

(15) " And he said unto them : With desire I have desired to eat this Passover with you before I suffer ; (16) for I say unto you, I will not eat it, until it be fulfilled in the kingdom of God. (17) And he received a cup, and when he had given thanks, he said : *Take this and divide it among yourselves :* (18) *for, I say unto you, I will not drink from henceforth of the fruit of the vine, until the kingdom of God shall come.* (19a) And he took bread, and when he had given thanks, he broke, and gave to them, saying : *This is my body,* (19b) *which is broken for you : this do in remembrance of me.* (20) And the cup in like manner after supper, saying : *This cup is the new covenant in my blood, that which is poured out for you.*"

It will be noticed that this longer form makes mention of two cups, and that the words relating to the second in verse 20a are identical with St. Paul's in I Cor. xi. 25a.

B. (i). In Codex D and in the Old Latin Codices *a d ff i l* there appears a shorter text, containing verses 15-19a of the above, but not 19b-20. This text mentions only one cup, and places it before the bread.

(ii) Two other Old Latin Codices, *b* and *e*, have the same short form, but in the following order of verses : 15-16, 19a, 17-18. In this arrangement the bread comes before the cup.

C. (i). In the Old Syriac Version known as the Curetonian, verse 20 is absent, and the other verses are in the order : 15-16, 19ab, 17-18. The bread here again comes before the cup.

(ii). In the other Old Syriac Version, the Sinaitic, verse 19b is absent, as well as verse 20, and after " divide it among you " in verse 17 the addition, "This is my blood, the new covenant," is inserted.

D. In the Syriac Vulgate or Peshitta we have a short text consisting of verses 15-16, 19-20, verses 17-18 being omitted.

There are two questions to which, in the light of the above documentary evidence, attention has now to be directed. These concern (1) the comparative value of the records before us, and the probabilities which exist with regard to the basic form of the tradition of the Institution, (2) the revelational aspect under which Jesus is presented by his actions and words at the Supper.

1. There is general agreement that the Pauline and Markan narratives, though similar in substance, emanate from independent sources of tradition. " The incidents are the same, and in the same order, but the language is wholly different." So,

perhaps a little too emphatically, Drs. F. G. Kenyon and S. C. E. Legg in an article on " The Textual Data " contributed to a recent work on the Sacraments in the Christian Church.[1] Certainly, if the Pauline features exhibited (a) in the explanatory statement " which is for you " after the words " This is my body," and (b) in the double injunction to repeat the rite in remembrance of Jesus had formed part of the tradition known to Mark, it is difficult to think that he would have left them out. But by its omission of these features the Markan narrative shows itself not only independent of the Pauline but less formal in character and to that extent entitled to rank as a relatively earlier form of tradition. The brighter colouring of the vision of the future in Mk. xiv. 25, as contrasted with I Cor. xi. 26, seems also to support the view that Mark embodies the older tradition.

More difficult is the question of the comparative value of the Markan and the Lukan traditions. The problem here is complicated by the variety of textual forms in which the Lukan account has come down to us. To which of the four types of Lukan text set out above is the priority to be awarded ? Since the Syriac texts C and D appear by various signs to be conflations of the A and B texts, the question reduces itself to that of the comparative merits of the two latter types. Has the longer "Neutral" text of אB A C W, which includes verses 19b-20, or the shorter " Western " text of D a d ff i l, which omits them, the better claim to represent what Luke originally wrote ? Here Dr. Hort declared unhesitatingly in favour of the shorter text. It is unthinkable—so runs the argument—that if verses 19b-20 had stood in Luke's original narrative of the Lord's Supper any later transcriber would have ventured to delete them. " The only motive that could apparently in any way account for the omission as a corruption would be a perception of the double reference to the cup. But this explanation involves the extreme improbability that the most familiar form of the Words of Institution, agreeing with St. Paul's record, should be selected for omission, while the vaguer, less sacred, and less familiar words, in great part peculiar to Luke, were retained." [2] On the other hand, the supplementing of the defects of a text, which was at variance with familiar (Pauline, Markan) tradition in the two important points of placing the cup before the bread and not giving it a precise relation to the blood of Christ, is easily understood. This argu-

---

[1] *The Ministry and the Sacraments*, edited by R. Dunkerley (1937), p. 280.
[2] Westcott and Hort, *The New Testament in Greek*, Vol. II, p. 63.

ment is a strong one, and the acceptance of it would mean that Luke started from a tradition which was very different from both the Markan and the Pauline and which, if its special features cannot be explained as secondary, must be seriously considered in any attempt to recover the original form of the Eucharistic rite.

This conclusion from the textual phenomena of the Lukan narrative is, however, resisted by those who, like Kenyon and Legg in the above-cited article, or like Goguel in a recent work,[1] contend that the Syriac texts C and D presuppose a knowledge of the longer A text. They take the position that all forms of the shorter text, including B, arose from the desire to eliminate one or other of the two cups which the A text mentions. The arguments which they adduce for this position, however, are not able to weigh down those by which Hort defends the priority of B. The conflate Syriac texts are of later origin than the Greek, whether as represented by B or by A, and nothing hinders the supposition that the Syriac reproduction of B was infected in one way or another by influences from the A text.

Even if it were otherwise, and if the longer text should be accepted as what Luke wrote, it would still be difficult for literary analysis to regard the narrative as a unity. Verses 19b-20a clearly point to the Pauline tradition in I Cor. xi. 24b-25a, while verses 17-19a as clearly point to another tradition which is guaranteed as a tradition of the Eucharist by the evidence of the Didache, where in chapter ix. 1-3 the prayer over the cup is given before the prayer with regard to the broken bread, and also by St. Paul's indirect allusions to the sacrament in I Cor. x. 21 and x. 26, where also the cup is mentioned first, the bread second.

We seem, then, to be left with two rival traditions as to the form of the institution, Mk. xiv. 22-25 and Lk. xxii. 17-19a. Can we determine to which of these oldest traditions the historical priority is to be assigned? The question is difficult because we do not know all the circumstances under which these two primary types were evolved. In other words, we do not know the precise relation of either tradition to history. Conceptual motives of the kind which Form-Criticism stresses have been appealed to, and may have played a part in the shaping of both narratives. It is argued, however, that if the question of priority is stated in the form of asking which of the two accounts is the more characterized by secondary features, the answer is simple. In the short Lukan narrative the cup which Jesus takes

[1] *Life of Jesus*, pp. 458-460.

is given no reference to his blood or to a covenant established by its effusion, but relates entirely to the consummation of the Messianic festival in the kingdom of God (Lk. xxii. 17-18). There is no parallelism, as in Mark, between the words about the cup and the words about the bread. Since, however, the natural tendency governing the formation of oral tradition lay more to the creation of parallelisms than to the suppression of them, it follows that the Markan narrative represents a distinctly more evolved phase of tradition than the Lukan, and therefore stands at a greater remove from the starting-point, in other words, from history.

Plausible as this reasoning is, it by no means takes account of all the facts, nor exhausts all the possibilities of the case. Underneath the preference given to the shorter Lukan tradition there lurks without disguise the idea that an emphasis on the world to come is the primary, and indeed exclusive, mark of the authentic mind of Jesus. A Eucharist which points forward purely to the Messianic festival in the kingdom of God is considered to bear a greater stamp of historicity than one which, as in the Markan and Pauline traditions, bends back to the sacrifice of Jesus, and makes that sacrifice the way to the kingdom. Here one should not forget what the emphasis on the world to come really signified as an expression of the mind of Jesus. If we have been right in the view maintained throughout this book that in the religion of Jesus, as in the prophetic religion of Israel, the apocalyptic vision was the projection upon the future of an intense realization of the divine righteousness in its bearing on history in a sinful world, it will not be imagined that the hope of the Messianic festival in the kingdom to which Jesus was looking forward would stand for him in no profound relation to the thought of sin and its forgiveness, or to the redemption of men's souls as precious. If he whose eyes were directed towards the glory of the Son of Man saw and taught that the Son of Man must first be slain, is it likely that at the Supper the symbols used to point forward to the consummation would not be given a relation to his sacrifice? For these reasons it will not do to draw too precipitate a conclusion in favour of the Lukan as against the Markan and Pauline traditions of the institution. The question has its difficulties, and if in recent days there are those who, like Otto, think they best approach the mind of Jesus from the Lukan standpoint, there are others who, like Vincent Taylor, are convinced upholders of the Markan tradition. Both points of view will require to be considered in the sequel.

2. It is not proposed to enter here into the vexed question of the historical occasion of the original institution of Jesus. The Markan tradition which Matthew and Luke have followed identifies the Supper at which Jesus presided and spoke with the Jewish Passover. But the difficulty of conceiving that the arrest, trial, and crucifixion of Jesus were carried out on the day of the solemn festival inaugurated by the Passover, coupled with the fact that the Fourth Gospel expressly represents the Passover celebration as synchronizing with, or following the *death* of Jesus (Jn. xviii. 28, xix. 31), puts serious obstacles in the way of accepting the Synoptic chronology. Though Dalman [1] and Billerbeck [2] still defend its correctness, most scholars now incline to the view that ideal motives rather than accurate historical reminiscence determined the Markan tradition at this particular point, and that the Supper in the context of which the Eucharist originated was one which took place, as the Fourth Gospel suggests, some twenty-four hours before the Passover proper, and which was either a Qiddush celebration [3] or, as Otto prefers, an ordinary religious fellowship meal of the company of Jesus. [4] No serious issue is raised by the controversy, but if reason should exist for holding that the Synoptic reckoning is the result of some confusion of ideas, it is a confusion which is easily explained. Jesus had suffered at the Passover season. The Passover rite was in his thoughts at the time of the institution. He was known to his followers as " our Passover " (I Cor. v. 9). What was more natural than that the ordinance which set forth his Passion should come to be regarded as the Christian Passover, and the Supper at which it was inaugurated identified popularly with the Jewish festival ?

Otto contends that the original meal which Jesus and his disciples gathered to celebrate was a *cheber* or *chaburah*, a religious festival with a ritual element, which the company of Jesus was accustomed to observe at stated times, and which had its analogies in contemporary Pharisaic practice. He thinks that the custom rested on ancient religious usage in Israel, finding traces of the latter in Ps. xvi. 5, where the convert to the religion of Yahweh says, " The Lord is the portion of mine inheritance and of my cup," and again in Ps. cxvi. 13, where one who has been greatly delivered says, " I will take the cup of salvation (*kos yeshu'oth*) . . .

---

[1] *Jesus-Jeshua*, pp. 86-184. [2] *Kommentar*, Bd. II, pp. 812-853.
[3] W. O. E. Oesterley, *The Jewish Background of the Christian Liturgy*.
[4] *The Kingdom of God and the Son of Man*, pp. 278-284.

I will pay my vows unto the Lord." The custom of consecrating or pronouncing a *berakah* over the food, the bread or wine which was consumed on such occasions was long established. It imported that those who partook of the food or of the cup of wine obtained a share in the blessing invoked by the prayer spoken over it. The Jews accordingly spoke of the cup mentioned in Ps. cxvi. 13 as ' the cup of David,' and connected it with the sure mercies of the covenant made with Israel in him. Otto therefore is firm that immemorial Jewish, not Greek, usage constituted the foundation of the sacramental rites at Corinth to which St. Paul alludes when he speaks of ' the cup of blessing which we bless.' The same usage underlies the forms of the Eucharistic prayers in the Didache, and he thinks that it dictated the form of the original institution of Jesus. Here the cup and the bread were elements already given, elements which had been sanctified by the history of religion, and what Jesus did was by special words to put a particular meaning upon them by which they became henceforth signs of the imminent Messianic kingdom and of the Messiah's sacrifice.

We are now to look at the two narratives in the light of these conceptions, and first at Lk. xxii. 15-19a. Here Otto argues that verse 19a was followed in the source by what is now found in verses 29-30, so that the story in the Lukan source ran as follows :

(15) " And he said to them, With desire I have desired to eat this Passover with you before I suffer ; (16) for I say to you, I will not eat it, until it be fulfilled in the kingdom of God."

(17) " And he took a cup, and after giving thanks said : Take this, and apportion it among yourselves ; (18) for I say to you, I will not drink from now of the fruit of the vine, until the kingdom of God comes."

(19a) " And he took bread, and after giving thanks he broke it, and gave to them, and said : This is my body. . . ."

(29) " And I dispose (or covenant) to you (διατίθεμαι ὑμῖν) a kingdom even as my Father has disposed to me ; (30) that you may eat and drink at my table in my kingdom, and sit on thrones judging the twelve tribes of Israel."

Otto urges that this account cannot have originated in the theology or practice of the Church. It reports " an event which had no organic connection with the life of the Church but only with that of Christ himself." [1] He goes on to add that all the essential constitutive elements in the other accounts are present

---

[1] *The Kingdom of God and the Son of Man*, p. 268.

in this archaic statement, and that the later narratives are poorer in point of the bearing which the act of Christ had upon the final coming of the kingdom of God.[1] He considers, however, that verses 15-16, or at least verse 16, came in as redactional matter, supplied to link the Last Supper of Jesus to the Passover observance. But is this last supposition necessary? May not the tradition in verse 15 have behind it the fact that Jesus up to the last night of his life on earth desired and hoped to partake of the approaching Passover, and only at the end saw that this hope was not to be fulfilled? The Supper at which he presided was a different meal. If so, the utterance of Jesus may well have been a factor in the process which linked the Supper to the Passover observance.

We come to the action proper. In verse 17 Jesus takes a cup, and after giving thanks offers it to the disciples with the words: "Take this, and divide it among yourselves." By giving them the cup Jesus confers on them a share in the blessing which the prayer has invoked. Nothing is said about the cup signifying his blood or mediating to the disciples a covenant established by its effusion. The words which accompany the distribution, the words, "I say to you, I shall not drink from now of the fruit of the vine until the kingdom of God comes," are farewell words which prophetically link the moment of separation on earth to the Messianic festival in the future when, according to the apocalyptic expectation in Enoch, the Son of Man as the One to whom all power will be committed will cause his elect to "eat, recline, rise up, and sit with him upon thrones."[2] The action with the cup, therefore, has its foundation in the thought of Jesus as the Son of Man, the final Redeemer, whose elevation to the throne marks the consummation of the Messianic salvation, of which the cup is the sign and pledge. Up to this point Jesus has held in reserve the character in which he is to be revealed as the Son of Man. This is now made explicit by his second action at the table. He takes a piece of bread, gives thanks, and solemnly breaks it: then gives it, thus broken, to the disciples with the words "This is my body." Anyone acquainted with Hebrew prophetic symbolism would have no difficulty in making out the meaning of this sign. Otto adduces for comparison's sake the act of the ancient prophet in Jer. xix. 1-3, 10-15, and understands Jesus to be saying in effect: "What has happened to this bread will happen to me." Vincent Taylor strongly supports the same

[1] *The Kingdom of God and the Son of Man*, p. 276.　　[2] *Ibid.*, p. 289.

idea of ' effective representation ' in the symbol.[1]   At the same
moment the disciples, by taking and consuming the broken bread,
obtain a share in the consecration and blessedness signified by the
sacrifice.   There cannot be the slightest doubt that here, by means
of a new and hitherto unused symbolism which the ritual apparatus
of the repast suggested, Jesus is saying and bringing to final point
and expression what he had otherwise taught with regard to
the Son of Man.   The Son of Man is the Isaianic Servant who
through suffering, rejection, and having his life taken from the
earth, attains to a glorious exaltation.

The reference of the action to the sacrifice of the Servant-Son
of Man is sustained and confirmed by the declaration in verses
29-30 if in the source-tradition, as Otto holds, these words immediately followed on the deliverance " This is my body."   So
precise a sequence cannot indeed be proved, but as there is no
sound reason for denying that the words in question occurred in
the source in the context of the Supper narrative, a direct connection between the ' covenant ' which Jesus here refers to and
the sacrifice which his actions at the table symbolized provides
the best explanation of them.   The word ' covenant ' (*diatheke*)
is not used, but the verb employed (*diatithemai*) is proof that the
covenant-notion was present to thought, so that the meaning
may well be that Jesus by the signs or token-actions which he has
used at the Supper has given his followers the covenant-assurance
of the kingdom of God, and by making them partakers in the cup
and in the bread he has consecrated them for that inheritance.
It will be remembered that the Isaianic Servant of the Lord
stands for a covenant of God with Israel, which the prophet
defines as the fulfilment of the sure mercies of David.

> " I the Lord have called thee in righteousness, and will . . . give
> thee for a covenant of the people. . . . Behold, the former things are
> come to pass, and new things do I declare ; before they spring forth
> I tell you of them " (Isa. xlii. 6, 9).
> " Thus saith the Lord. . . . In a day of salvation have I helped
> thee ; and I will preserve thee, and give thee for a covenant of
> the people. . . . They shall feed in the ways, and their pastures shall
> be in all high places.   They shall not hunger nor thirst " (Isa.
> xlix. 8-10).
> " I will make an everlasting covenant with you, even the sure
> mercies of David " (Isa. lv. 3).

---

[1] *Jesus and His Sacrifice*, pp. 119-120.   Cf. Otto, p. 302.

At the Supper Jesus finally accepts this covenant office and responsibility, and *thus the rite for ever presents him as the Servant of the Lord who by his great humiliation and vicarious sacrifice consummates the salvation of his people, as promised long ago to David, and attains to the glory of the Son of Man.*

It cannot but be acknowledged that the short Lukan narrative so explained offers a very vivid and impressive presentation of the origin of the rite of the Lord's Supper. If reasons are admitted for holding that it stands nearer to original tradition and fact than the other narrative, that of Mark, the explanation of such variations as the latter presents will be sought not in an originally different apprehension of the historical act of Jesus but in developmental tendencies natural to the reflective process and agreeable to the laws governing the growth of a tradition. But is this a satisfactory account of *all* the features of the Markan representation? It is remarked by Kenyon and Legg in the article already mentioned that the differences of Mark from Luke, if we make the slight change of placing verse 19 in Luke before verses 17-18, reduce themselves almost to a single point.

Mk. xiv	Lk. xxii
(22) "And as they ate he, taking bread, after blessing, broke and gave to them, and said : Take, This is my body."	(19*a*) "And he, taking bread, after giving thanks, broke and gave to them, saying : This is my body."
(23) "And, taking a cup, he, after giving thanks, gave it to them, and all drank of it."	(17) "And, receiving a cup, he, after giving thanks, said : Take this, and divide it among yourselves."
(24) "And he said to them : This is my blood of the covenant, which is shed for many."	
(25) "Amen I say to you, that further I shall not drink of the produce of the vine until that day when I drink it new in the kingdom of God."	(18) "For I say to you, From now I shall not drink from the produce of the vine until there comes the kingdom of God."

A glance at the above conspectus, in which I have given effect to the suggestion of Kenyon and Legg, reveals, however, a very significant difference between the traditions in the point that Mark has, and Luke has not, the word (Mk. xiv. 24) which makes the cup a representation of Jesus' *blood* as covenant-blood which is shed for many. Is it enough to say that Mark's account here

has simply arisen from the tendency to establish a formal parallelism of significance between the bread and the cup, the cup
being given a relation to the blood of Jesus which in Luke's
account is absent ?   While it is to be admitted, on the strength
of the differences between the Markan and the Pauline accounts,
that the tradition of the words spoken over the cup was not so
uniform or constant as that of the word about the bread, does it
really follow that the feature in which the Markan and Pauline
accounts are agreed, namely, the giving to the cup of a relation
to the blood of Christ, is of secondary origin ? or that in the
earliest tradition the bread alone signified the sacrifice of Christ,
the cup being merely a cup of farewell which, while it marked the
separation of Jesus from his own, pointed forward only to the
advent of the kingdom and the glory of the Son of Man ?   While
it is natural for liturgical usage to develop its elements of speech
and action, it cannot by any means be assumed that such developments alone led to the defining of the covenant which Jesus made
with his own (Lk. xxii. 29 f.) as a covenant in his blood, or that
Goguel is right in saying that the elimination of the marked
reference of the rite to the future kingdom in the Pauline narrative
in I Corinthians is due, not to a fading out of interest in the last
events, but to " the tendency to place the two constituent elements
of the Communion in exact parallelism, in order to make of them
two expressions of the same ideas and the same sentiments." [1]

Such considerations, combined with those already advanced
at an earlier point,[2] may well put us on our guard against too
precipitate a dismissal of the Markan in favour of the Lukan
tradition.   There are those, as we have seen, who consider the
short text of Luke to represent not an independent original
historical source, but a literary revision of what Luke first wrote.
But other reasons exist against allowing too great a weight of
authority to attach to the short text, and here reference may be
made in particular to Dr. Vincent Taylor's penetrating study of
the subject in his book, *Jesus and His Sacrifice*.   While Otto holds
that the breaking of the bread by Jesus is not merely an act
exhibitory of his Passion but signifies that Jesus wills to communicate to the disciples " a share in the power of that which is
represented, namely, the expiatory power of the broken Christ,"
Taylor presses the sacrificial implications of the symbolism to still
more definite conclusions.   In explaining the bread to mean his
body " Jesus has sacrificial practice in mind. . . . It is difficult

---

[1] *Life of Jesus*, p. 446.   [2] See above, pp. 137-138.

not to think of the sacred meal which normally was the final stage in the Old Testament sacrifices. . . . We must infer that Jesus uses the term ' body ' because he looks upon his Passion as an offering for men in which they are invited to share." [1] This is strongly brought out in the Markan narrative by the words " Take ye " at the giving of the bread, which are absent in Luke. Thereby any conception of the Passion which views it merely as a martyrdom or merely as a revelation concerning God and sin is shown to be inadequate.[2] But the analogy of the sacrificial rites of Israel goes further, and in Dr. Taylor's opinion creates a strong presumption in favour of the historicity of the words spoken over the cup. A feature so central to the Markan and Pauline traditions is not to be rejected on the sole ground of its absence from the short text of Luke. Nor is it intrinsically probable that it developed simply in accordance with certain laws governing the growth of a tradition. St. Paul at any rate has no hesitation in claiming dominical authority for the rite as he interprets it, and certainly if a sacrificial connotation was given by Jesus to the bread which he broke, there appears no reason why it should not also have covered the cup which he dispensed. Dr. Taylor finds the real background of the original act in Exod. xxiv. 1-11, culminating in the words : " Behold the blood of the covenant, which Yahweh has made with you concerning all these things."

Here, it is pointed out, there are two sprinklings of blood, one upon the altar, the other upon the people. " The former is the symbol of the people's obedience ; it is their offering to God, confirmed by the words : ' All the words which Yahweh has spoken will we do.' The latter, the blood sprinkled upon them, is dedicated blood which Yahweh has accepted, and the sprinkling means that the people now share in the blessings and powers which it represents and conveys." [3]

So Jesus, giving the cup with the words : " This is my blood of the covenant," means that " as of old dedicated blood was applied in blessing to the people of Israel, so now his life, surrendered to God and accepted by Him, is offered to, and made available for men." [4] And thus, for Christianity, Jesus steps into the place of the ancient sacrifices of Israel. He represents the fullness, the consummation of sacrifice, by which the new covenant is inaugurated.

---

[1] *Jesus and His Sacrifice*, p. 121.   [2] *Ibid.*, p. 125.
[3] *Ibid.*, p. 137.   [4] *Ibid.*, p. 138.

10

It may be felt, upon a review of all the evidence, that the question of the original form of the institution is not one which can be settled by the methods of literary or of form-criticism. In view of the marked discrepancy of the traditions, a certain shadow of doubt must always persist with regard to the original symbolism of the cup. As regards Dr. Vincent Taylor's argument, it is by no means certain that Jesus, when he spoke of his sacrifice and of the institution of the new covenant, had Exod. xxiv. 8 in mind, and not rather Deutero-Isaiah's language about the Servant. In one point, however, both of the traditions and also their expositors are agreed, and that is in the objective significance of the broken bread. This stands for the vicarious sacrifice of the Son of Man as something not only offered to God on behalf of men, but —in accordance with the true meaning of sacrifice now at last perceived—offered in their stead. The Son of Man came not only to give his life a ransom for men, but to make them sharers of his sacrifice, and so to claim, commit, and consecrate them for the Kingdom of Heaven.

Chapter VIII

EPILOGUE : JESUS MESSIAH

In the preceding chapters it has been sought to show with what materials Early Christianity, starting from the basis of its Messianic confession, built up its tradition of the revelation of God in Christ. It has been a governing assumption of the inquiry that the historical events in which Christianity took its rise can be approached through the Synoptic tradition by a just and patient evaluation of its terms. The impulse to avoid this critical process and to strike for the goal by the method of historical intuition is, of course, a strong one, and makes a powerful appeal to the imagination. But while intuition has a place in history, its function is a subordinate one, and brilliant improvisation which by-passes the problems of the Synoptic tradition is never immune from the charge that what it offers represents a short-circuiting of thought, an over-simplification of the facts.

It is worthy of notice that, wherever the intuitional method is favoured, the tendency has been to take the origins of Christianity back to an *idea* in the mind of Jesus, and therefore to assume that an ideal unity and simplicity will have characterized the original terms of his message and of the earliest Christian kerygma. From such a standpoint the complications and involvedness of the Synoptic tradition cannot but be suspected and deplored. But if the actual starting-point of the Christian confession and of the Christian conception of the revelation of God in Christ was not an idea but a life, a spiritual history, a drama of divinely inspired and guided personality, the case is different. The probability is that the testimony borne to Jesus from the start will have exhibited elements as various and as heterogeneous as those which within a generation are found entering into the composition of the Q source and of the Gospel of Mark.

It needs to be remembered in this connection that Christianity did not originate in a vacuum but at the heart of the most highly developed and self-conscious religious system which the world had known. A glance at Deut. iv. 7 f. or 32 f. will reveal the nature of the self-consciousness of Israel by which Jesus was environed :

" What great nation is there, that hath God so nigh unto them, as the Lord our God is whensoever we call upon him ?   And what great nation is there, that hath statutes and judgements so righteous as all this law ? "

" For ask now of the days that are past, which were before thee, since the day that God created man upon the earth . . . whether there hath been any such thing as this great thing is, or hath been heard like it ?   Did ever people hear the voice of God speaking out of the midst of the fire, as thou hast heard, and live ?   Or hath God assayed to go and take him a nation from the midst of another nation . . .? "

The reactions of Jesus of Nazareth to such an environment could not but be as multiform and as various as were the ideas and the situations with which he was confronted in Judaism, and any tradition which reproduced objectively the character of his teaching and activity under these conditions would have for its unity not the singleness of an idea but of a spirit.   While, therefore, with the progress of time developments would undoubtedly occur within the tradition to augment its complexity, there cannot have been any stage at which it did not exhibit many seemingly unrelated or even contradictory features.   The Church was content to find the source of all this manifold in Jesus.   So in the New Testament as a whole the subject of the Christian message is nowhere a doctrine but a person, " in whom," to use the language of St. Paul, " all the treasures of wisdom and knowledge are hidden " (Col. ii. 3), and in whom all Christian life has its ultimate ground (Col. iii. 3).   It would be easy, of course, to imagine a faith of a different complexion, in which the convictions and hopes of the adherents were grounded not on a person but on the truth or consistency of an idea or of a system of ideas, but such a faith would not be that of the New Testament or of early Christianity, which has no unifying focus for its religious conceptions except the one thought that God has interpreted His power, His wisdom, and His love in the man Christ Jesus.

The complexity of the Synoptic tradition is not therefore a reason for denying to it, à priori, the claim to be substantially an historical record or for withholding from it the patient critical investigation to which all documents making that claim require to be subjected.

It is time to stand back a little from the details of the tradition and to contemplate Jesus and his work more generally as they appear against the background of Jewish history and religion. When we do so, the effect is greatly to enhance our sense of the intensely personal character of the revelation in which Christianity was born.

I. PERSONAL CHARACTER OF THE REVELATION IN JESUS

We see a little group of adherents of Jesus, who had followed him from Galilee, overtaken at Jerusalem by the disaster of his death, yet within a very few days rising up and proclaiming the ' good news ' that through this Jesus God is now to bring about what Josephus calls ' the revolution of the ages.' [1] What explains that these disciples did not abandon their faith in Jesus after his death or indeed surrender the whole idea of a personal Messiah ? " Did not the deaths of both John the Baptist and Jesus show "—so Dr. Johannes Weiss states the issue—" that men ought to look for the coming of God's kingdom, but not in dependence upon any human persons ? " [2] Such was the position to which Judaism for its part eventually came. Speaking of the repeated disappointments sustained by the Jews during the century of turmoil which preceded the final insurrection under Bar Kokhbah, Dr. Joseph Klausner remarks :

" The Jews expected the Messiah any time. Every day there were false Messiahs, visionary patriots, stout-hearted but feeble-handed, who passed away like a shadow once the Romans or the Herodians had made an end of them and their deeds. Sometimes the Pharisees and Tannaim supported them, as Rabbi Akiba supported Bar Kokhbah ; but, as a rule, the Pharisees dreaded the difficult consequences of the Messianic belief in practice. Hence in the older Talmudic literature we find an ambiguous attitude towards the Messianic promises : there is a certain wariness as touching the persons of the Messiahs, but a deep and enthusiastic belief in the Messianic hope itself." [3]

If by contrast the faith of the first Christian group did not fade out after this manner, or succumb to " the difficult consequences of the Messianic belief in practice," or drop to the disillusioned level of Talmudic Judaism, plainly the reason is that Jesus had inspired in his followers something more than a Messianic *hope*. He was the source of an experience of which that hope was but the efflorescence. He had proclaimed the advent of the world

---

[1] *Jewish War*, III, 374. Cf. *C. Apionem*, II, 28.
[2] *History of Primitive Christianity*, Vol. I, pp. 21 f.
[3] *Jesus of Nazareth*, p. 402.

to come, but unless the tradition wholly misleads us, he had brought it as a moral and religious reality within the orbit of their spirit and in a way which henceforth linked their whole hope in God with him. Only thus do we explain how, when death overtook the person of their Master, it did not move these followers from their confidence, and how no comparable interests appeared from the side of Judaism to draw their eyes backwards to the past or to divide their affections. We see the Jewish ideas of the Messiah and of the World to Come being bent to take the shape of the fortunes of Jesus and so transmuted. *It was not a case of an ardent Messianic hope leading men to believe in Jesus but of an ardent faith in Jesus leading them to believe in the Messianic hope.* He was the creator of their Messianic hope. Thus the way to the kingdom of heaven becomes for them the holding on to faith in Jesus.

"The certainty of belonging to the Messiah," says Dr. Oscar Holtzmann, "and of participating with him in an eternal and blissful life in the future, and the duty of living, for the sake of this hope, a pure and holy life in the footsteps of Jesus, confident that God would one day both remove the taint of sin from the members of the Messianic community, and bestow on them the holiness of perfection—these were the permanent ideas which survived the disappointment of the first Messianic hopes."[1]

It is some measure of the incomparable spiritual impression made by Jesus on the first circle of his followers that he who had taught them in lowliness on earth remains their beloved teacher and master even when he is exalted to the Messianic throne, and that the 'following' of Jesus continues for ever to form the pattern and to point the direction of the religious life.

II. The Transcending of Apocalyptic Dualism

We revert to the 'signs' which play so conspicuous a part in the earliest tradition of the revelation of God in Jesus. As Jesus speaks of his exorcisms and other similar acts, they are not merely symptomatic of the near approach of the Reign of God but definitely mark its entrance into time, and we have seen how powerfully the phenomena in question influenced the mind of Jesus in determining his thoughts of his destiny to a Messianic form and conclusion. Here, too, it is impossible not to recognize the transforming effects of the personality of Jesus. For these

[1] *Life of Jesus*, p. 507.

exorcisms and mighty works done to rescue and redeem the souls of men were not something new and unheard-of either in Judaism or in the wider world. They had an abundance of parallels in the miracle-literature of the period. What was new and epoch-making in the history of religion was the significance which Jesus attached to these acts, the realism of faith by which he saw in the redemption of the souls of men from sin and Satan the fulfilment of Israel's hope of the final salvation of God. Judaism both in its moralistic and in its apocalyptic directions had virtually put the God of salvation beyond the bounds of the existing world-order. God's demand on the world remained, but His presence and power were in principle restricted to the world to come.

That thereby religion had dropped from the level of its own highest norm in Israel is acknowledged by Rabbinical theology when it asserts that Israel went astray on the day when men began to speak of the *malkuth* or reign of God in future tenses.[1] Such words are an admission within Judaism that the apocalyptic world-dualism of the post-exilic period was in contradiction with a vital apprehension of God's presence in history. Yet this particular development of religious thought was necessary if the prophetic conception of the transcendent holiness of God was to come to its full expression. The advance which here dates from Jesus in the history of religious thought consists in the fact that he takes this fully developed transcendent conception of God, and he brings it again into vital relation with the life of the world, and this not by any qualification of the holiness or ' otherness ' of God and of His kingdom but by the bringing of the present world under the form and power of the world to come. " If I by the finger of God cast out the demons, then has the kingdom of God unexpectedly reached even to you."

In the religion of Jesus ' eschatology,' the Jewish doctrine of the last things, becomes the sign or token of the inner transformation of men and of world-history.

The significance of this element in the revelation of God in Jesus must not be undervalued or ignored. Rabbinical theology in its effort to resolve a contradiction existing in late Jewish religion comes down ultimately on what virtually is the side of this world and its values. It does so by condemning the apocalyptic literature and proscribing its doctrines. To this extent it makes the present order of things the measure of the order to

[1] Mechilta 44*a*, a saying of R. Jose of Galilee. Cf. S. Schechter, *Some Aspects of Rabbinic Judaism*, p. 86.

come. In this connection the central word of the apostolic
religion of the New Testament is perhaps St. Paul's declaration
in II Cor. v. 19 : " God was in Christ reconciling the world
unto Himself." Here the world has become again the stage of
the divine redeeming love and purpose. God is restored to his
world, but as the transcendent, all-holy Redeemer. Apocalyptic
Judaism in despair of the world had thrown the whole centre of
our life's meaning into the future age, looking to find there the
resolution of all its discords and the reward of all its strivings. It
cannot be said that Christianity has abandoned this apocalyptic
opposition of the then and now. It looks for the consummation
of redemption to take place only in the world to come. But
a change has, nevertheless, come over its attitude to the present
sphere of existence in that this shadowed world of sin is now seen
under the immediate sign and power of the world to come. *The
future and higher sphere of glory already in a real sense penetrates and
intersects this sphere of humiliation through the power of the Spirit.*
Something has crossed the dividing-line, and this not merely a
Vox, a summons from the world beyond to repent and believe,
but a higher manifestation. While much of the traditional
apparatus of apocalyptic ideas is retained in the Synoptic records
and in the New Testament, the thing which is new and distinctive in the Christian revelation of God is the experience which expresses itself already in the words of Jesus about his mighty works :

" The kingdom of God has come upon you."
" The kingdom of God is in your midst."
" The kingdom of God is as if a man should cast seed into the
ground."

This is not all an enthusiastic prolepsis of the things to come. It
means that the world is not left wholly to itself but stands, despite
all demonism, under the power and, by grace, within the range
of the salvation of God, and this would seem the first of the
certitudes for which Jesus the Messiah stands.

III. ETERNAL NATURE OF OUR RELIGIOUS DEPENDENCE ON
JESUS

In the teaching of Jesus the essential fact which confronts us
is *a spiritual encounter of our souls with him in which Jesus of Nazareth
so interprets and represents to us the meaning of the Eschaton or Reign of
God that henceforth there can be for us no separation of the Messianic
good from the revelation of God in the spirit of Jesus.* If anywhere the

revelation of God in the Christian Redeemer asserts over us an entirely personal and unique ascendancy, it is in the domain where he is teacher. For here the starting-point is not a declaration of abstract truth but a particular, existential summons to our spirit, by which we are called primarily not to thought but to action, and to action *vis-à-vis* with God. In listening to Jesus we are not set in a situation in which to compare or contrast his teaching with other teaching—at least not for very long—or even to think of it primarily as a system of thought. We are brought face to face with *God*, and what we experience as the critical and momentous new thing is the direct and inexorable quality of the issue put before us—for or against God's will to reign ! The first hearers of Jesus did not receive new *ideas* of the kingdom of God—they had these ideas before—but they were made to feel the tremendous moral actuality of God's claim on their obedience, with the result that, as we have seen, for the first time in their experience the kingdom of God as object of religious faith and aspiration came into direct, verifiable, and transforming relation to their lives. The teaching of Jesus throws us not primarily upon ideas but upon God. It passes us on from itself to God. Something is wrought by this teaching as the result of which the hopes and ideals associated with religion are taken out of the realm of anticipation, in which they have hitherto existed, and enter on a crisis or actuality phase. " The law and the prophets were until John."

What is of concern to us at present, however, is the uniquely and irreducibly *personal* aspect of this revelation, the element in the encounter which binds our souls to permanent and boundless religious dependence on Jesus. At first sight no necessity of this kind of personal nexus appears to be involved in the nature of the experience. Indeed, conclusions of an opposite character might at first be drawn, and have been drawn from the actual terms in which Jesus addresses us. For in this matter of revealing to us the will of God Jesus not only declines to allow the finality of the traditional regulations formulated by the Mosaic system of religion but gives us no alternative code of his own in which the measure of our duty to God is objectively and completely stated. The purpose of his comments on the Law and on the righteousness which God requires is primarily to lead us face to face with God and to leave us there. But it is just here that the principle which binds our souls in religious trust to the person of the Revealer comes into view. The spirit of Jesus becomes the determining factor in our vital communion with God. If Jesus Christ had given us rules in which the total measure of our duty to God in any situation was exhaustively stated, we might conceivably have gone off with these rules and abstracted ourselves from him and from God. But because the object of his teaching is the vital one of bringing us face to face with God in all situations, the limit of our dependence on him is not and cannot be restricted to the revelation occurring at any given moment. It is realized as continuous.

" Lord, to whom shall we go ? Thou hast the words of eternal life."

The principle which binds us here to Jesus Christ as personal spirit revealing God may be expressed thus, that *he who has said so much to us about our life must needs say more. He who by his moral disclosures has taken us so far into the knowledge of God must take us all the rest of the way.* At the point to which he brings us in the Sermon on the Mount, so far beyond the limit of the world's ideas and so far beyond the reach of its safeguards and securities, the soul stands alone with him. The words of other teachers, breaking in at such a moment, cannot but appear an intrusion and an impertinence. *What Jesus has said to us about ourselves and about God is so drastic and unanswerable as revelation that it leaves us waiting upon him for the next word, indeed for everything that we shall henceforth know of God.* Above all, because his revelation of the perfect will of God is inevitably and at the same time the revelation to us of our *sin*, we are left waiting upon him for the next word there. What has he to say to us about the situation in which we now know ourselves to stand as sinners before a holy God ? Has he the adequate word of release for us in this situation, the word which, since the unity of our existence has been shattered by the break-up of our spiritual self-sufficiency, can provide also for its re-integration upon a sufficient foundation by the communication of assured forgiveness, of the right to hope, and of the power to live ? The questions with which our souls beset all prophets or hierophants who confront us with accusing truth from God press with their maximum force and intensity around the person of one who in the matter of God's judgement upon us and of God's requirement at our hands has gone beyond all other religious teachers. *In this way, salvation in the Christian sense reveals itself as bound up for us in the end with the complete significance of Jesus in divine-human relations.*

Here instincts deeply rooted in the past history of religion contributed to the form in which the first followers of Jesus expressed their dependence upon his person. This was a dependence not limited to the words or revelations of the moment but which took in the full scope and implications of the redemptive purpose of God in history. Jesus was the Messiah ! In actual point of fact, revelation, at the intense level of significance which had come to attach to that conception in the history of Israel, had never been construed in terms of word simply but in terms of spirit and of power. The Messiah who was to come was one who was not only to declare the righteousness of God but to put it into force, gathering together a holy people whom he should lead in righteousness.[1] The 'justification' which the prophetic religion had denied to the existing world and to those living in it was to be a gift of the divine order of the future. In agreement with this idea, Jesus' requirement of righteousness takes the fullest account of God's purpose now to institute His reign, and this is a point which, if the full reality of the instincts impelling Christians from the beginning to an unlimited religious dependence upon his person is to be appreciated, must not be dropped from view.

In other words, if the ethical absolute of Jesus which brings us to our knees in total confession of sin is not to leave us in despair or to make us cry like St. Peter, " Depart from me, for I am a sinful man, O Lord," it must be because of the perceived larger context of divine grace which is behind the imperative, and which finds expression, for example, in the beatitudes upon the poor, the humble, and the penitent. In crises of the kind exemplified in the experience of Peter the Christian salvation can only be conceived possible if there is something in the revelation made in Jesus which holds and draws us on despite our clear knowledge of our sin, and which so holds and draws us on because it is predictive and significant of a whole new world of love and power in which our guilt and weakness are transcended. And such, when we look at it as a whole, as the presentation of the kingdom of God, is the teaching of Jesus. God's coming to reign involves not only His judgement on us but His will to forgive, to bless, to save us. Thus the significance of Jesus the Teacher is enlarged to include for us the significance of the whole divine purpose in history. We are thrown on aspects of the revelation which go beyond the ethical absolute of the teaching, though they are not

[1] Psalms of Solomon, xvii. 28.

separable from it, and which minister to hope by creating a faith in manifestations of grace and power which are not yet seen in all their fullness.

In consequence, the formula for Christian life from the beginning takes the shape of adding to the moral imperative of Jesus the calling : " And come, follow me ! " Christian men believe that the resolution of their conflict can only come through him who has revealed it in all its sharpness. The conditions under which the divine forgiveness which Jesus announces to men is mediated are not yet fully apparent as Jesus discourses in Galilee. What is, however, apparent and must not be overlooked is that *no real salvation or life is possible for sinful men which takes the form of going backwards out of the light of the moral absolute of Jesus and not rather of going onwards to the last consequences of truth in him*, waiting on him at every point for the next word, nay, for all the words of this life. In this manner, in the end, the teaching, the person, and the cross of Jesus become integrated for us in the one experience, and the religious life comes to be bounded by him or, as St. Paul says, to be hid with Christ in God.

IV. The Transvaluation of Christology

In our review of the Son of Man logia in Chapter VI reason was found for considering that the Messianic language used by Jesus for the explication of his destiny came as the final stamp upon an extraordinary sense of engagement to bring his nation to God. It did not indicate the entrance of Jesus on a new conception of his destiny, but served rather to bring to historical definition a consciousness of vocation which had inspired all his work and teaching. It marked, however, a new understanding of the Messianic concepts Son of God and Son of Man. All this may be expressed by saying, as we have already done, that the Messianic ideas of Israel functioned as the historical reagent which brought out the final significance of the revelation concerning God with which Jesus believed himself to be charged.

The results of our inquiry into the inner nature of the encounter of our souls with Jesus in the all-important matter of his teaching will by now have confirmed the rightness of this observation. It is the significance which Jesus has for us as spirit which lifts him above all legislators and prophets and sets him in a unique and unsurpassable place as the Mediator to us of God. Whether or not the Synoptic tradition says it in so many words,

we may say that, because through the spirit of Jesus the kingdom
of God, otherwise a dream, attains to a state of actuality for us
and cannot be separated in our experience from the revelation
made in Jesus, Jesus is for us the Messiah, the Son of Man who
is Lord of the future.

But the same reasoning will also have made it plain that
the Messianic confession of Christianity remains anchored to
the historical personality and character of Jesus. It is the
human figure of the Man of Nazareth that gives its peculiar
point and pathos to the evangelical doctrine of redemption and
that gives it also its historical reality. So patent is this to
Christian religious feeling that the writer to the Hebrews can
project the idea backward into the eternal counsels of God, and
speak of what it " behoved " the author of our salvation to be.

" Verily not of angels doth he take hold, but he taketh hold of
the seed of Abraham.   Wherefore it behoved him in all things to
be made like unto his brethren, that he might be a merciful and
faithful high priest in things pertaining to God " (Heb. ii. 16-17).

Jesus has transmuted the language used by Judaism in its doctrine
of the Messiah and of the last things. *It is not a case of the human
personality of Jesus being swallowed up in a Messianic conception, but
of all Messianic conceptions being absorbed into the sphere of his spirit.*
The fact that in occasional passages in the early Christian literature, such as II Thess. ii and the Revelation of St. John, the
traditional language of Jewish apocalyptic Messianism breaks
through and even occludes the human lineaments of the Saviour
should not mislead us. In such purely apocalyptic pronouncements the re-entrance of the older language was only to be
expected, but it impresses us as amazingly out of keeping with the
general New Testament presentation. Christian instinct has
never finally suffered the human personality of Jesus to be
absorbed or lost in supernatural conceptions of his function.

But the principle which has been stated goes further and helps
to explain the new developments on which Christology enters
when the gospel passes beyond the Palestinian-Jewish frontiers
and lays hold on the language of the wider world of the Diaspora.
Here under different intellectual and religious conditions the
human personality of Jesus maintains its essential dominance
over thought. It is not swallowed up in Messianic or quasi-
Messianic conceptions but all such conceptions are subordinated
to the spirit of Jesus. Just as the Man of Nazareth had taken

over the Messianic categories of Palestinian Judaism in order to express and interpret his unique historical sense of mission, so now his followers appropriate to him the attributes of the Hellenistic-Jewish Wisdom or Logos of God, but always in essential subordination to the personal and historical character in which Jesus had taken his place in humanity.

Already in St. Paul the term Messiah or Christ as applied to Jesus has shrunk for the most part to an appellative or personal name. So completely has the personality of Jesus absorbed the Messianic idea ! So little was Christianity concerned to insulate and objectify for its thought the specifically national or political connotation of the Jewish concept ! Similarly, if Jesus bears everywhere in St. Paul the Messianic title of the Son of God, the emphasis is upon the ' spirit ' in which Jesus revealed, and in which he guarantees to our spirit, the Fatherhood of God (Gal. iv. 6 f., Rom. viii. 15). Here was an opportunity for Hellenistic thought to bring to the interpretation of the Christian mystery its own peculiar resources of religious thought and imagination, and Hellenistic Christianity was not slow to do so ; but it is the Jesus who lived, loved, laboured, taught, suffered and was crucified on earth whose significance is thus developed. So also, if St. Paul constantly thinks of Jesus as the Son of Man—and he does so even where he makes no use of that particular title—it is because Jesus is the ' one man ' who by his obedience or ' righteous act,' i.e. by his acceptance of death in the stead of men, has cancelled the effect of Adam's transgression, and become the head of a new humanity (Rom. v. 12-21). The emphasis is not upon the glory of a coming apocalypse, though that is not excluded, but upon the completeness with which Jesus on earth identified himself with men in their state of sin and death. St. Paul, in fact, is bringing out the intensely human and historical character of the claim of Jesus to the apocalyptic title. It is true that, taking advantage of the *à priori* suggestions of the title in the Enoch-literature, St. Paul insists on Christ's pre-existence as the Son of the Father, but this pre-existent being who was in ' the form of God ' has stooped to the nature and to ' the likeness of men ' that, as man, he might serve and redeem his brethren (Phil. ii. 5-11). The emphasis is throughout upon the human life, the human drama ; the Christological language is but the vehicle of the historical-suprahistorical meaning which Jesus as personal spirit has for faith.

If thus the personality of Jesus by its spiritual revelational

quality absorbed into itself the Messianic conceptions of Palestinian Judaism, was there any reason why it should not equally
and for the same reason attract and absorb those other forms in
which the idea of divine-human mediation or mediatorship had
taken shape in Judaism? We find in Philo the recognition that
' the man after the Image '—really a variant form of the idea of
the Heavenly Man or Son of Man—is one of the multiple names
of the Logos of God.[1] If the association of the Heavenly Man
with the Logos or Wisdom of God had thus already taken place
in the Jewish-Alexandrian theology, was there any reason why
St. Paul, in whose theology the pre-existent Son of God is manifested on earth for our sakes as the Second or Heavenly Man
(I Cor. xv. 45-47), should not also lay hold of the Logos idea for
the bringing home to his converts of the supreme revelation-value
of the person of Christ? We are not concerned here with the
details of the cosmological expansion of Christology which has
taken place in the Pauline doctrine, nor with its consequences.
Enough that the desire to present the full religious implications
of the revelation made in Jesus led the missionary apostle to
make for him the transcendent claim which he states. To take
the clearest example, in the Letter to the Colossians we find the
apostle praying that the Christians whom he is addressing, and
who already abound in faith, love, and hope, may grow in the
knowledge of God and understand the ' mystery ' of God, namely
Christ, in whom all the treasures of wisdom and knowledge are
hidden (ii. 2-3). These are words which recall the language
used by an earlier writer of the apocalyptic Son of Man. " This,"
says the writer, " is the Son of Man who hath righteousness,
with whom dwelleth righteousness, and who revealeth all the
treasures of that which is hidden, because the Lord of Spirits
hath chosen him " (I Enoch xlvi. 3). What concerned the
apostle in the Colossian epistle was the propaganda at Colossae
of a subtle form of syncretistic religion which, while giving a place
to the Christian Redeemer in the mediating of the mystery of
God to men, contended that there were whole areas of divine-
cosmic relation which the Christian gospel of forgiveness did not
touch, in which, therefore, other spiritual intermediaries between
God and man were to be recognized and worshipped. St. Paul's
answer is to claim all such areas and functions of mediatorship
for Jesus, and to do so on the ground that " it was the divine
good pleasure that in him the whole Pleroma should dwell "

[1] De Conf. Ling. 146.

(i. 19), that in him " the whole Pleroma of the Godhead dwells bodily " (ii. 9). The meaning is that in the person of Jesus Christ and in his historical work we have the perfect revelation of the mind of Him who is at once our Creator and Redeemer. We cannot anywhere or ever think of God's relation to His world except in terms of Christ.

What made it easier and more instinctive for St. Paul to transpose the Christology of the primitive Church into a doctrine involving the cosmic mediatorship of Christ was the circumstance that in the thinking of Diaspora Judaism the principle of the Wisdom or Logos of God had developed the qualities of a virtual substitute for the Palestinian conception of the Messiah. The religious mind of the Diaspora was interested in the coming of the Gentile world to the knowledge of God ; it was not interested to the same extent in a nationalist programme of political domination for Israel. While, therefore, in Judea the thought of God's redemptive purpose for the world continued to express itself through the activistic and futuristic categories natural to the Hebrew mind, in Alexandria it had concentrated more particularly around the self-manifestation of the divine Wisdom or Logos in the realm of spirit. That Greek influences contributed to this determination of the Diaspora mind need not be questioned. But the fact that in first-century Judaism there existed two great parallel lines of religious idealism may not be ignored. It made it possible, for profounder minds at least, to pass from the one series of conceptions to the other without any undue jolt or sense of strangeness. Wisdom could be clothed with Messianic, and the Messiah with sapiential attributes. In this way Jesus, without ceasing to be the personal Messiah or Son of Man of the Church's primitive confession, could be presented in his critical significance for faith by the aid of forms of thought embodying a Logos-Christology.

V. The Fullness of Sacrifice

The historical character of the Church's gospel comes finally to expression in the central place which is given to the death of Jesus and in the unique redemptive value which is attached to that event.

For this event is no historical accident which can be separated off in thought from the manifestation of God in the mind and life of Jesus, but an event which, as the tradition is concerned to show, stands in the intimatest relation to the purpose which Jesus came to serve. It develops with an inward necessity from his sense of destiny, and marks the final consequence of his extraordinary consciousness of engagement to bring his nation to God.

Yet to the sub-Christian or non-Christian mind of the age the same event is a paradox, insupportable from the standpoint of the existing ideas of God. To the Jews it is a stumbling-block, an insurmountable offence to Jewish preconceptions of divine omnipotence and glory, and to the Gentiles it is foolishness, a blank negation of the Greek idea of a reasonable principle at the heart of things. Only to Christians, enlightened by the Spirit, does the event appear as what it truly is, the manifestation of divine omnipotence and of divine wisdom. The judgement of St. Paul at this point—a judgement which is corroborated later by the rise of the Docetic heresy among the Greeks and by the sustained refusal of the Jews, as shown by Justin's *Dialogue*, to accept the doctrine of a crucified Messiah—indicates how small was the part which ideas played in fixing for the Christian mind the significance of the Cross. Plainly the Christian doctrine of salvation did not originate in general ideas of redemption being applied to the death of Jesus in order to veil its offence or to resolve its mystery, but in the stark fact of such a death coming to one in whom God had been so signally manifested for the reconciling of men to Himself. This gave rise to new and revolutionary thoughts of God, and it transformed the whole idea of the Messianic salvation.

The contrary view, if we should suppose it extractable from Pauline or other New Testament statements, proves itself on a closer approach to be fallacious. In the opening chapters of Romans, it is true, St. Paul appears to be arguing that the guilt of the world before God points to the necessity of the expiatory sacrifice of the Messiah, but in reality the order of his thought is different. The sequence of ideas in an argument by no means always reflects the order in which things have been apprehended by the mind, nor can it have been the intention of the apostle to rationalize in any way the supreme paradox of grace. Most of the difficulties of the Pauline theology arise from an imperfect appearance of a will to rationalize on the part of the apostle. As a matter of fact, the real starting-point of the Pauline gospel and theology is not the sin of the world but the cross of Jesus the Messiah, as appears by the admission that " All have sinned and come short of the glory of God, being justified freely by his grace

through the redemption which is in Christ Jesus " (Rom. iii. 23 f.).
It is the death of the Messiah, with the meaning attached to it
in the Christian tradition from the beginning (I Cor. xv. 3), that
has brought home to the apostle the reality and the totality of
the guilt of the world.   It has revolutionized his conception of
God.   It has given him a new axis and co-ordinates for com-
puting God's relation to the cosmos.   It has transformed his
understanding of the Messianic salvation (II Cor. v. 16).   *What
we have here therefore is not the triumph of ideas over history, but the
triumph of history over ideas.*   It is the victory of the element of the
personal and the factual in Jesus over the world's preconceptions
of God and salvation, the subordination of all Messianic categories to the order of realities in the mind and life of the man of
Nazareth.

When we speak of history as forming the substance, the warp
and the woof of the gospel, it is important that we understand
our terms.   To history belongs not the suffering of Jesus only
but the mind with which he approached that suffering and the
interpretation which he put upon it.   At the heart of the Synoptic
tradition there stands, as we have seen, an irreducible core of
words of Jesus about the ' cup ' which he must drink, the
' baptism ' which he must undergo, the rejection and death which
the Son of Man must endure, and so forth.   Words such as these
are not easily put down to *ex post facto* invention on the part of
the Christian community, nor can this be done without the consequence of denying to Jesus all part in the making of Christianity.
What, then, is the nature of the necessity which the mind of
Jesus recognized as attaching to his rejection and death ?   Here
various lines of approach to the subject will suggest themselves.

In a famous passage of the *Republic* of Plato (Bk. II 360D—
362C) an argument is put into the mouth of Glaucon which
concerns the fortunes of the just man whose life is inspired by the
pure love of righteousness and not by any consideration of its
rewards.   In his zeal for this pure aim the just man refuses in
any way to compromise with injustice.   What will his fate in the
world be likely to be ?   The answer has a truth and validity
which are independent of the purely captious argument which
Glaucon is briefed by Plato to defend.   It is that the just man
will be flogged, tortured, kept in chains, and after suffering
every kind of evil he will be impaled (361E).   So great is the
human hatred and intolerance of righteousness that the just man
must look to be crucified !

Not of this kind is the necessity which either the New Testament as a whole or the tradition of the words of Jesus in particular ascribes to the event on Calvary. The New Testament in its characteristic expressions does not say merely that Jesus the Righteous One met death through the hostility and evil will of men : that is true, but it is not the whole truth, nor is it the truth which the gospel is concerned principally to defend. The Christian message is that Jesus suffered as 'a sacrifice for sins' ($\pi\epsilon\rho\grave{\iota}$ $\dot{\alpha}\mu\alpha\rho\tau\iota\tilde{\omega}\nu$), as 'the just for the unjust,' that he might bring us unto God (I Pet. iv. 18). The redemptive significance of his death lies not in its effects, in the spiritual reactions induced in our souls by the tragedy, but in the prevenient will or intention by which Christ related his dying to our forgiveness at a time when, in St. Paul's words, " we were yet sinners." At this point the New Testament goes beyond Isa. liii, for while the latter represents the Servant of God as suffering the consequences of our transgressions, and to that extent taking our sins upon himself, it nowhere suggests that the Servant willed to do this beforehand. If then the New Testament as a whole and such Synoptic words as the 'ransom' saying in Mk. x. 45 and the 'blood of the covenant' saying in Mk. xiv. 24 in particular are not to be denied a basis in authentic deliverances of Jesus, we have to ask whether the necessity which Jesus recognized as attaching to the death of the Son of Man is not to be approached along another line than that of the righteous man's taking the consequences of his righteousness. God's ought-to-be, as Jesus declared it, plainly includes more than the revelation of the ethical imperative embodied in the Sermon on the Mount. It includes the translation into action of God's immediate gracious will to forgive and to redeem a lost humanity. It was to save the 'many,' to make the grace of God an instant and indefeasible reality in the lives of the 'lost sheep' of Israel, that Jesus preached and taught, laboured, hungered, and suffered. In following out this purpose we find him ruthlessly setting aside the barriers which Jewish moralism had interposed between the righteous and 'sinners.' The hedge of the Law, so sacrosanct to Pharisaic piety, is not permitted to interfere with the entrance of the lapsed into the kingdom of God. It is in a context of grace also that, as we have seen, the Synoptic tradition sets Jesus' presentation of the perfect norm of righteousness in the Sermon on the Mount. The crisis to which he there brings the soul is part of the larger crisis indicated by the approach of the kingdom of

God with all that that kingdom means of divine love, grace, and power. This being so, it needs to be asked whether it is not in this domain of his soul's absorption in the task of rescuing, forgiving, restoring, and redeeming sinful men that we are to look for the peculiar necessity which Jesus recognized as belonging to his death when that event projected its shadow on to the scene.

To this question there can only be one answer. The Synoptic tradition makes it plain that *the acceptance by Jesus of death was the price not simply of his fidelity to truth but of his carrying through to the end his task of reconciling the many to God and his conviction of herein serving the will of the Father in heaven.* For an exposition of the nature of this task and of the conviction with which it was associated the writer would take the opportunity of referring to Dr. A. B. Macaulay's recent work on *The Death of Jesus.* Premising that Jesus in his earthly life was *viator* only, not as St. Thomas Aquinas thought both *viator* and *comprehensor*, and that his death was the climactic and all-determining moment in the realization of a supreme passion to reconcile Israel to God, Dr. Macaulay finds along two lines the possibility of a psychological approach to the crisis of Gethsemane and Calvary. First, it is fundamental to the understanding of the mind of Jesus that from the start he accepted the Isaianic ideal of the Servant of the Lord, the one on whom the sins of Israel were laid, as the norm of righteousness. The adoption of this norm preceded and led up to the acknowledgment of his Messianic vocation, and involved that the Servant's task of reconciling the many to God was the key to the Messianic salvation and the condition of the coming of God's heavenly reign. Secondly, the approach of death at the hands of those whom he came to save revealed its proper relevance to his particular sense of destiny by its direct challenge to his redeeming purpose. It was fundamental to his sense of calling that he should bring men to repentance and to the state of forgiveness. This meant that their forgiveness was possible and had for it the will of God. Now, however, this consciousness was confronted with the double temptation (*a*) in face of the appalling revelation of human sin which met him at his trial and at the cross, to doubt the redeemability of humanity, (*b*) in face of the same spectacle, to doubt that in his passion to redeem he had the mind of God. The only way to go through with his calling, therefore, was to accept death as the price, and thus through death as " a perfected personal experience of the enmity of the carnal mind to God " Jesus established the objective validity of his commission

at once to call men to God and in God's name to declare forgiveness to men.

Whether or not we can trace in this way or by so many steps
the process by which Jesus came to the integration of suffering
and death into his sense of his redemptive calling, it is clear that
the self-dedication implied in the ransom-word and in the coven-
ant-word in the Synoptic tradition is sacrificial in its character.
In his unlimited passion to bring the sinful sons of men to God
and to forgiveness Jesus in effect identified himself with them to
the extent of taking the curse of their sin upon his spirit, and
making his soul an 'asham for them. That he should make such
an experience, that he should know himself to be doing what
Moses and David in critical hours had wished to do for their
nation but could not do, need not, when taken together with the
purity and intensity of his apprehension of God in relation to
man, be thought to exceed the limits of what was possible, psycho-
logically and historically, for his pure spirit. The radical character of his apprehension of God is stamped on all his work and
teaching, and now it provides a background to the Cross. Thus
to the Christian mind the vicarious self-devotion of the Son of
Man has revealed itself from the beginning as having the reality
of a complete and perfect sacrifice. To it the souls of men have
turned, lifting from all other *piacula* and means of atonement.
In the blood of Christ they have found a cleansing of conscience
such as no other rites have accomplished, and a supreme verifica-
tion of God to their spirits.

And here also the eternal nature of the dependence of our
souls on Jesus comes to final expression. We saw how the
encounter of our souls with Jesus in his revelation of the will of
God brings us to a point where, if the truth which he declares is
accepted, it leaves us waiting on him for the next word, and for
all the words of life. It is now seen into what ultimate character
of life this waiting upon Jesus leads us. It is into an existence
conditioned by trust in, and determined by gratitude towards
one in whom, as nowhere else, the redeeming love of God towards
sinful man has actualized itself in a way which meets our need.
" The life which I now live in the flesh," so runs one of the most
classical of statements of the conception, " I live by faith in the
Son of God who loved me and gave himself for me." In such
an orientation of life the Christian soul has never had any doubt
of being in contact with eternal spirit and of being reconciled
to God.

APPENDICES

A

THE APOLLOS EPISODE IN ACTS XVIII, 24-28

THE exegetical difficulties presented by the passage are concentrated in the single verse, xviii. 25, and reduce themselves to the problem of explaining how one who is there stated (*a*) to have been instructed in ' the way of the Lord ' and to teach with accurate knowledge ' the things concerning Jesus ' is at the same time said (*b*) to understand only ' the baptism of John.' Theories which assume the apparently contradictory elements to be due to conflation of sources on the part of the writer of Acts are not satisfactory in the point that they ignore the possible complexities of Christian history in the apostolic age.

1. H. H. Wendt in the Meyer-Kommentar on Acts (9th ed., 1913) proposes to regard the whole of verse 25 as an expansion of the source-narrative by the writer of Acts. The source-narrative presented Apollos simply in the character indicated in verse 24, as an Alexandrian-Jewish scholar who had come to Ephesus. The author of Acts, influenced by the next section in the source which spoke of disciples of John at Ephesus (Acts xix. 1-7), understood Apollos to be an adherent of that sect and, as such, to possess a real, though as yet only an imperfect, knowledge of ' the way of the Lord ' and of Jesus. In this expansion of his source the writer of Acts was governed by the idea—opposed to the primary tradition in Mk. i. 1-11 and Mt. xi. 2-6, Lk. vii. 18-23—that the Baptist knew Jesus to be the Messiah and had proclaimed him as such. A very real objection to this view is that it does not explain why the writer of Acts, supposing him to have inferred from his source that Apollos was a disciple of John, was at such pains to describe him as possessing a knowledge of Christianity and of the things pertaining to Jesus. No motive appears for this elaboration unless the source in some manner suggested it. Verse 25, therefore, is not a pure addition by the writer of Acts.

2. Prof. Kirsopp Lake, in his *Earlier Epistles of St. Paul* (2nd ed., 1914) accepts verse 25 as original tradition, and attributes the seeming contradiction of terms between (*a*) and (*b*) to the writer's inexact use of language. Apollos was a genuine adherent of the sect of John the Baptist, who had taken up and continued John's proclamation of the advent of the Coming One or Messiah, a message which, as John and Apollos preached it, had no reference to Jesus. With this message on his lips Apollos wanders unwittingly into the Christian circle in the synagogue at Ephesus, and is there put right as to the true meaning

of ' the way of the Lord.' When the writer of Acts introduces him as a preacher of ' the things concerning Jesus,' he ought properly to have said ' the things concerning the *Christ*.' The statement is " quite intelligible," Lake holds, " if we take the phrase to mean the Messianic passages in the Old Testament, which to the Christian writer of Acts were τὰ περὶ 'Ιησοῦ (cf. Lk. xxiv. 27), though, as a matter of fact, Apollos did not, until he met Aquila, know to whom they referred except that he, whoever he was, was the Messiah " (p. 109). This theory, while not incredible, is not necessary if there is reason to consider that the writer's words, literally taken, reflect an actual historical situation.

3. More satisfactory is the treatment of the passage by the same scholar and Dr. H. J. Cadbury in the Commentary on Acts which forms Vol. IV of the work, *The Beginnings of Christianity* (1933). According to these scholars the meaning of the passage is either (*a*) that " Apollos knew and taught accurately the story of Jesus, but knew nothing of Christian baptism," his instruction in ' the way of the Lord ' being to this extent imperfect, or (*b*) that Apollos knew and reproduced in his preaching the historical teaching of Jesus in such points as judgement to come, the need of repentance, and the nature of the righteousness which God required for entrance into the approaching Kingdom, but he did not know the disciples' teaching that Jesus was the Messiah. According to the first of these interpretations the purpose of the Apollos section and of the section which follows it in Acts xix. 1-7 is " to illustrate the way in which Christian baptism supplanted John's baptism." It is against this view, however, that the narrative concludes, not with any mention of Apollos receiving Christian baptism, but with the statement that he now preached that " the Christ is Jesus " (Acts xviii. 28), which is what we would expect if the second view were right. We seem, therefore, justified in giving the second view the preference. It is not, however, either necessary or right to assume with Lake and Cadbury that Jesus did not historically teach that he was the Messiah, but only that this doctrine was not part of his *public* deliverance. Apollos knew by report the public teaching of Jesus, but the inner secret, constituting the more perfect knowledge of ' the way,' he learned only from the Christians of Ephesus.

The idea put forward by Reitzenstein in *Das Iranische Erlösungsmysterium* that Apollos after his enlightenment remained in the camp of John, since there is no reference to his being baptized as a Christian, has nothing to support it except the necessity which that ingenious scholar feels to press everything and everybody into the service of his Redemption-Myth theory. John the Baptist and Apollos were, according to this theory, really pre-Mandæans.

B

THE TARGUM ON ISAIAH LII, 13—LIII, 12

The Aramaic text of the Targum is printed in Walton's *Biblia Sacra Polyglotta* (1657), Vol. III ; in P. de Lagarde's *Prophetæ Chaldaice*, pp. 278-279 ; and in Driver and Neubauer's *Jewish Interpreters of Isaiah liii.* Latin translation in Walton ; German in Strack-Billerbeck's Kommentar, Bd. I (1922), pp. 482 f. ; English in Driver and Neubauer.

The following conspectus exhibits in parallel columns (*a*) the text of Isaiah in selected verses according to the English Revised Version, and (*b*) the corresponding sections of the Targum according to Driver and Neubauer's translation. Comparison will reveal how the Targum diverts the element of humiliation, suffering, and death from the person of the Servant-Messiah and transfers it to Israel or to the heathen nations.

(*a*) Text	(*b*) Targum
lii. 13. Behold, my Servant shall deal wisely, he shall be exalted. . . .	lii. 13. Behold, my Servant Messiah shall prosper, he shall be high. . . .
14. As many were astonished at thee, his visage was so marred more than any man, and his form more than the sons of men :	14. As the house of Israel looked to (or for) him during many days, because their countenance was darkened among the peoples, and their complexion beyond the sons of men :
15. So shall he sprinkle many nations ; kings shall shut their mouths at him. . . .	15. So will he scatter many peoples ; at him kings shall be silent.
liii. 1. Who hath believed our report ? and to whom hath the arm of the Lord been revealed ?	liii. 1. Who hath believed this our glad tidings ? and the strength of the mighty arm of the Lord, upon whom as thus hath it been revealed ?
2. He grew up before him as a tender plant and as a root out of a dry ground : he hath no form nor comeliness ; and when we see him, there is no beauty that we should desire him.	2. The righteous will grow up before him, yea, like blooming shoots, and like a tree which sends forth its roots to streams of water will they increase—a holy generation in the land that was in need of him : his countenance no profane countenance, and the terror of him not the terror of an ordinary man . . . and all who see him will look wistfully for him.
3. He was despised and rejected of men ; a man of sorrows and acquainted with grief : and	3. Then he will become despised, and will cut off the glory of the kingdoms : they will be

(a) Text

(b) Targum

as one from whom men hide their face he was despised, and we esteemed him not.

prostrate and mourning like a man of pains and like one destined for sickness : and as though the presence of the Shekhinah had been withdrawn from us, they will be despised and esteemed not.

4. Surely he hath borne our griefs, and carried our sorrows : yet we did esteem him stricken, smitten of God, and afflicted.

4. Therefore for our sins he will pray, and our iniquities will for his sake be forgiven, although we were accounted stricken, smitten before the Lord, and afflicted.

5. But he was wounded for our transgressions, he was bruised for our iniquities : the chastisement of our peace was upon him ; and with his stripes we are healed.

5. But he will build up the Holy Place, which has been polluted for our sins and delivered to the enemy for our iniquities : and by his instruction peace shall be increased upon us, and by devotion to his words our sins will be forgiven us.

6. All we like sheep have gone astray . . . and the Lord hath laid on him the iniquity of us all.

6. All we like sheep had been scattered . . . but it was the Lord's good pleasure to forgive the sins of all of us for his sake.

7. He was oppressed, yet he humbled himself, and opened not his mouth : as a lamb that is led to the slaughter . . . he opened not his mouth.

7. He prayed, and he was answered, and ere even he had opened his mouth, he was accepted : the mighty of the peoples he will deliver up like a sheep to the slaughter . . . there shall be none before him opening his mouth or saying a word.

8. By oppression and judgement he was taken away ; and as for his generation, who considered that he was cut off out of the land of the living ? for the transgression of my people was he stricken.

8. Out of chastisements and punishments he will bring our captives near ; the wondrous things done to us in his days who shall be able to tell ? for he will cause the dominion of the Gentiles to pass away from the land of Israel, and transfer to them the sins which my people have committed.

9. And they made his grave with the wicked, and with the rich in his death ; although he had done no violence, neither was any deceit in his mouth.

9. He will deliver the wicked into Gehinnom, and those that are rich in possessions into the death of utter destruction, in order that those who commit sin may not be established, nor speak deceits with their mouth.

(a) Text	(b) Targum
10. Yet it pleased the Lord to bruise him ; he hath put him to grief : when thou shalt make his soul (or, when his soul shall make) an offering for sin, he shall see his seed, he shall prolong his days, and the pleasure of the Lord shall prosper in his hands.	10. But it is the Lord's good pleasure to try and to purify the remnant of his people, so as to cleanse their souls from sin ; these shall look on the kingdom of their Messiah, their sons and their daughters shall be multiplied, they shall prolong their days, and those who perform the law of the Lord shall prosper in his good pleasure.
11. He shall see of the travail of his soul, and shall be satisfied : by his knowledge shall my righteous Servant justify many : and he shall bear their iniquities.	11. From the subjection of the nations he will deliver their souls, they shall look upon the punishment of those that hate them, and be satisfied with the spoil of their kings : by his wisdom he will hold the guiltless free from guilt, in order to bring many into subjection to the law : and for their sins he will intercede.
12. Therefore will I divide him a portion with the great, and he shall divide the spoil with the strong : because he poured out his soul unto death, and was numbered with the transgressors : yet he bare the sin of many, and made intercession for the transgressors.	12. Then will I divide for him the spoil of many peoples, and the possessions of strong cities shall he divide as prey, because he delivered up his soul to death, and made the rebellious subject to the law ; he shall intercede for many sins, and the rebellious for his sake shall be forgiven.

It would scarcely be possible to conceive a more complete perversion of the whole central idea of the Hebrew prophet's vision than is here revealed in the Targum. The latter recognizes the Servant as the Messiah (xlii. 1, xliii. 10, lii. 13, liii. 10), but deliberately contorts everything in Isa. liii. into conformity with the worst excesses of Jewish nationalistic doctrine. The Servant-Messiah is to scatter and crush the wicked Gentiles (lii. 15, liii. 3, 7, 8, 11, 12), to emancipate Israel (liii. 8), to rebuild the Temple which for Israel's sins has been delivered to the enemy (liii. 5), to bring Israel by instruction to increase of peace (liii. 5), and to subject many rebels to the Law (liii. 11, 12). The disfigurement, the oppression, the humiliation, and the penal suffering for guilt, of which the passage speaks, are transferred from the Servant-Messiah either to Israel (lii. 14, liii. 2, 4, 10) or to the wicked nations or kingdoms (liii. 3, 7, 8, 9, 11). In place of the prophet's " He was cut off out of the land of the living : for the transgression of my people was he stricken," the Targum indulges the sadistic reflection that the

Messiah, in freeing Israel at last from the dominion of the Gentiles, will transfer to them the sins which Israel has committed—a new doctrine of vicarious atonement !

C

INTERCONNECTION OF THE CONCEPTS DAVIDIC MESSIAH, SERVANT OF THE LORD, AND HEAVENLY SON OF MAN

We have noted in the text the recurrence of a certain common pattern of thought, embodying the ideas of divine exaltation, gift, and inheritance, in association with the Davidic Messiah, the Suffering Servant of Deutero-Isaiah, and the apocalyptic Son of Man. We take opportunity here to notice the coincidences in expressions of detail which characterize these three phases of the Jewish Messianic idea. The matter will be presented in parallel columns.

I. SERVANT OF THE LORD (A) AND DAVIDIC MESSIAH (B)

A	B
Isa. xlii. 1. " Behold my *Servant*."	Ezek. xxxiv. 23 f. " My Servant David " ; Zech. iii. 8. " I will bring forth my Servant, the Branch."
Isa. xlii. 1. " I have put my *Spirit* upon him."	Isa. xi. 2. " The Spirit of the Lord will rest upon him, the Spirit of wisdom, etc."
Isa. xlii. 3. " He shall bring forth *judgement*."	Isa. ix. 7. " Of the increase of his government . . . there shall be no end upon the throne of David . . . to uphold it with judgement." Jer. xxiii. 5. " I will raise unto David a righteous Branch, and he shall reign as king . . . and shall execute judgement."
Isa. xlii. 6. " I the Lord . . . will give thee for a *covenant* of the people."	Ps. lxxxix. 3. " I have made a covenant with my Chosen . . . sworn unto David my Servant." Ezek. xxxiv. 23 f. "I will set up . . . my Servant David . . . and I will make with them a covenant of peace." Cf. xxxvii. 24, 26.
Isa. xlii. 6. " for a *light of the Gentiles*." Cf. xlix. 6.	Isa. ix. 1-2. " No gloom to her that was in anguish. . . . A great light. . . ."
Isa. xlii. 7. " to bring out the *prisoners*."	Ezek. xxxiv. 27 (a Davidic passage). " When I have broken the bars and delivered them, etc."

A

Isa. xlix. 1. "The Lord hath called me from the womb."

Isa. xlix. 2. "He hath made my *mouth* like a sharp sword."

Isa. xlix. 6. "to raise up *the tribes of Jacob*, and to restore the tribes of Israel."

Isa. xlix. 7. "Him whom man *despiseth* . . . whom the nation *abhorreth*."

Isa. xlix. 7. "*Kings* shall see and arise ; princes, and they shall worship." Cf. lii. 15. "Kings shall shut their mouths at him."

Isa. lii. 13-liii. 12. The *sufferings* and *reproaches* which fall on the Servant.

Isa. liii. 2. "He grew up as a tender *plant* and as *a root* out of a dry ground."

Isa. liii. 2. "He has no form . . . *no beauty*."

Isa. liii. 6. "All we like *sheep* have gone astray."

Isa. liii. 8. "As for his generation, who considered that he was cut off out of the land of the living ? "

B

Isa. vii. 14 f. and ix. 6. "Unto us a Child is born."

Isa. xi. 4. "He shall smite the earth with the rod of his mouth."

Jer. xxiii. 8 (a Davidic passage). "As the Lord liveth which brought up . . . the seed of the house of Israel . . . from all the countries whither I had driven them."

Ps. lxxxix. 50 (The Anointed, God's Chosen, speaks). "Remember, Lord . . . how I do bear in my bosom (the reproach of) all the mighty peoples ; wherewith thine enemies have reproached, O Lord, wherewith they have reproached the footsteps of thine Anointed."

Ps. lxxxix. 27. "I will also make him the highest of the kings of the earth " ; lxxii. 10 f., "All kings shall fall down before him " ; ii. 10., "Now, therefore, be wise, O ye kings. . . . Kiss the Son."

Ps. xviii. 4-6, cxxxii. 1. "David and all his afflictions " ; lxxxix. 38, "Thou hast cast off and abhorred, thou hast been wroth with thine Anointed " ; lxxxix. 41, "He is become a reproach to his neighbours."

Isa. xi. 1. "There shall come forth a shoot out of the stock of Jesse, and a branch out of his roots shall bear fruit." Jer. xxiii. 5. "I will raise unto David a righteous Branch."

Ps. lxxxix. 44. "Thou hast made his brightness to cease, etc."

Ezek. xxxiv. 22-24, Jer. xxiii. 3-5. Israel, the scattered sheep of God, is to come under the rule of "David, my Servant."

Ps. lxxxix. 45. "The days of his youth thou hast shortened . . . " ; 47 f., "O remember how short my time is."

A	B
Isa. liii. 10. "He shall see his *seed.*"	II Sam. vii. 12, 16. The promise to David's house. Ps. lxxxix. 4. "Thy seed will I establish for ever"; 36 f., "His seed shall endure for ever, etc."
Isa. liii. 12. "Numbered with the transgressors."	Ps. lxxxix. 50. Quoted above in the parallel to Isa. xlix. 7.

II. Son of Man, Davidic Messiah, and Servant of the Lord

We take here the evidence of I Enoch xxxvii-lxxi, commonly known as the Similitudes of Enoch, in which Dr. R. H. Charles thinks we ought to distinguish two sources : a ' Son of Man ' source, which we shall here indicate by S, and an ' Elect One ' source, which we shall indicate by E.

Enoch xlvi. 3 (S). "This is the Son of Man who hath *righteousness* "; xlviii. 4, "He shall be a staff to the righteous whereon to lean themselves "; lxii. 2 (E), "The Spirit of righteousness was poured out upon him "; lxxi. 14 (S), "The Son of Man who is born unto righteousness, etc." For righteousness as a divine endowment of the Davidic Messiah compare Isa. ix. 7, xi. 4-5, Jer. xxiii. 5-6, Zech. ix. 9, Psalms of Solomon xvii. 25, 28, 29, 31, 42, 46, xviii. 8 : and for the righteousness of the Servant of the Lord compare Isa. xlii. 6, liii. 11.

Enoch xlvi. 3 (S). "The Lord of Spirits hath *chosen* him," and his lot "hath the pre-eminence ever." Compare God's choice and exaltation of the Davidic Anointed in Ps. ii. 6 f., and lxxxix. 27, and of the Servant in Isa. xlii. 1.

Enoch xlvi. 4 (S). The Son of Man "shall raise up the *kings* and the mighty from their seats "; lxii. 3 (E), the kings and the mighty " shall see and recognize how he sits on the throne of his glory "; lxii. 9 (S), the kings and the mighty "shall fall down before him on their faces and worship . . . that Son of Man." See also xlviii. 8. For the worshipful homage of kings to the Davidic Messiah compare Ps. ii. 2 f., 10-12, lxxii. 10-11, lxxxix. 27, etc., and towards the Servant, Isa. xlix. 7 and lii. 15.

Enoch xlviii. 4 (S). "He shall be *the light of the Gentiles.*" This is an explicit ascription to the Son of Man of the function assigned to the Servant in Isa. xlii. 6 : " I will give thee for a light of the Gentiles." For the illumination of the nations in the times of the Davidic Messiah compare Isa. ix. 1-2.

Enoch xlviii. 4 (S). "He shall be . . . the hope of those who are troubled in heart." Compare Isa. l. 4, which predicates of the Servant a divine endowment " to sustain with words him that is weary," also Isa. lxi. 1-2, which possibly refers to the Servant. Compare the words of Jesus in Mt. xi. 28-30.

Enoch xlviii. 10. " The Lord of Spirits and *his Anointed* " ; lii. 4, " the dominion of his Anointed that he may be potent and mighty on the earth." For the same epithet applied to the Davidic prince see Ps. ii. 2, and for its use possibly with reference to the Servant compare Isa. lxi. 1 f., " The Spirit of the Lord is upon me, because he has anointed me, etc."

Enoch xlix. 3 (E). " In him dwells the spirit of *wisdom*, and the spirit which gives insight, and the spirit of understanding and of might, etc.," to which is added " and the spirit of those who have fallen asleep in righteousness." Charles comments on the first part of this statement that it enumerates " endowments of the Messiah after Isa. xi. 2," and on the addition that " the eschatological hopes of all the faithful in the past are realized " in the Son of Man. For the wisdom of the Servant of Yahweh compare Isa. l. 4-5, lii. 13, liii. 11, " by his knowledge shall my righteous Servant justify many."

Points of comparison might be indefinitely multiplied, but enough evidence has been adduced to show that the concepts of the Davidic Messiah, the Suffering Servant, and the pre-existent Heavenly Man, however disparate in origin they may have been, have in the religious thought of Israel been conformed to the same type, and are to be recognized, therefore, as far as the religion of Israel is concerned, as *successive phases of the Messianic idea, which connect respectively with Israel as nation, Israel as Church, and Israel as final, perfected elect of the supernatural Reign of God.*

D

THE HEAVENLY MAN REDEMPTION MYTH

(The question is discussed in Bousset-Gressmann's work, *Die Religion des Judentums* (3rd ed., 1926), also in Bousset's *Hauptprobleme der Gnosis* (1907), pp. 160-223, 238-276, but for the fuller speculative development of the theory reference should be made to the various works of Dr. R. Reitzenstein, including his *Poimandres* (1906), *Die Göttin Psyche* (1917), *Das Mandäische Buch des Herrn der Grösse* (1919), *Das Iranische Erlösungs-mysterium* (1921), and *Die Hellenistischen Mysterien-Religionen* (3rd ed., 1927). See also H. Gressmann's *Der Messias* (1929), A. F. von Gall's *ΒΑΣΙΛΕΙΑ ΤΟΥ ΘΕΟΥ* (1926), and J. Héring's *Le Royaume de Dieu et Sa Venue* (1937). For criticism of the theory reference may be made to M. J. Lagrange's *Le Judaisme avant Jésus-Christ* (1931), and to J. M. Creed's article on " The Heavenly Man " in the *Journal of Theological Studies*, Vol. XXVI, pp. 113-136.)

Attention has been directed at various points in the present work to the theory that a widely diffused redemption myth of Oriental provenance and centering around the conception of a Primal or

Heavenly Man was current in the period of Christian origins and exercised a formative influence on the development of the New Testament doctrine of Christ. An outline of the alleged myth, as it offers itself to us in the speculative constructions of Dr. Reitzenstein, has been given in Chapter I, and reasons have been there formulated against accepting the view that suggestions from this quarter gave rise to the primitive Christian confession of Jesus as the Messiah. As, however, this disclaimer does not close the door to the wider possibility that Oriental ideas of the Man from Heaven, percolating into Judaism, influenced the interpretation which Jesus placed upon the destiny of the ' Son of Man ' and assisted the development of the Pauline doctrine of Christ in certain of its most important directions, it becomes necessary to consider at somewhat closer range the kind of evidence upon which the case for the alleged penetration of Judaism by these ethnic ideas has been held to rest. It will be convenient, in the interests of clearness, to subdivide the inquiry under the following series of heads :

    I. New ideas emerging in the later Jewish doctrine of the Last Things.

    II. The glorification of the First Man in apocryphal Jewish and Jewish-Christian literature.

    III. The existence, in the background of Judaism and Christianity, of an Indo-European myth of the First or Heavenly Man.

    IV. The source of the ' Son of Man ' conception in Daniel and in I Enoch 37-71.

    V. The teaching of Jesus with regard to the Son of Man's lowly fortunes and exaltation.

    VI. St. Paul's conception of Christ as ' the Man from Heaven.'

    I. It is matter of general agreement that from the Persian period onwards the Jewish doctrine of the Last Things takes to itself new powers of expression and incorporates a series of ideas which have their closest analogies in certain features of the dualistic religion of Zoroaster. The judgement of the God of Israel on the nations assumes in this period the dimensions and the character of a final cosmic and supra-historical event. The divine sovereignty over the world appears in the sharpest opposition to the power of Satan, and as God has His entourage of angelic and heavenly spirits, so Satan has his hierarchy of evil principalities and demons. A great gulf separates the kingdoms of the world, now subject to the powers of sin and death, from the bliss of the coming Reign of God. The final judgement of the world is associated with a resurrection of the dead. It is customary to see in all this the influence on Jewish apocalypse of Zoroastrian ideas which, working on the mind of Israel in the centuries succeeding the Exile, turned the religion of Israel in certain quarters into a religion of dualism or at any rate powerfully reinforced the dualistic tendencies already latent in the prophetic doctrine of God. The ideas of the two world-æons and of the resurrection of the dead are unknown to the older Biblical religion, but as they are organic to the religion of Persia, it is considered that without difficulty they may be traced to a source in that religion, and a similar explanation is offered for the change which comes over Jewish Messianism in what we call the apocalyptic literature.

In the Jewish apocalyptic writings the old national expectation of a Messianic king from the house of David has sunk beneath the horizon. In some of these books, e.g. in parts of I Enoch and in the Assumption of Moses, the Messiah does not appear at all, the judgement of the world and the final deliverance of Israel being wholly reserved to God. But in other parts of the literature there emerges a transcendent figure with wholly celestial attributes, for whose appearance we are not prepared by anything in the older religion of Israel. He comes into view first in the famous vision in Dan. vii, where under the form of one like ' a son of man ' or man—' Son of Man ' is the ordinary Aramaic expression for man—he arrives with the clouds of heaven before the Ancient of Days, and is given an everlasting kingdom and dominion. In Daniel this celestial figure is not invested with any of the titles or attributes of the Jewish Messiah. Within the limits of the vision he functions merely as a symbol or personification of the Jewish nation, the people of ' the saints of the Most High,' for whom an everlasting kingdom is intended (Dan. vii. 18, 22, 27). It does not follow, however, that the religious significance which the Heavenly Man conception possessed for the writer of Daniel is exhausted in the purpose to which the idea is put in his particular representation, much less that the Man himself was a pure creation of the apocalyptist. The idea as it came to him may well have had a larger force and range of meaning than he has chosen to give to it in his seventh chapter, and in that case we should expect a fuller expression of the idea to occur in other quarters.

Such a fuller expression we do actually find in I Enoch xxxvii-lxxi and in parts of IV Ezra. There the Son of Man reappears, but no longer for the mere purpose of symbolizing the saints of the Most High. He is a pre-existent heavenly being, who as the Elect or Righteous One of God has been hidden with God from before the creation of the world, and is now revealed to the saints by the wisdom of the Lord of Spirits (I Enoch xlviii. 7). In Enoch also, as the preceding Appendix will have made clear, the same angel-like figure is invested with the attributes and glories of the Jewish Messiah. He is destined to sit on a throne of glory, and to have the sum of judgement committed into his hands (I Enoch lxi. 8, lxix. 27, 29).

What then is the origin of this remarkable conception, in which two different forms or principles have obviously been run together and conflated, on the one hand the Jewish Messiah, on the other hand a heavenly spirit in the likeness of man who has been with God from before the ages ? Is it possible to regard the Enochian representation as merely an imaginative development from the basis provided by Daniel's vision ? In favour of this view is the fact that the writer of the Similitudes obviously has his eye on the picture in Daniel, and as an illustration of the instinct to advance upon the latter, reference might be made to the Septuagint version of Daniel itself, where, in place of the original, " There came with the clouds of heaven one like a son of man, and he came even to the Ancient of Days " (Dan. vii. 13), there is substituted : " There came on the clouds of heaven as it were a son of man, and *he came as one ancient of days.*" It might be argued that this Septuagintal rendering was but an imaginative gloss on the text before the translator. But the attribution of eternity or pre-existence to the Son of Man in the Septuagint of Daniel and in Enoch is also capable of the explanation that behind Daniel, and behind his Greek translator and the Similitudes of Enoch, there existed the fully-formed conception of a heavenly Man with soteriological functions, whose form has been appropriated by Daniel only so far as was rendered necessary by the particular purpose of his vision, but who in the later writers is re-invested with a larger measure of the attributes and qualities pertaining to him. Obviously the decision between these alternative explanations will depend largely on what other evidence is forthcoming as to an attraction exercised over Judaism, apart from Daniel, by the idea of the Heavenly Man.

II. We find in late Jewish and Jewish-Christian literature a glorification of the first man Adam which is not explained by anything in the older religion of Israel but for which we must seek another cause. Thus in the Latin Vita Adae xii-xvii [1] it is taught that Adam was created in the image of God in order to be worshipped by all angels. " Michael went out and called all the angels, saying : ' Worship the image of God as the Lord God hath commanded.' And Michael himself worshipped first." The devil, however, refused to worship this first man, and by his arts he overcame Eve. So in II (sometimes called Slavonic) Enoch, a strongly syncretistic work which Bousset assigns to the Herodian period, we read in Chapter xxx. 11-12 that God created Adam " a second angel, honourable, great, and glorious," and appointed him to rule on earth and to have God's wisdom, no creature being worthy to be compared to him. In xxxi. 6 we hear that the devil seduced Eve, " but he did not touch Adam." But the supreme illustration of this tendency to exalt the First Man above the human measure is in the pseudo-Clementine literature, originating in Jewish-Christian circles about the end of the second or the beginning of the third century of our era. Here, as Bousset observes, the historical first man has been taken up and identified with another and

[1] This work is assigned by R. H. Charles, as regards the bulk of the material, to a first Christian century date, while Bousset carries it as far back as Herodian or post-Herodian times.

heavenly figure who, like the prince of darkness, is a son of God, and to whom belongs the rule of the world to come (Homilies xx. 2 ff.). The fall of Adam and the other features of the Genesis story are rejected in favour of the idea that under the rule of the first man as vehicle of the pure and perfect revelation of God the world enjoyed a blessed and glorious age. With this glorification of the first man there goes in the Clementine representation the idea that the divine principle of revelation who appeared in Adam has made himself known in a whole series of later successors or representatives, Enoch, Noah, Abraham, Isaac, Jacob, Moses, etc., Jesus Christ being the last and supreme instance of his manifestation. Finally, as in II Enoch and in the Adam-literature, the first man has his express counterpart and enemy in the devil who wills to wrest from him the rule of the world to come. It will be seen that the whole representation lies far away from the conception of the Old Testament Adam.

How do we explain this singular development? It might be supposed to be the result of an unassisted working of the Jewish imagination on the Old Testament material in Genesis. Against this, however, is the fact that the idea of a primal or heavenly man occurs elsewhere than in Judaism, and in forms and contexts of religious thought to which the hypothesis of Biblical influence is wholly inapplicable. We find it in the Hermetic religion of Egypt, in the doctrinal system of the Naasenes as described by Hippolytus in his Refutatio v. 6 ff., possibly in the Attis-cult, and on a grandiose scale in the Manichæan system of religion. In all of these, though the evidence is for periods much later than the origin of Christianity, the figure of the original Man takes forms which cannot by any stretch of imagination be traced to purely Jewish or Christian inspirations. One would therefore need, as Bousset says, to draw one's circle very wide to include the whole history of the ' Son of Man ' conception. But if the ethnic interest in the first man thus points to the influence of ideas lying altogether beyond Judaism, the same influences may well account for the singular developments of the Adam-conception in Jewish Midrash and in Jewish-Christian heresy. Here, if anywhere, we see a magnetization of the Jewish mind in a direction away from its original basis and towards the conflation of its own Adam with a Heavenly Man of other extraction.

Even in Philo of Alexandria the clear traces of such an attraction are discernible. Philo, as is well known, starts from the creation not of one man but of two : the first, a spiritual and heavenly man, a principle of the purely rational or ideal world ; the second, an earthly and sensual man, who belongs to the world we know. The material basis for this distinction lies in the dual narratives of the origin of man in Gen. i. 27 and ii. 7 : the formal criteria enabling the distinction to be interpreted are supplied by the Platonic philosophy which is fundamental to Philo's thinking. But neither Philo's Biblical starting-point nor his Platonic philosophy account for his peculiar idealization at certain points of the *earthly* principle, Adam. That he should exalt the spiritual Adam, calling him " Father, not mortal but immortal, Man of God, who, being the Logos of the Eternal, is necessarily imperishable " (De Conf. Ling. 41), is natural and to be expected from his Platonic premises. That he should glorify the earthly Adam is neither required by his Biblical authority nor to be expected from the standpoint of his Platonic philosophy. Yet Philo does it. He says that Adam excelled all who came after him in the transcendent qualities of both soul and body, that he represented the acme of humanity, that the divine Spirit had flowed into him in full current, and that he may be described as heavenly (De Opif. Mund. 136, 140, 144, 147). Such aberrations of Philo's thought from its ordinary orbit may be taken to indicate the presence to his mind of ideas not dissimilar to those which we have seen at work in the Adam-literature of Judaism.

III. The cause to which an influential group of scholars in recent days have proposed to carry back the phenomena we have been considering is, as has been stated, a diffused Oriental belief in a Primal or Heavenly Man which Reitzenstein considers to have been developed both in a cosmological and in a soteriological direction, and which he takes back to a root in the Zoroastrian myth of Gayomart, the first man. Gayomart is not mentioned in the Gathas, the original sermon-poems of Zoroaster, but at a few other points in the Avesta he and his ox appear, and he is represented as the first believer in the truth, " who first hearkened to the thoughts and teachings of Ahura Mazda," and from whom " Ahura Mazda brought forth the families of the Aryan lands," the generation of the Aryan peoples (Yast 87). In the Avesta also we find occurrences of the phrase " from the man Gaya to the victorious Saoshyant," an expression which covers the Zoroastrian span of history. The Avesta literature, as we have it, is a very late recension of Zoroastrian tradition. Eduard Meyer,[1] who attributes the Gathas to the prophet himself, brings down the bulk of the work to Arsacid and later times in the third and fourth Christian centuries, and some authorities would descend still further for the final recension. There is, however, no reason to doubt that the Avesta and the still later Pehlevi literature preserve a mass of ancient material. Ideas integral to the doctrine of the latter, such as the division of time into a series of world-periods and the dogma of resurrection, seem to have been known in Greek circles as early as the age of Theopompus (*c.* 350 B.C.).[2] Certainly there need be little disposition to question the primitive character of the Avesta references to the first man. His name—Gaya Maretan, meaning " mortal life "—is a characteristic Zoroastrian abstraction, which probably covers an older heathen

---

[1] *Ursprung und Anfänge des Christentums*, Bd. II, p. 58, n. 1, and p. 74.
[2] Von Gall, *ΒΑΣΙΛΕΙΑ*, pp. 148-150.

name. The conception of this original man as the first believer may well represent a Zoroastrian appropriation for religious purposes of a primitive myth. And it may also be a mark of the prophet's teaching that the Avesta makes no reference to the man Gayomart as having descended from heaven.

In the later Pehlevi literature, however, Gayomart appears as " a heavenly being who falls a victim to the powers of evil, and from whose seed the human race is derived." [1] The Bundahish, the Dinkard, and the other writings in which his story is told, date in their present form from a period not earlier than the seventh Christian century, yet here again many traditions may well go back to ancient times, indeed it is more than probable that a resurgence of old pagan tradition has to a great extent overlaid the figure of the Zoroastrian Gayomart.

Be that as it may, the myth presents itself now with a definitely cosmological aspect or significance, and as it is also taught that Gayomart will be the first to be raised when the Saoshyant, the Persian Messiah, brings about the resurrection at the end of the world, it is seen that the conception of Gayomart admits of developments by which it becomes associated not only with the origins but with the final destinies of the human race.

According to the Dinkard iii. 82, Gayomart is the son of Ahura Mazda, the Father of all, by his daughter Spendarmad, the earth : this genealogy is taken by von Gall to represent a genuinely ancient tradition. In the Bundahish iii. 19 ff. we hear how at the close of the second great period of world-history, when for 3000 years the righteous Gayomart and his labouring ox had held the evil spirit and his demons at bay, the evil spirit achieved his ruin and death. The story is obscure and need not be discussed except to say that the theory that it presents a parallel to the Greek story of the fall of Narcissus into matter [2] is now discredited. It relates that the ox perished first, and from its seed sprang beasts, birds, fishes, and plants. Gayomart also was slain, and from his body the metals were created, while from his seed, miraculously preserved by an angel and Spendarmad, there arose in course of time a plant, and from the plant the first human pair, Mashya and Mashyana. If here we have the relation of Gayomart to the origins of man and of the world which man inhabits, his significance for the final destiny of man and the last things is given, as already stated, in the belief that, at the end of this world-æon, the bones of Gayomart will first be raised, then those of Mashya and Mashyana, then those of the rest of men. The religious emphasis upon the first man, characteristic of Zoroaster's teaching, remains a feature of the myth through all these developments. Gayomart is

---

[1] J. M. Creed, " The Heavenly Man," p. 123. To this article, to Bousset's *Hauptprobleme*, and to von Gall's *ΒΑΣΙΛΕΙΑ* I am indebted for the summary of details in this and in the preceding and following paragraphs.

[2] So Bousset, following Windischmann. See his *Hauptprobleme*, pp. 203 ff.

" the pure man," the " first reasonable high-priest " of wisdom, " in whose protection was the whole creation of holy natures from their beginning to the final consummation of the world." As one who looked to God, Gayomart stands with Zoroaster and the Saoshyant. He is the precursor of all men in the true life, and in the end he attains to the rank of the archangels. From certain expressions in these later books, in which the religion of Zoroaster is identified with the nature of Gayomart, it becomes possible to say that man's spiritual life is what he holds of Gayomart.

From such ideas, assumed to have been current for centuries before the Bundahish and similar books existed, and by calling in the aid of Babylonian and Syrian speculations, Reitzenstein elaborates the religious significance of his Iranian myth. According to this, the soul or spiritual part of man is a divine principle which man has by his descent from the first God-man. This principle the evil spirit by his victory over Gayomart has imprisoned in a world of darkness, and for its final release and redemption it is dependent upon Gayomart's exaltation. According to the developed myth, the Heavenly Man was rescued from the powers of darkness after his death, and the soul of man, which is part of him, will be saved by rising in reunion with him. Reitzenstein has not chapter and verse for all this in Zoroastrian tradition, but he finds the myth reflected in the Gnostic and Hermetic speculations of the early Christian centuries, and above all he finds it in its concretest form in the Manichæan and Mandæan religions.

Such sweeping generalizations call for closer criticism than is possible here. But certain considerations thrust themselves to the front. It may be admitted that in the ferment of ideas giving rise to religious syncretism and Gnosticism in the Orient the Iranian religion was a powerful organizing factor, but this is not to say that it was the only factor. Bousset, for example, sees behind the Persian Gayomart the Indian myth of Purusha, the man whom the gods sacrificed and from whose dismembered body arose the world and its order. He would also derive from Indian sources the idea, reflected in the Manichæan and in the Jewish-Christian Clementine literature, of a god or man who from the beginning wanders through the world and reveals himself in ever new incarnations.[1] It is not, therefore, clear that the myth which Reitzenstein so elaborately reconstructs derives the mystical and inward character, on which he lays so great a stress, from its Iranian root.

The Manichæan and Mandæan religions, on which he relies so greatly for the proof of his theory, are highly syncretistic and composite products. Mani declared himself expressly to be a follower of the Buddha and of Jesus as well as of Zoroaster, and, in point of fact, we can neither trace the whole development of thought from Zoroaster to Mani, nor fully analyse the complex system of Manichæan ideas. Many factors, including Jewish and Christian ideas, may have contributed to the formation of the Manichæan mythology, so that features of the latter on which Reitzenstein fastens as indicative of the source of certain elements in the New Testament doctrine of Christ may themselves be of Christian origin.

Nor again is it by any means clear that those features of the Hermetic and Gnostic religions, which Reitzenstein considers to reflect his myth, are Iranian and not rather Egyptian or Greek in origin. The similarities which exist between the various religious systems may be the result not of the victorious progress of one particular myth but of the common tendency of all peoples, face to face with the one mystery of life and death, to cast their thoughts about the soul's relation to its environment into the same or similar moulds.

It is not necessary to the present purpose to examine in detail the common pattern of ideas which Reitzenstein finds in the various religious systems which he reviews. A useful summary will be found in the late Prof. J. M. Creed's article on " The Heavenly Man " as already cited. I cannot, however, conceal my conviction that the terms in which Reitzenstein states the spiritual import of the myth are to a large extent Greek rather than Oriental. More important is it to decide in what relation the conception of redemption embodied in the myth stands to Jewish and Christian ideas. We saw that through the Zoroastrian derivation of the world of men and things from the seed of the divine man Gayomart a cosmological and anthropological interest attaches to the myth which wraps itself around him. The spiritual part of man's being, the element of light within his darkness, is what he holds of Gayomart, is indeed the nature of Gayomart. Correspondingly, the belief that Gayomart will be the first to be raised at the resurrection gives the myth the possibility of being intimately related to man's final redemption and to the last things. But in the actual course of its development, to judge from Reitzenstein's outline of the full-grown myth, the idea of redemption has swung away from the last things and attached itself essentially to an event lying before the beginning of human history and of the world.

It is very definitely so in Manichæism. According to the latter, the primal God-Man, the son of the Father of light, who is ensnared and overcome by the power of darkness, is at the same pre-cosmic stage delivered and raised up by the Father. Though the soul of man, derived as it is from the light-elements which the Primal Man left behind him in the world of chaos, has to be redeemed in time, the ground on which its redemption rests is an event which is anterior to all time. The Redeemer, as Reitzenstein continually insists, is one who has been himself redeemed. The same pre-cosmic idea of redemption characterizes the Gnostic systems generally ; and this feature, as it shows how far the development of thought has travelled from its starting-point in the Persian story of Gayomart, reveals also how very different is the orientation of the myth from that of the Jewish and Christian doctrines which it is supposed to have influenced.

IV. It may be that the conception of the Heavenly Man or Son of Man, of which we get a visionary glimpse in Dan. vii and a fuller and more substantial picture in the Similitudes of Enoch and in IV Ezra xiii, came into Judaism, together with other component ideas of the later Jewish doctrine of the last things, from Persia. An admission of this may even seem to underlie the statement in I Enoch xlviii. 6 f. that the Son of Man has been hidden with God from before creation, and only now has " the wisdom of the Lord of Spirits revealed him to the holy and righteous." But if the conception has been taken over from the Persian thought of the Heavenly Man, it is with a significant difference.

No cosmological interest of any kind attaches to the Son of Man in Daniel or in I Enoch or in IV Ezra. Nor is there any suggestion in these books that man's soul or spiritual part is, as in the Persian story, something which by nature he has derived from the Son of Man. The Jewish apocalyptists, however hospitable they may have been to other Iranian ideas, give no kind of countenance to this. On the contrary, the figure of the Heavenly Man, if it has been in any way appropriated from a Persian source, has been turned to account purely in connection with the last things. The Son of Man enters on his functions not at the beginning but at the end of world-history, and if his appearing, which is a sign of judgement for the world, is also a token of redemption for the righteous, it is in virtue not of any *pre-cosmic* exaltation, as in the Iranian mystery, but of an exaltation which is yet to be.

The apparition and the glory of the Son of Man belong to the last things, and for this there can only be one explanation. Either the conception of the transcendent Son of Man in Judaism was a spontaneous product of the native Messianic idealism, or, if it came into Judaism from the outside, it was swept into the current, and subdued to the purpose of that central imperious direction of thought and interest. In either case, it is through his identification with the Messiah that the Heavenly Man in Judaism as in Christianity becomes a sign of our salvation.

V. It is not necessary to restate the argument advanced in Chapter I against the hypothesis that the Heavenly Man idea of the Iranian myth suggested or gave form to the primitive Christian confession of Jesus as the Son of Man. The Synoptic evidence is entirely against the probability that the idea of a Heavenly Man who descends to earth to suffer and die before attaining to his glory was known to the first disciples of Jesus. It may be argued, however, that what was unknown to these simple followers may well have been familiar to Jesus himself, coming to him as part of some religious doctrine—possibly propagated by John the Baptist,[1] possibly current in apocalyptic or Rabbinical circles—in which the Son of Man conception had been developed to conclusions not reached in Daniel or in Enoch. In this connection attention has been directed in particular to two features of the teaching of Jesus about the Man. These are (a) the idea of the Son of Man as homeless and a wanderer on earth who has not where to lay his head, and (b) the idea of the Son of Man as overborne and slain by the powers of evil.

Before, however, any decision can be taken on the question of the source or ground of these ideas, the relation of the teaching of Jesus as a whole to the Iranian myth of the Heavenly Man needs to be considered, and here the evidence is not at all encouraging to the defenders of the myth-hypothesis. Nowhere in the Synoptic tradition is the Son of Man given any kind of ontological or cosmological relation to the world or to humanity. Nowhere does the soul or spiritual part of man appear as a nature derived or descended from the Son of Man, and saved by being re-united to him. Nowhere is the Son of Man presented as pre-existent or as owing his redeeming status to a pre-cosmic event. Nowhere does the Redeemer come before us as one who has been himself redeemed. That is to say, all the distinctive characteristics of the Heavenly Man of the Iranian mystery are absent. The orientation of the mind of Jesus is entirely to the future.

Even those words of Jesus which make use of the formula ' I came ' or ' the Son of Man came ' constitute no exception to this rule. For what they define in their contexts is not the functions or the consequences which flow to the Son of Man from his status of pre-cosmic Redeemer, but rather the historical conditions and necessities under which he labours in order to attain Redeemership at the end.

This being the general relation of the Synoptic presentation of Jesus to the Iranian doctrine of the Heavenly Man, it becomes us to be very cautious in allocating to that source, directly or indirectly, any even of the special features which characterize the utterances of Jesus regarding the Son of Man. To take the particular cases alluded to above, the sayings which speak of the Son of Man as a wanderer on earth and those which speak of his appointment for suffering and rejection, must we assume that, because these features are absent from the representation in Daniel and in Enoch, they must therefore have been drawn by Jesus from sources offering larger helpings of the Iranian myth ? Is nothing of the Christian mystery to be accredited to Jesus himself and to his personal interpretation of history ? On this subject a few observations fall to be made.

In the first place, when we read the sayings in question, when we

[1] According to Reitzenstein, John the Baptist was a Mandæan, whose message was that of the Heavenly Man Redeemer.

hear of the Son of Man not having where to lay his head or of his being set for suffering and death, it is not possible to keep out a feeling of the paradox which the situations so described involved even for the mind of Jesus. Nothing could be less like the recital of a set of ideas derived from a tradition or myth than these words, spoken as Jesus spoke them. But to admit the element of paradox here is to admit the possibility that not tradition or myth but history in the sense of Jesus' own experience of God and life was the real factor which carried his thought of the Son of Man beyond its Jewish and Biblical starting-point. The admissibility of such an explanation is decidedly strengthened when we consider, in the second place, what the real ground of the Saviour's sense of vocation from the beginning actually was. If the central thesis of this book is correct, it was not any doc-trinal presuppositions regarding the kingdom of God or the Son of Man but an extraordinary sense of engagement to bring his nation to God in preparation for the kingdom that led Jesus to define his calling ultimately in terms of the vision in Daniel's seventh chapter. Conse-quently, when he speaks of the Son of Man as being homeless and a wanderer or as destined to be rejected and slain, we do not need to think of him as formulating doctrinaire ideas on the subject of the Son of Man. There exists the alternative explanation that he is simply accepting by completest faith in God the moral and logical consequences of the historical mission in which he had found his Christhood.

> " The kingdom that I seek
> Is Thine, so let the way
> That leads to it be Thine."

On this view all necessity to invoke ethnic or esoteric ideas for the explanation of any part of his teaching disappears. While the Son of Man conception may have come to Daniel and the writer of Enoch from an Iranian source, to Jesus its presence in Daniel made it part of Holy Writ, and, as such, to be received and understood in the light and context of all that is made known to him in his personal history concerning the Will of God.

It remains to add that A. F. von Gall's attempt to trace the con-ception of the Isaianic Servant, towards which Jesus turned for the confirmation of his own deepest intuitions, to an origin in the Persian Gayomart and so to bring in the Iranian myth by another door, makes too many demands on our credulity to be impressive, and, so far as we know, has no point of contact in the thought-world of Jesus.

VI. When we pass from the Synoptic tradition to the teaching of St. Paul, we feel ourselves to be in a different world. The influence of Midrashic ideas upon the mind of the Apostle is too various and abundant to permit the supposition that, if doctrines of the Heavenly

Man such as have left their mark on the Adam-literature of Judaism were current in the Rabbinical circles in which he moved, we should not find traces of them in his thinking. As a matter of fact the evidence of the Pauline theology at this point is of an extraordinarily interesting but at the same time ambiguous order.

The doctrines of Christ and of man, and of Christ in relation to man, exhibit striking resemblances to the pattern of things in Reitzenstein's myth, but they also exhibit striking differences. Thus —to take the positive side of the case first—it cannot be said of the Pauline teaching, as of the Synoptic tradition, that the Christ whom it presents to us (*a*) did not exist before creation, or (*b*) has not a cosmological significance for the world and for humanity, or (*c*) is not already the victorious Redeemer who has been raised from death at the hands of the principalities and powers of darkness, or (*d*) is not the Man from Heaven, or (*e*) is not the source and ground of our spiritual part in the sense that all that we have as Christians of divine or heavenly life is derived and held from him. In all these points, which differentiate the Pauline doctrine of Christ from the simpler Messianic terms of the Synoptic teaching, we have to recognize a marked approximation to the form of ideas set forth in Reitzenstein's myth.

On the other hand, a closer examination reveals the most pronounced differences within this general agreement, as the facts now to be stated will make sufficiently plain.

(*a*) The Christ of St. Paul pre-exists creation, but " in the form of God " (Phil. ii. 6) or as the Son of God (Col. i. 13-17), not as man or in the form of man.

(*b*) He has a cosmological relation to the world and to men, but this he has as the instrument or organ of creation (δι' οὖ, I Cor. viii. 6), not as the ontological source of being (ἐξ οὖ).

(*c*) He is already the triumphant Redeemer, *Christus Victor*, but he does not possess this rank from before the foundation of the world. He has attained it only in the last days, in what St. Paul calls " the end of the ages " (I Cor. x. 11).

(*d*) He is the Man from Heaven, not, however, because he pre-existed as man, but because he assumed our nature in his incarnation and retains it in his heavenly life.

(*e*) We are united to him in the life of salvation, but by a " new creation " of his producing (II Cor. v. 17), not by the possession of a divine principle or nature in ourselves which Christ simply awakens and recalls to its source.

These differences between the Pauline doctrine of Christ and the Iranian myth are very fundamental, and taken together with the agreements noted above, they raise in a very real way the question of the truth or error of Reitzenstein's hypothesis.

Reitzenstein has not the slightest doubt that the myth influenced

St. Paul. From the moment of the Damascus experience, when the persecutor was called out of his darkness into the light of the knowledge of Jesus Christ, the apostle's thoughts of religion cast themselves into the one mould of a mystical faith directed towards the heavenly Man who, as victor over sin and death, had revealed himself as the second Adam, the inaugurator of the æon of righteousness and life. Here was the chance to lay hold of whatever elements of Midrashic thought on the subject of the Son of Man had established themselves in Rabbinical doctrine, and St. Paul was not slow to do so. Reitzenstein instances the cosmological functions ascribed to the Christian Redeemer as a proof that the apostle was influenced, through Jewish Messianic theology, by Iranian beliefs.

As an even more impressive sign of the same influence he cites the conception of the Christian life, so characteristic of St. Paul and so remote from the language of Jesus, which takes shape in the expressions " Christ in me," " I in Christ." He says of this determination of religious sentiment : " Only mystery-ideas can explain it, and of these none so clearly as the (Iranian) idea of a God-man, who is at once our inner man and the divinity of which our souls are parts." He thinks it is from such a starting-point that St. Paul's ideas of dying and living again with Christ come into possession of their full reality, and these are the ideas which form the kernel, the innermost thing in the Pauline religion. He also cites as marks of Iranian influence the Pauline conceptions of Christ as awakening the slumbering soul, of present existence as a ' body of death,' of the redeemed as wearing heavenly garments or a ' spiritual body,' and in general the whole dualism implied in the Pauline doctrine of flesh and spirit. Neither " the spirit of original Christianity, as for example in the message of Jesus " nor " any deepening of ethical consciousness in Paul, a factor which every one of us will gladly admit " is, he thinks, equal to the explanation of St. Paul's complete fusion of the notions of flesh, sin, and death in that which is contrary to God. There is another factor to be recognized, the Iranian dualism. In Philo the kernel common to these ideas has been obscured through his alliance with Greek philosophy, in St. Paul it is refashioned for a new purpose.

Before coming to a judgement on Reitzenstein's hypothesis, it will be worth while to study St. Paul's teaching on the person of Christ a little more fully.

(1) St. Paul nowhere directly names Jesus the Son of Man, but that the title was known to him and influenced his thinking appears by manifold signs. For example, in I Cor. xv. 25-28 where he is making the point that " Christ must reign till he has put all enemies under his feet," he quotes Ps. viii. 6 (LXX) in confirmation. But in this Psalm the words, " Thou hast put all things under his feet," refer to man or the son of man as the object of the divine regard (Ps. viii. 4-6). If the apostle was not thinking of Christ as the Son of Man, it

would not have occurred to him to base Christ's universal sovereignty on this text. Again, in Rom. v. 14-15 we have the marked emphasis of the designation Man as applied to Jesus Christ over against its use with reference to the first Adam, described as the type of the Man to come, and in v. 16-21 we have the impressive parallel between the solidarity of the race in sin and death with Adam and the solidarity of the new humanity in righteousness and life with Christ.

But while Christ is thus for the apostle the Son of Man or Heavenly Man, and while as such he has Lordship or sovereignty over all things under God, it is not at all apparent that it is with this rank or dignity that St. Paul connects the cosmological functions of Christ (I Cor. viii. 5-6, Col. i. 15-17), though this is what we should expect if with Reitzenstein we regarded the Iranian myth as the underlying pattern of the Pauline doctrine of Christ. As a matter of fact, the Pauline Christ pre-exists the world not as Man, but " in the form of God " (Phil. ii. 6) or as the eternal Son of God (Col. ii. 13-17). His cosmological significance, therefore, does not pertain to him as Man. In addition, the language used by the apostle to bring out the connection of Christ with creation is that ordinarily employed of the Logos or Wisdom of God in Hellenistic Judaism, which suggests the ascendancy over his mind at this point of one or other of those conceptions.

It has to be recognized, indeed, that in a famous passage of Philo the names Logos and Heavenly Man are bracketed together as different designations of one and the same principle : this principle is at once the Logos and the Man after the Image of God (De Conf. Ling. 146). But an examination of the passage shows that Philo, in thinking of the Logos, connects him more closely with another conception—that of the Son of God. The passage is as follows—I quote from the translation in the Loeb edition :

> " But they who live in the knowledge of the One are rightly called ' Sons of God,' as Moses also acknowledges when he says ' Ye are sons of the Lord God.' . . . But if there be any as yet unfit to be called a son of God, let him press to take his place under God's First-born, the Word, who holds the eldership among the angels, their ruler as it were. And many names are his, for he is called ' the Beginning' and ' the Name of God,' and his ' Word,' and ' the Man after his Image.' . . . If we have not yet become fit to be thought sons of God, yet we may be sons of his invisible image, the most holy Word. For the Word is the eldest-born image of God " (De Conf. Ling. 145-147).

For Philo, then, the Heavenly Man is identified with the Logos, but the Logos is primarily conceived as the First-born or Son of God. In St. Paul, as we have seen, Christ as the Man from heaven is but the manifestation in the flesh of the eternal Son of God.

(2) The revelation of Christ as the Man from heaven is the special subject of the exposition in I Cor. xv. 45-49. It is the point of

St. Paul's argument that Christ, though the Man from heaven, is not the first, but the second or last Man : " Not first that which is spiritual, but that which is psychical ; thereafter that which is spiritual " (I Cor. xv. 46). It is usually considered that the apostle is here polemising against the teaching of Philo, whose first man, created according to Gen. i. 27, is spiritual and heavenly, whereas his second man is, according to Gen. ii. 7, ' psychical ' and earthly. It is not necessary, however, to suppose that Paul had read Philo, for Philo's doctrine may conceivably have owed something to Jewish Midrashic notions of the first man, influenced possibly by Oriental speculations, with which St. Paul also was acquainted : in which case St. Paul is reacting against Rabbinical doctrine in the defence of his Christian faith.

However that may be, the apostle names Christ as the Man from heaven and, in contrasting him with Adam, designates him as the second or last Man simply because in these latter days, when the fullness of the time was come, God sent forth His Son to be born of woman and to redeem to Himself a new humanity consisting of the sons of God (Gal. iv. 4). Existing in the form of God, this Son divested himself of heavenly glory, and took his place in history in the likeness of men, in order to suffer and to die (Phil. ii. 6-8). It is obvious that if St. Paul, whether through Rabbinical speculation or under other influence, was conversant with the form of ideas in the Iranian mystery, he is protesting against it at this point in the name of the Christian order of revelation.

(3) St. Paul certainly represents the Christian life as a life ' in Christ ' and derived from Christ. He not only speaks of Christ as in us and of us as in Christ, but he speaks of Christians as having in baptism ' put on ' Christ (Gal. iii. 27), and he travails in birth-pangs for his converts until Christ be ' formed ' in them (Gal. iv. 20). So also the Christian life is presented as a dying with Christ and a rising with him to newness of life (Rom. vi). The forms of language here employed are ordinarily put down to modes of thought characteristic of mystery-religion, and Reitzenstein, as we have noted, puts in his claim for the Iranian mystery as that which best accounts for the particular determinations of St. Paul's thinking. But, save in form, there is no agreement at this point between the Pauline and the Iranian doctrine. The two conceptions of salvation are not in the least degree *in pari materia.*

The Christian redemption, as taught by St. Paul, does not consist, like the Iranian, in the release and sublimation of a divine nature which is inherent in us and which the Man from Heaven awakes and recalls to himself. It is not any transaction in the realm of nature that the apostle has in his mind, but the divine miracle of a ' new creation ' wrought by Christ upon us and coming out in a new determination of our life by the Spirit of God. Hence, as often as he elucidates for us the meaning of his mystical phraseology, it is by translating it back into terms of faith. " I have been crucified with Christ," he writes, " and it is no more I who live, but Christ lives in me." Then he at once adds the explanation : " The life which I now live in the flesh, I live by faith in the Son of God who loved me and gave himself for me " (Gal. ii. 20. Cf. Rom. vi. 8-11).

Summing up, we may say that if ideas of Iranian provenance, coming into Judaism with the conception of the Son of Man, obtained a foothold in Rabbinical circles and were there employed, with or without a consciousness of their source, for the speculative development of the matter of Daniel's vision, it is not at all improbable that they would be known to St. Paul and would contribute features to the schematization of ideas in his doctrine of the person and work of Christ. That such ideas did actually establish themselves in Jewish quarters seems practically certain from the development of Daniel's figure of the ' one like a son of man ' in Enoch and in IV Ezra, and also from certain tendencies in the Adam-literature of Judaism. But such formal influences, if they impressed a stamp on St. Paul's doctrine of Christ, do not extend to the whole range of his matter, and in view of the character of the latter they can only be called secondary. Heavenly Man is not for the apostle the supreme or ultimate category of the Redeemer's significance, but rather Son of God, and where the Heavenly Man conception comes explicitly to the front, it is in a form which definitely opposes itself to the order of ideas in the Iranian myth. Above all, the inward relation of Redeemer and redeemed in the Pauline religion is of a nature which has no parallel in Jewish Midrash or in its remoter sources. Hence, while it is possible and indeed likely that traditional or received ideas helped the apostle here, as at other points, to self-expression, the matter of his gospel must be pronounced independent of extraneous influences, based as it is on Christian historical revelation and on the Christian experience of God.

SHORT BIBLIOGRAPHY

ABBOTT, E. A.   The Fourfold Gospel (1913, etc.).

ABRAHAMS, I.   Studies in Pharisaism and the Gospels (1917, etc.).

ARVEDSON, T.   Das Mysterium Christi (1937).

BACON, B. W.   Jesus and Paul (1921).

BOUSSET, W. and GRESSMANN, H.   Die Religion des Judentums (3rd ed., 1926).

BOUSSET, W.   Hauptprobleme der Gnosis (1907).

—— Kyrios Christos (2nd ed., 1921).

BULTMANN, R.   Die Geschichte der Synoptischen Tradition (2nd ed., 1931).

—— Jesus and the Word (1935).

BURKITT, F. C.   Christian Beginnings (1924).

—— Church and Gnosis (1932).

—— The Religion of the Manichees (1925).

BUSSMANN, W.   Synoptische Studien, Bd. I-III (1925-1931).

CHARLES, R. H.   Apocrypha and Pseudepigrapha of the Old Testament, Vols. I-II (1913).

—— Critical History of the Doctrine of a Future Life (2nd ed., 1913).

—— The Book of Enoch (1912).

CLEMEN, C.   Religionsgeschichtliche Erklärung des Neuen Testaments (2nd ed., 1924).

CREED, J. M.   " The Heavenly Man " ; article in Journal of Theological Studies, Vol. XXVI.

DALMAN, G.   The Words of Jesus (1909).

—— Jesus-Jeshua (1929).

DENNEY, J.   Jesus and the Gospel (1908).

DIBELIUS, M.   From Tradition to Gospel (1934).

—— Gospel Criticism and Christology (1935).

DODD, C. H.   The Apostolic Preaching and its Development (1936).

—— History and the Gospel (1938).

DRIVER, S. R. and NEUBAUER, A.   The Jewish Interpreters of Isaiah LIII, Vols. I-II.

EASTON, B. S.   The Gospel According to St. Luke (1926).

—— Christ in the Gospels (1930).

EICHRODT, W.   Die Theologie des Alten Testaments, Bd. I (1933).

FASCHER, E.   Die Form-geschichtliche Methode (1924).

FOAKES-JACKSON, H. and LAKE, K.   The Beginnings of Christianity, Vols. I-V (1920-1933).

GALL, A. F. VON.   ΒΑΣΙΛΕΙΑ ΤΟΥ ΘΕΟΥ (1926).

GOGUEL, M.   Critique et Histoire (1928).

—— Life of Jesus (1933).

GRESSMANN, H.   Der Ursprung der Israelitisch-jüdischen Eschatologie (1905).

—— Der Messias (1929).

HARNACK, A. VON.   What is Christianity ? (1901).

—— The Sayings of Jesus (1908).

HEBERT, A. G.   The Throne of David (1941).

HÉRING, J.   Le Royaume de Dieu et Sa Venue (1937).

HOLL, K.   Urchristentum und Religionsgeschichte (1927. Eng. trans. by N. V. Hope, " The Distinctive Elements in Christianity," 1937).

HOLTZMANN, O.   Life of Jesus (1904).

HOSKYNS, E. and DAVEY, N.   The Riddle of the New Testament (2nd ed., 1936).

KITTEL, G.   Die Religionsgeschichte und das Urchristentum (1931).

KLAUSNER, J.   Jesus of Nazareth (1925).

LAGARDE, P. DE.   Prophetae Chaldaice (1872).

LAGRANGE, M. J.   Le Judaisme avant Jésus-Christ (1931).

LAKE, K.   The Earlier Epistles of St. Paul (1914).

LEGGE, F.   Forerunners and Rivals of Christianity, Vols. I-II (1915).

LIGHTFOOT, R. H.   History and Interpretation in the Gospels (1935).

MACAULAY, A. B.   The Death of Jesus (1938).

McNEILE, A. H.   The Gospel according to St. Matthew (1915).

MANSON, T. W.   The Teaching of Jesus (1931).

MENZIES, A.   The Earliest Gospel (1901).

MEYER, E.   Ursprung und Anfänge des Christentums, Bd. I-III (1921-1923).

MICHEL, O.   Prophet und Märtyrer (1932).

MOFFATT, J.   Jesus Christ the Same (1942).

MONTEFIORE, C. G.   The Synoptic Gospels, Vols. I-II (2nd ed., 1927).

MOORE, G. F.   Judaism, Vols. I-II (1927).

NIEBUHR, R.   An Interpretation of Christian Ethic (1936).

NORDEN, E.   Agnostos Theos (1913).

OESTERLEY, W. O. E.   The Jewish Background of the Christian Liturgy (1925).

OGG, G.   The Chronology of the Public Ministry of Jesus (1940).

OTTO, R.   The Kingdom of God and the Son of Man (1938).

RASHDALL, H.   Conscience and Christ (1916).

RAWLINSON, A. E. J.   The New Testament Doctrine of the Christ (1926).

REITZENSTEIN, R.   Poimandres (1906).

—— Die Göttin Psyche (1917).

—— Das Mandäische Buch des Herrn der Grösse (1919).

—— Das Iranische Erlösungsmysterium (1921).

—— Die Hellenistischen Mysterien-Religionen (3rd ed., 1927).

SCHECHTER, S.   Some Aspects of Rabbinic Judaism (1909).

SCHWEITZER, A.   The Quest of the Historical Jesus (2nd ed., 1911).

SCHWEITZER, A.   The Mystery of the Kingdom of God (1925).

SCOTT, E. F.   The Validity of the Gospel Record (1938).

SMITH, B. T. D.   The Parables of the Synoptic Gospels (1937).

STRACK, H. L. and BILLERBECK, P.   Kommentar zum Neuen Testament aus Talmud und Midrasch, Bd. I-IV (1922-1928).

STREETER, B. H.   The Four Gospels (1924).

TAYLOR, V.   Behind the Third Gospel (1926).

—— The Formation of the Gospel Tradition (1935).

—— Jesus and His Sacrifice (1939).

WALTON, B.   Biblia Sacra Polyglotta (1657).

WEISS, J.   Das Älteste Evangelium (1903).

—— Christ : the Beginnings of Dogma (1911).

—— The History of Primitive Christianity, Vols. I-II (1937).

WENDT, H. H.   Die Apostelgeschichte (1913).

—— The Teaching of Jesus, Vols. I-II (1893).

WERNLE, P.   The Beginnings of Christianity, Vols. I-II (1903).

—— Jesus (1917).

WINDISCH, H.   Der Sinn der Bergpredigt (2nd ed., 1937).

—— Paulus und Christus (1934).

INDEXES

I. BIBLICAL AND NON-CANONICAL PASSAGES

(a) OLD TESTAMENT AND JEWISH LITERATURE

(b) New Testament

II. AUTHORITIES CITED

III. GENERAL SUBJECT-INDEX